DAY OF INFAMY

At 0745 on the bridge of the carrier *Akagi* 180 miles north of Pearl Harbor, Admiral Nagumo waited nervously with Kusaka, his chief of staff. They waited in total silence.

Then came the signal from Fuchida, flying with the high-level bombers above Oahu. As the Japanese squadrons dove on their respective targets, Fuchida grabbed his microphone. *Tora-Tora-Tora!* The American fleet is present. Total surprise has been achieved.

Nagumo and Kusaka turned toward each other, smiled and wordlessly shook hands. The die had been cast. There was no turning back.

THE WORLD-AT-WAR
From those who experienced it

THE NAVAL AIR WAR IN VIETNAM (1749, $3.95)
by Peter B. Mersky and Norman Polmar

With more than 200 photographs you'll see the Vietnam war from the cockpit, just as the fliers who were there saw it. And you'll discover the exhilaration and tragic dimensions of the war we did fight.

GREEN KNIGHT, RED MOURNING (1626, $3.50)
by Richard Ogden

In Vietnam Richard Ogden suffered the death of his friends and killed the enemy with both his M-79 and his bare hands. This is a memoir of blood and fire, tears and torture ... and the vivid truth of men at war.

VICTORY AT GUADALCANAL (1684, $3.95)
by Robert Edward Lee

For six months and two days combined U.S. Army and Marine forces held off the Japanese assault on Guadalcanal. It was the longest single battle in the history of American warfare and marked the end of Japanese advances in the Pacific.

ESCAPE FROM LAOS (1113, $2.95)
by Dieter Dengler

In February, 1966, Navy Lieutenant Dieter Dengler crawled out of the twisted wreckage of his Skyraider and into an epic struggle for survival in a Hoi Het prison camp. The only thing that kept him alive—and sane—was one thought: escape.

AND THE WALLS CAME TUMBLING DOWN
by Jack Fishman (1444, $3.95)

The Resistance men awaiting execution in Amiens prison were vital to the entire D-Day operation—they had to be rescued. The Allies' only chance was to blow up the prison ... and pray they didn't blow up the very men they were trying to free.

Available wherever paperbacks are sold, or order direct from the Publisher. Send cover price plus 50¢ per copy for mailing and handling to Zebra Books, Dept. 1887, 475 Park Avenue South, New York, N.Y. 10016. Residents of New York, New Jersey and Pennsylvania must include sales tax. DO NOT SEND CASH.

THE GREAT BATTLES OF WORLD WAR II
VOLUME II:
THE PACIFIC NAVAL BATTLES

BY CHARLES E. PFANNES AND VICTOR A. SALAMONE

ZEBRA BOOKS
KENSINGTON PUBLISHING CORP.

ZEBRA BOOKS

are published by

Kensington Publishing Corp.
475 Park Avenue South
New York, NY 10016

Copyright © 1986 by Charles F. Pfannes and Victor A. Salamone

All rights reserved. No part of this book may be reproduced in any form or by any means without the prior written consent of the Publisher, excepting brief quotes used in reviews.

First printing: August 1986

Printed in the United States of America

To my brother Frank J. Salamone

Though we have lived miles apart, we are always close at heart.

TABLE OF CONTENTS

INTRODUCTION: The Breaking of The Japanese Code 13
CHAPTER ONE: Pearl Harbor 27
CHAPTER TWO: The Battle of The Coral Sea 85
CHAPTER THREE: The Battle of Midway 117
CHAPTER FOUR: The Naval Battles in The Solomons 161
CHAPTER FIVE: The Battle of The Philippine Sea 225
CHAPTER SIX: The Battle of Leyte Gulf 269

Preface

From the high tide of victory at Pearl Harbor to the shattering of the Japanese fleet at Leyte Gulf, this book examines the great Pacific naval battles. In Volume I we studied the Pacific Island Battles. This particular volume is an excellent companion to the first one. In conjunction with our *Great Commanders and Admirals* series these volumes capture the essence of the Pacific War.

Chapter one studies the infamous attack on the American Naval Base at Pearl Harbor. Chapter two examines the first Pacific carrier battle of World War II, the Battle of the Coral Sea. In the next chapter the Japanese debacle at Midway is examined. Chapter four looks at the many Solomon naval battles. The Battle of the Philippine Sea is studied in chapter five. In the last chapter we examine the largest naval battle in world history, the Battle of Leyte Gulf.

We wish to thank our wives Lillian and Susanne, and our children Tom, John, Jennifer, Charles and

Victor, for their love and support. We also thank our faithful readers and wish them all well. Vic wants to thank in a special way the Diaconate Class of 1986 of which he is proud to be a member.

> Victor A. Salamone
> Poughkeepsie, New York
>
> Chuck Pfannes
> Cold Spring, New York
>
> April 7, 1986

INTRODUCTION

THE BREAKING OF THE JAPANESE CODE

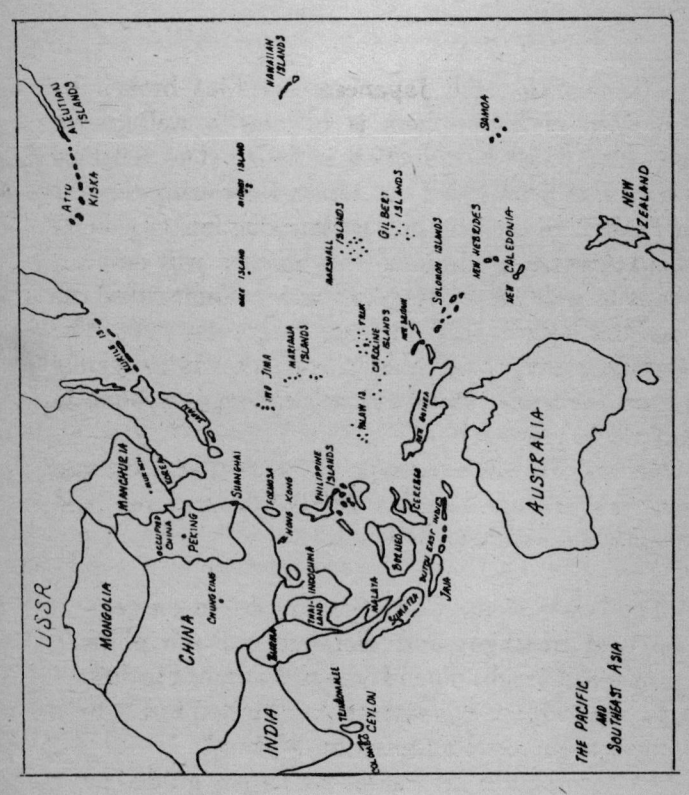

The fact that the Japanese code was broken by American cryptographers is by now a well-known fact. This brief introduction is designed to tell how Magic and Ultra aided the Americans during the war in Pacific. Since it is but an introduction to a book about American admirals, this chapter will only attempt to give the briefest summary. The text of the book that follows will elucidate the greater story. The overriding purpose of this introduction is to merely inform the reader about this all-important weapon in America's arsenal.

General Marshall perhaps said it best in a letter to New York Gov. Thomas Dewey during the 1944 presidential campaign.

The battle of the Coral Sea was based on deciphered messages and therefore our few ships were in the right place at the right time. Further, we were able to concentrate our limited forces to meet their naval advance on Midway.

Operations in the Pacific are largely guided by the information we obtain of Japanese deployments. We know their strength in various garrisons . . . we check their fleet movements and the movements of their convoys . . . we know the sailing dates and routes . . . and can notify our submarines to be in wait at the proper points.[1]

Therefore, the fact that the code was compromised was of extreme importance.

Magic refers to all the information gathered from the encipherment of the Japanese diplomatic signals, while Ultra (not to be confused with the German Enigma encipherments) was the name given to the intelligence gathered by the codebreakers of the Japanese naval and army signals. Combined with Magic, Ultra provided the American high command with an excellent insight into Japanese intentions and plans.

The story of the breaking of the Japanese code is a lengthy, circuitous one. Certain personalities stand out above all others. Codebreaking has been accomplished for as long as man has attempted to deceive his fellow man by the use of cryptic statements. Even during the American Civil War codes predominated. Perhaps the most celebrated of the American codebreaking organizations was the American Black Chamber made famous by Herbert Yardley. In 1921 Yardley's Black Chamber broke the then-existing Japanese code. This effort had a great bearing on the Washington Naval Conference that settled the issue of a 5:5:3 ratio of capital ships between the United States, Great Britain and Japan respectively.

The man most celebrated as the breaker of the Japanese diplomatic code, however, was William F. Friedman. By the fall of 1940, Friedman and his group of cryptanalysts had solved some of the highest grade cryptographic systems of the Japanese Foreign Office. The Signal Intelligence Service constructed four machines, called Purple, to decipher the secret Japanese diplomatic traffic. At that time, the military codes remained undecipherable.

The U.S. government quickly reaped the benefit of these intercepts. When the new Japanese ambassador to the United States, Admiral Nomura, presented himself to Cordell Hull, the United States secretary of state, his pacific attitude was welcomed as a sign of a positive prospect for peace. The intercepts, however, helped Hull and Roosevelt to establish the actual Japanese intention hidden by the cosmetics of Nomura.

An immediate question poses itself here. Since the codebreakers had broken the diplomatic code, why was the attack on Pearl Harbor a surprise? Two recent books have been published, each taking a different side of the question. John Toland in *Infamy* states emphatically that President Roosevelt had advance notification of the approach of the Japanese Task Force and, beyond that, prior to this notification, vital Japanese intercepts were neither handled properly nor sent to the necessary people.

In *The American Magic*, Ronald Lewin presents an excellent case of exonerating the president and the military chiefs in Washington. Both eminent scholars have convincingly argued their point and both portray what might be the "truth." The authors of this chronicle merely direct the readers to these two outstanding books and will let them draw their own conclusions. Will the truth ever be known?

After Pearl Harbor the Japanese war machine spread its mighty tentacles throughout the Pacific and Southeast Asia. In time their victories swelled the

Japanese with a deep sense of pride which was later translated into "victory disease." Having conquered an empire with so little loss, the Japanese were hesitant to swing over to the defensive. Australia, a potential base for an Allied counterattack, had to be eliminated. In addition, the American aircraft carriers which had, fortunately for the Americans, escaped destruction at Pearl Harbor, had to be dealt with. This gave rise to two possible Japanese offensives: one toward Port Moresby and the other toward Midway.

It was up to Cmdr. Joseph Rochefort of the Fleet Radio Unit, Pacific (FRUPac as it was called) to piece together the many enemy intercepts in an attempt to determine the Japanese intentions.

The Japanese naval code, JN 25, was attacked by Rochefort and his men more extensively than earlier codes. JN 25 presented them with a host of problems. Naval Intelligence in Washington, Op-20-G, also put its expertise to work attempting to crack the Japanese naval code.

Aiding the codebreakers was the fact that the Japanese were fattened by their easy victories and by the vast multiplication of bases throughout the Pacific. That caused an intelligence problem. To maintain a code's integrity it must be changed frequently. To overuse a code might easily expose it to decipherment. The extent of the Japanese Empire, however, mitigated against rapid disbursement of new code books. This resulted in the retention of codes like JN 25 for dangerously long periods of time. This allowed the American intelligence teams the time to crack the code. Consequently, both the Port Moresby operation and, more important, the Midway offensive were disclosed to Admiral Nimitz.

With the knowledge provided by Ultra, Nimitz was able to position Fletcher's carriers at the right place in the Coral Sea. So too at Midway, the intelligence allowed Nimitz to stay one step ahead of the Japanese.

> Shapes and patterns gradually emerged to be confirmed in the end by intercepts so specific in detail and so conclusive in their significance that Nimitz, on the eve of his next great battle (Midway), had a more intimate knowledge of his enemy's strength and intentions than any other admiral in the whole previous history of sea warfare.[2]

Midway was as much a victory for the cryptographers as it was for the brave pilots who risked their lives to sink the Japanese carriers.

In June 1942, just prior to Midway but too late to foil the Americans, the Japanese changed the JN 25 code system. Not because they suspected its integrity but simply as part of the normal routine. This necessitated the codebreakers beginning their efforts all over.

W. J. Holmes of FRUPac commented on the plight of a codebreaker.

> Progress on the five digit code that the Japanese had been using since 1 June 1942 was slow. It was August before any light began to dawn. That same month the code, having been in effect only a little more than two months, was changed again.[3]

It was unfortunate for Nimitz that the change occurred just as the invasion of Guadalcanal (August 7, 1942) was about to commence. Though cryptanalaysis was temporarily blind, radio intercepts (traffic analysis) was still functional. Through this Nimitz discovered in June that the Japanese were constructing an airfield on the jungle-clad island of Guadalcanal in the Solomons. This news impelled the admiral to quickly schedule Operation Watchtower before the Japanese could make the airfield operational. Holmes comments again:

> Until the Battle of Midway, communications intelligence completely dominated combat intelligence, but when the action shifted to the Solomons there was also a change in the nature of combat intelligence. The Japanese, being now on the defensive and having their forces concentrated in Rabaul, no longer needed to transmit their plans by radio and this, together with the change in their code, made it impossible for radio intelligence to determine specific details of their dispositions and timing. We could still read some minor codes . . . with this information and traffic analysis, it was frequently possible to detect a buildup of Japanese naval strength.[4]

Thus, until the codebreakers could open that elusive window again, traffic analysis, aerial reconnaissance, and the daring and brave coastwatchers had to supply the necessary eyes and ears for the Americans.

The debacle at Savo Island could have been linked to the fact that the Japanese code could not be read at that time. Throughout most of the campaign, therefore, only low-grade codes were penetrated. However, through these low-grade codes, combined with the aforementioned traditional methods of intelligence gathering, the job was done. In part, eventual victory was aided as much by these advance warnings as by the blood of the Army, Navy and Marine forces.

When the new year of 1943 dawned, FRUPac was again reading the Japanese code.

Meanwhile, in the Southwest Pacific, through traffic analysis, MacArthur received advance warning of the Japanese attack on Port Moresby. The valuable information disclosed the Japanese intention to utilize the Kokoda Trail across the Owen Stanley Mountains, the spiny backbone of Papua, New Guinea. Thanks also to Ultra, in March 1943, during what would later be called the Battle of the Bismarck Sea, Army Air Force planes of the Fifth Air Force flew four hundred sorties with a loss of but five aircraft. The Japanese, on the other hand, lost an entire convoy loaded with reinforcements and supplies destined for New Guinea. Ultra told the American pilots where to be and what time to be there in the Bismarck Sea.

The next coup credited to Ultra intelligence was none other than the assassination of Admiral Yamamoto. His itinerary, showing just where the admiral would be on April 18, was intercepted and deciphered four days prior to the trip. The Americans prepared a trap and the brilliant designer of the Pearl Harbor attack was killed.*

*See *Great Commanders of World War II Volume IV: The Japanese*, chapter 2.

Ultra also provided Admiral Nimitz with a fairly accurate estimate of Japanese forces on the many islands invaded in the Central Pacific. However, it could not make the job any easier for the combat troops.

Decoded signals translated into Ultra could provide and often provided abundantly precise information concerning the enemy's capability on an island about to be assaulted. The name, the strength and the location of individual units, the amount of ammunition or rations available . . . all these and many other valuable details came to the Americans from the fountain of Ultra. But what signal intelligence could not do was to provide topographical knowledge, nor could it penetrate the camouflage of those defensive positions so secretly and so skillfully devised by the Japanese.[5]

Ultra could only provide so much. It had its limitations which the assault forces dramatically discovered on their bloody trail across the Central Pacific.

As the reader will discover in the forthcoming chapters on Nimitz, Spruance and Turner, Ultra intelligence convinced Nimitz that Kwajalein Atoll in the Marshalls should be invaded directly even though his principal commander opposed that move. From intercepts Nimitz knew that the Japanese expected an attack on the perimeter islands in the Marianas and were deploying their forces to meet just such a threat. They ignored Kwajalein.

By the spring of 1943 the Japanese army code, which had eluded the codebreakers, was finally broken. From then until the end of the war, the wealth of Japanese intelligence compromised by the Americans was enormous. The Maru* code was also broken in 1943. Thus, through Ultra, the Japanese homeland was quickly cut off from the natural resources of its empire. With the knowledge provided, American submarines found the Japanese merchant ships and sent them to Davy Jones' locker. As Holmes explains, "There were nights when nearly every American submarine on patrol in the Central Pacific was working on the basis of information derived from cryptanalysis."[6]

With the aide of Ultra, by the middle of 1943, the submarines had doubled their kill ratio. The information was so accurate that not only were the names of every ship known, but also their numbers, cargoes and routes. Even their precise noontime position for every day of the voyage was disclosed. The tonnage of Japanese losses was astounding. Over seventy percent of all Japan's shipping losses was the result of U.S. submarine attacks, an awesome achievement when the size of the Pacific Ocean is considered. Thanks to Ultra, the submarines were at the right spot at the right time.

Though the Japanese military cipher eluded the codebreakers for the early months of the war until the major breakthrough in 1943, excepting the periods

*Merchantman cypher.

prior to the Coral Sea and Midway battles, the Japanese diplomatic code, Purple, continued to supply Washington with a clear insight into the Japanese political scenes throughout the war. In fact, it even gave the codebreakers an insight into the German situation as Japanese diplomats diligently reported Germany's military and economic situation to their home. This added bonus filled many gaps in the knowledge already gained from the breaking of the German Enigma code*.

For example, on December 10, 1943, the Japanese ambassador to Germany, Baron Oshima, described the Atlantic Wall for his superiors in Japan. He gave an accurate description of the German defensive systems, placement of divisions and much additional useful information.

Thanks to the efforts of the codebreakers, the daily policies of the Japanese government were known in Washington. This was of inestimable value during the final months of the war as Japan attempted to bring about a favorable settlement. Their policy toward Russia was made clear to the Washington planners, as was the Soviet position as they reacted to the Japanese overtures.

Truly Magic and Ultra were America's greatest allies in the Pacific War. However, the final outcome still boiled down to bitter fighting against a determined foe, which Allied combat troops were forced to endure. But without Ultra, that enemy would have

*See *Great Commanders of World War II Volume II: The British*, introduction.

been better fortified. Their supply ships would have reached their destinations unscathed.

The authors would like to recommend the books listed in the bibliography of this introduction for the serious reader who would like to pursue this topic in depth.

NOTES

1. Ronald Lewin, *The American Magic*, p. 8
2. *Ibid*, p. 92
3. W. J. Holmes, *Doubled Edged Secrets*, p. 107
4. *Ibid*, p. 110
5. Lewin, *op cit*, p. 188
6. Holmes, *op cit.*, p. 128

BIBLIOGRAPHY

1. Clark, Ronald. *The Man Who Broke Purple*. Little Brown & Co., Boston, 1977.
2. Holmes, W. J. *Doubled Edged Secrets*. Naval Institute Press, Annapolis, 1979.
3. Kahn, David. *The Code-Breakers*. Weidenfeld and Nicolson, London, 1967.
4. Lewin, Ronald. *Ultra Goes to War*. McGraw-Hill, New York, 1978.
5. Lewin, Ronald. *The American Magic*. Farrar Straus Giroux, New York, 1982.
6. Pfannes, Charles and Salamone, Victor. *The Great Commanders of World War II Volume II: The British*.

Zebra Books, New York, 1981.
7. Toland, John. *Infamy*.
   Doubleday & Co., New York, 1982.
8. Van Der Thoer, Edward. *Deadly Magic*.
   Charles Scribner's Sons, New York, 1978.

CHAPTER ONE

PEARL HARBOR

"Air raid, Pearl Harbor. This is no drill." That earth-shattering signal reverberated through the air waves, reaching every outpost in the Pacific. At first, those on the receiving end questioned the accuracy of the message. Had the Japanese really struck the mighty United States naval base in Hawaii? Indeed they had.

The following day, President Franklin D. Roosevelt responded with his now-famous declaration, "Yesterday, December 7, 1941, a date which will live in infamy." America was at war, embroiled in a conflict with a tenacious foe who had ignobly launched the surprise attack, killing over two thousand Americans and leaving the U.S. Pacific fleet in shambles.

How could something of this magnitude happen? It was the result of the diplomatic failure of a foreign policy, a fiasco that drove a wedge between America and Japan to such an extent that the latter felt it had no alternative but to strike with a vengeance at America. The principal character in the episode was Japanese Adm. Isoruku Yamamoto, a man who was reluctant to go to war with the United States. Yamamoto's plan of battle coupled with the aforementioned failure in diplomacy led to the notorious attack and propelled Japan into the largest war in its history.

The year 1867 marked Japan's entry into the modern era. With the overthrow of the shogunate and the restoration of the monarchy to full power, Japan cast off its Middle Ages mentality and entered the modern world of industry and power politics.

Raw materials and markets are the bread and butter of any industrial nation. As a result Japan embarked on an ambitious policy of overseas expansion. In 1895 it went to war with China. The outcome saw Japan receive Formosa and China expelled from Korea. During the course of the war Japan also invaded Manchuria where her forces occupied and held onto the southern portion of that area. Germany, France, and Russia responded in opposition immediately. Those countries feared a strong Japanese presence in Manchuria. The Japanese government had little option but to back down in the face of this superior foreign threat. The resulting loss of face was accepted with rage by the military, who accused the politicians of knuckling under to foreign pressure. An important lesson was learned, however. If Japan were to hold its head high among other nations of the world, its military might would have to grow along with the rest of the country. Therefore, she set out to become a power to be reckoned with. Accordingly, the army and navy ministers assumed a greater stature within the government. The longterm effect of this move was the eventual erosion of civilian control as the generals and admirals appropriated more and more control of the government.

In 1904 Japan found itself at war again, this time with Czarist Russia. The *causa belli* was Korea. The Koreans were unhappy with the Japanese protectorate and called for autonomy. Meanwhile, from their bases in Manchuria, Russian troops moved into northern Korea under the pretext of providing security for a forestry concession granted them by the Korean government.

After the humiliation of having to back down in 1895, Japan was not about to do so again. Instead, without any declaration of war, on February 8, 1904, the Japanese battle fleet struck the Russian Pacific squadron which lay at anchor in Port Arthur. The similarity to the future attack on Pearl Harbor was noteworthy. At that particular time, Japanese diplomats were negotiating in Moscow just as they would be in Washington on December 7, 1941.

The Russo-Japanese War was brilliantly conducted both on land and at sea by the Japanese. In Japan itself, the war was enthusiastically accepted. The decisive victory of the legendary Admiral Togo over the Russian fleet at the Straits of Tsushima was hailed as a great naval feat. Young Lieutenant Yamamoto, the future architect of the Pearl Harbor attack, was actively involved in that historic battle and saw the Russian fleet totally destroyed.

Though outwardly it appeared enormous, economically the Japanese victory proved a great drain. The great loss of life made the victory more Pyrrhic than glorious. As Japan's army was bled white, the emperor's government bowed to the inevitable, a negotiated peace, with President Theodore Roosevelt of the United States volunteering his services as mediator.

When the Treaty of Portsmouth was signed on September 5, 1905, the Japanese people were appalled by the fact that Russia was not required to pay an indemnity. It appeared to the ultranationalists that even though Japan had won a great victory, once again she was being awarded the short end of things. As a consequence, right-wingers turned their fury against the United States, resulting in widespread street riots. The unrest was quelled only by declaring martial law.

World War I brought even more aggrandizement to Japan. But in the 1920s, the country again felt the oppression of foreign interference.

The 1920s was a decade of optimism. Nations tried to outlaw war with ineffectual paper documents and endeavored to limit naval development in an effort to avoid the pitfalls of the armament races so typical of the pre-World War I years. Japan was no exception. In 1922 she signed a naval limitation treaty in Washington that limited her navy to a 5:5:3 ratio of capital ships to that of the United States and Great Britain. The army was reduced by four divisions by the civilian government. There was also talk among the politicians of disbanding the costly Kwangtung Army which was stationed in northern Korea and Manchuria. In 1929, Prime Minister Hamaguchi initiated a friendship policy with China in hopes of working out an equitable solution to both Chinese and Japanese claims to Manchuria. This attempt was met with a heated response from both within and outside the military.

Many ultranationalists were up in arms over the prospect of a negotiated compromise. They firmly believed that it was Japan's right to rule not only Manchuria, but all of Asia. These extremists believed that the country should be purged of weak-kneed civilians, with government control placed in the hands of soldier administrators who would bring Japan to its rightful place in Asia.

That same year the Great Depression hit Japan exceptionally hard, causing widespread suffering. Countless factories shut down, resulting in a high rate of unemployment. The closing of the factories coincided with a disastrous crop failure that created famine. Huge numbers of Japanese looked to the leftwing parties such as the Communists for answers to their plight. The solutions proposed by the Communists did not sit well with the right-wing elements who felt that expansion was Japan's only answer to the Depression.

To the men of the Kwangtung Army the solution to the nation's woes was simple. Manchuria! Its wilderness contained the potential for transformation into a civilized and prosperous region. Japan's unemployment problem could be solved there, while those suffering from the effects of overpopulation would be able to find a new home there. Development of Manchuria might also guarantee the homeland new markets and raw materials.

The Depression had also unleashed many pent-up hostilities within Japan. One of the victims of this hostility was Prime Minister Hamaguchi, who was struck down by a bullet fired by a right-wing fanatic on November 14, 1930. With Hamaguchi perished any hope of a soft approach toward China. The army could not help but benefit by the assassination. It was Hamaguchi who had advocated a reduction in the army's size along with a non-aggressive attitude toward its traditional enemy, China.

At this point the Kwangtung Army, acting unilaterally, moved against Marshal Chung Tso-lin, the Chinese war lord in Manchuria. Without Tokyo's blessing, Japanese forces attacked a Chinese garrison after a contrived bombing incident. The army's action was totally without sanction. Any protest or warning from Tokyo was ignored. Claiming that the Chinese had struck first, the army justified its action by stating that the Japanese were merely defending themselves.

Within a few months, the Kwangtung Army had reached the Great Wall of China. Manchuria, now renamed Manchukuo, was solidly in Japanese hands. The Kwangtung Army declared the area to be an independent state under Japanese protection. No politicians in Japan dared to interfere for fear of assassination.

Luckily for Japan the Manchurian incident ended successfully and both the people and the government accepted the army's action as a *fait accompli*. In addition, there was a great sense of relief caused by the fact that the West failed to react in a hostile manner toward Japan's obvious aggression. The denouncement by the League of Nations was ineffectual.

In 1936 Japan underwent one of its worst waves of political assassinations. It appeared that anyone who interfered with the expansionist policies became a prime target. The job of prime minister became the "most dangerous job in the world."[1]

Numerous political factions tore at the fabric of Japanese life. There was one common denominator, however, that united all the various factions. That was the belief that Japan was destined to rule Asia. The majority of Japanese, even the moderates, believed that the Greater East Asia Co-Prosperity Sphere was no different from what the British believed their empire to be. If the British could rule vast numbers of colonies, then why not Japan as well?

In June 1937, a man came to the fore who was looked upon by all groups as the right man at the right time. Prince Funinaro Konoye, a member of an ancient nobel family, became prime minister. Konoye appeared to be the ideal choice. Ultranationalists viewed him as a sympathizer while liberals considered him an intellectual who would lead Japan to friendship with the West. Within a month of Konoye's assumption of office, on July 7, 1937, a Japanese army detachment, carrying out night exercises near the Marco Polo Bridge near Peking, was allegedly fired on by Chinese troops. Settlement of the issue might have been immediate and swift, but Japanese expansionists considered this an ideal time to further the nation's claims and provide Japanese Manchuria with a buffer against communist Russia and the Chinese Communists proliferating in the North. The army promised the Konoye government that the war could be swiftly concluded for Chiang Kai-shek's forces were inferior to those of the Kwangtung Army. Believing that the army would conclude the war rapidly and hoping to protect the settlers in northern China, the Konoye government gave its sanction for reinforcements to be sent to China.

The war, however, dragged on. In January 1939 Konoye resigned as prime minister and was replaced by Baron Hiranuma, an ultranationalist. The baron's government collapsed after the Germans concluded a non-aggression pact with Russia. Hiranuma's government was succeeded by one headed by General Abe. This regime lasted from August until January when it was replaced by yet another government, this one headed by Admiral Yonai, a known moderate.

Yonai's government was doomed from the outset. Ultranationalists resented his position of opposing any alliance with the Axis powers. Hotheads planned his assassination, but, thanks to a timely warning, the admiral was saved. Under army pressure, however, Yonai was forced to resign in mid-July 1940, and for the second time, Prince Konoye was handed the Imperial Mandate.

For foreign minister Konoye chose Yosuke Matsuoka, and for war minister, Gen. Hideki Tojo. By this time the latter had become one of the most powerful individuals in the army bureaucracy. The prime minister and war minister began their relationship in an affable manner. Both accepted as a primary goal the satisfactory conclusion of the China incident.

Konoye's cabinet was officially invested on July 22, 1940. At a series of meetings that began a few days later, the cabinet ministers reviewed in detail the important issues affecting Japan's future. A draft study was prepared entitled "Main Principles of Japan's policy for coping with the situation in accord with World Developments." In this study, Japan's conflict with China was discussed in broad terms. Essentially, the plan considered the escalation of the China conflict into a Greater East Asian War. Both Matsuoka and Tojo were in accord with its contents. Japan, the plan said, faced encirclement unless it could present a firm stand. The European war presented Japan, it went on, with an ideal opportunity to look southward to Indochina and the East Indies. With the European powers preoccupied with their own war, now was the time to strike.

The foreign minister, meanwhile, was laying the groundwork for bringing Japan closer to the Axis. He was mouthing a sentiment advocated by the military leaders and hawkish government officials. Germany also desired an alliance in hopes that Japan could tie the British down in Southeast Asia. Besides, the Germans said, an alliance would restrain the United States.

While treaty talks with Hitler's government continued, Japan forced the impotent government of Vichy France to sign a convention allowing it to occupy northern Indochina. This gave Japan air bases for attacks against China in the south. This move angered the United States who felt that besides being imitative of Hitler's bluster, the move threatened the Burma Road over which America was sending supplies to China. The United States therefore initiated an embargo of vital materials such as scrap iron and aviation fuel to Japan. This action and the pressure exerted by pro-German elements served to throw Japan firmly into the Axis camp. On September 27, 1940 this became a reality as the Tripartite Pact was signed. American reaction was that three gangster nations were out to conquer the world.

In the first article of the Tripartite Pact, Japan recognized the leadership of Germany and Italy in the establishment of a new order in Europe. The second article accorded Japan that same right in Asia. Articles

III through VI pledged the Axis partners to assist each other for the next ten years with all the political, economic and military means each one possessed should one of them be attacked by the United States.

Early in 1941, foreign minister Matsuoka visited Germany and formally ratified the alliance. Enroute home he stopped over in Russia where a Treaty of Neutrality was signed with Stalin's government. This treaty was aimed at freeing Japan to expand southward without concern about an attack by the Soviets.

On June 22, 1941, Germany attacked Russia. A shock wave of alarm swept through Japan. She had hoped that Germany's conflict with Britain would dilute British strength in the Far East. Now, free from the threat of German invasion thanks to Hitler's latest aggression, England was more able to defend its interest in Asia. There was also concern that a quick German victory over Russia might deny Japan a share in the victory and result in German presence in the Pacific. Matsuoka, who had recently concluded the neutrality pact with the Russians, advocated an immediate attack into Siberia. Wiser heads prevailed and this attack never came off. Instead, Japan's interest was focused in a different direction: south.

Tojo's tenure as war minister was fraught with tension between Japan and the United States. As relations between the two countries deteriorated daily, Tojo began to seriously contemplate the prospect of a war with America. The United States had already placed an embargo on iron and steel and had threatened to extend the embargo to include oil if Japan persisted in its aggression. What the United States viewed as aggression, however, the Japanese considered a divine mission.

Consequently, Japan grew to realize that the oil of the East Indies was essential to offset any embargo. Therefore, attempts to negotiate with the Dutch were initiated, but to no avail. Thus plans for a military move into the East Indies were drawn up but Japan also realized that any aggression in this area would have to include the Philippines and Malaya as well. This would of course embroil Japan in a war with the United States and the British Empire.

Already, on May 3, 1941, Tojo had stated that operations against the Indies and Malaya would require bases in Thailand and Indochina. In order to ensure this he gave his consent for the occupation of the latter. On June 16, he said, "If we don't finish the job before year's end, we will have to abandon our policy of establishing the Greater East Asia Co-Prosperity Sphere."[2]

Germany's attack on Russia had left Japan with a host of options. Tojo, however, was against involvement in Russia even though Foreign Minister Matsuoka firmly advocated it. Instead, Tojo was concerned about China and the United States. What would be America's reaction to a move against the Soviets? How could Japan move simultaneously northward and to the south? Therefore, he said, the movement to the south had to take priority because Japan urgently needed the vital natural resources of that region.

At an Imperial Conference on July 2, Tojo laid down the policy to be followed. First of all, he said, the Japanese must continue to apply pressure on the Chinese nationalist regime in order to bring about its overthrow. Secondly, war preparations must be made in the event of a war against America and Great Britain. Finally, he went on, Japan had to place heavy emphasis on Indochina and Thailand.

The significant point of these recommendations was that Russia was not considered the main threat. Instead, the two western democracies were viewed as the major enemies. An immediate reaction to the conference was the reinforcement of the Kwangtung Army with an additional three hundred thousand men, bringing its strength up to seven hundred thousand.

For Japan the die was cast. The direction of her energies would be to the south.

Before the end of the month, Japan extended its protection to include the rest of Indochina. The decrepit Vichy government had no choice but to accept the *fait accompli*. Within forty-eight hours of the Japanese occupation, the United States, Holland and Great Britain embargoed all trade goods, particularly oil, and froze all Japanese overseas assets. This economic blockade was tantamount to war since without oil, Japan was doomed. The only option short of loss of face was seize their own oil supplies in the Dutch East Indies.

Tojo and the Army General Staff were irate over the harsh western reaction. The army gave Konoye until October to resolve the deadlock via diplomatic means. After that, the war machine would swing into action.

Konoye made every attempt to convince the Americans that the occupation of French Indochina was not a military operation but rather a mutually accepted agreement reached with the Vichy authorities. After a taste of Hitler's methods, the United States refused to buy that reasoning and demanded an immediate Japanese withdrawal.

Although the prime minister did not desire trouble with the United States, the economic boycott was quickly leading to an irrevocable rupture of relations between the two nations. Konoye even went so far as to propose a summit conference with President Roosevelt aimed at reaching some form of an agreement.

Tojo placed little faith in a one-on-one summit if and when it did take place. At first Roosevelt reacted favorably to the proposal but was quickly convinced by Secretary of State Cordell Hull that many prior meetings would be necessary before any such conference could actually take place. Hull was in no mood to appease the Japanese, not after the British failure of appeasement at Munich in 1938.*

The freezing of assets and the oil embargo was the last step toward the encirclement of Japan, a denial of her rightful place as the leader in Asia, and a challenge to her very existence. Therefore, she was determined to take action. At another Imperial conference on September 6, a general plan of national policy was agreed on. Its policy statement read, "For the self-defense and self-preservation of our empire, we will complete preparations for war, with

---

*Britain allowed Germany to occupy the Sudetenland in Czechoslovakia in return for assurances that Hitler had no additional territorial demands in Europe.

the first ten days of October as a tentative deadline, determined, if necessary, to wage war against the United States, Great Britain, and the Netherlands."[3]

Negotiations were to continue, but a deadline had now been set. After that deadline expired, negotiations would cease and Japan would proceed with its last alternative: war. The emperor emphasized that every effort should be made to bring about a diplomatic settlement. He then read a poem composed by his grandfather, Meiji:

All the seas, everywhere,
   are brothers one to another,
Why then do the winds and waves of strife,
   rage so violently through the world?[4]

Tojo considered the decision reached at the conference to be an Imperial decree. If no breakthrough were made by mid-October, he was ready to proceed with war.

On September 18, an assassination attempt was made on Prime Minister Konoye. Although he was unhurt, the incident left him shaken. The army pressured him to make preparations for war. Konoye in turn reminded Tojo that he was still striving to keep negotiations open with the United States. Although Tojo was all for that, he declared that the October 15 deadline must not be violated.

The navy also felt that time was running out for them. Oil was necessary to keep the ships at sea. If the navy did not act soon, it would not have the ability to act in the future as its stocks were being rapidly depleted. Lack of oil would allow the American fleet to roam freely. Admiral Nagano, chief of the Naval General staff, said, "We are growing weaker while the enemy is growing stronger. . . . When there is no hope for diplomacy and war cannot be avoided, we must be ready to make up our minds quickly."[5]

Why were the negotiations deadlocked?

China was the crux of the problem. The United States wanted Japan to withdraw completely from there. Japan refused to make such a pledge except in the most vague terms. On the other hand, Japan's minimum demands included British and American restraint from interfering with the Japanese in China and the cessation of aid by the two nations to the Chinese nationalists. The Japanese were willing to make one concession, though, not to press beyond Indochina except for China, and even to pull its military out of the former French possession after a just peace had been established in the Far East. Beyond that, Japan would not do anything for the time being. To pull completely out of China would endanger her security and open Asia to the forces of communism, not to mention a loss of face if she bowed to the demands. The Japanese considered themselves the bulwark against communism in Asia.

Tojo believed that war with the United States was inevitable. Japan and its empire, he felt, would be placed in a desperate situation unless the United States altered its stance. His country, he reasoned, was being forced to take the ultimate step to war in order to defend itself and assure its preservation. He believed that making concessions by abandoning a portion of their national policy for the sake of a peace would not placate America. The United States would simply continue to demand more and more until Japan ceased to amount to anything in the world. Japan would therefore find herself a mere puppet subject to the whim of the American government. At least war offered a fifty-fifty chance of victory. To sit back and do nothing would only lead to slow strangulation.

Tojo exerted pressure on Konoye to take the necessary steps, to accept the risk. America was rich but lacked Japan's fighting spirit, he emphasized. The United States, he went on, would keep the negotiations open since she realized that her greatest ally was delay, for in time, Japan would not be in any position to resist.

The prime minister continued to press for keeping the negotiations open with no deadline attached, but Tojo reiterated that Japan could not afford to wait much longer before taking action. On September 25 he re-emphasized to Konoye that the armed forces' chiefs would hold to the Imperial Decree of September 6 designating October 15 as the final day to reach a peaceful settlement. As far as Tojo was concerned, the specified deadline was an Imperial Degree that could only be changed by the emperor himself. Anything else would be a violation of the emperor's wish. The army, he stated, would not deviate from the agreed-upon stance. If negotiations proved fruitful, fine. If not, then the decision for war would be made at the expiration of the allotted time.

Tojo was becoming highly upset with Konoye's faintheartedness. Imperial decisions could not be made light of. To do so would be to insult the emperor. Tojo said that if Konoye was too weak to stick to a promise (the deadline date), then he should resign.

Konoye invited his war minister and the naval minister, Admiral Oikawa, to a special meeting at his residence on October 12 in order to review the diplomatic impasse with the United States. Time was growing short and the prime minister was becoming worried. Konoye said that he could not possibly agree to Japan's being engaged in an even greater war than the one in China. Hostilities against the United States had to be avoided at all cost, even if it meant the temporary evacuation of China. Tojo angrily shot back that if Japan gave in to the Americans now, she would be doomed. He went on to state that in all good conscience, he could not agree to the evacuation of China. That act would simply demoralize the military in addition to exposing the country to the dangers previously stated.

Konoye thus found himself in a bind. Recently he had asked the commander-in-chief of the Combined Fleet, Admiral Yamamoto, what he thought were the chances for naval victory in a war with Britain and the United States. The reply was disheartening. Yet, at the October 12 meeting and at another one two days later, Admiral Oikawa, the naval minister, failed to express these sentiments in the presence of Tojo.

At the October 14 cabinet meeting, the issues were once again debated. Tojo was the master debater and held center stage. Again he argued the familiar points. To continue with the stalled negotiations in Washington required great confidence in the fact that they would eventually prove successful, he said. Did the foreign minister have such confidence? Admiral

Toyoda, who had been foreign minister since the spring, said that the biggest problem still revolved around the issue of China. If Japan evacuated China, then the talks would more than likely be a success. Tojo replied that Japan would not kowtow to the American demands. The long and expensive conflict in China would have been for nothing, Manchukuo and Korea would be jeopardized, and North China exposed to communism. "Withdrawal from China meant dishonorable defeat."[6] Morale would also be crippled.

Japan had been willing to compromise, it was the United States who was not. Japan would not capitulate! Tojo forcefully repeated his statement of a few days earlier: the cabinet should resign.

Konoye's position was untenable. Tojo had seen to that. The cabinet resigned on the sixteenth.

Who was to become the next prime minister during this most crucial period? What was obviously needed was someone strong enough to deal with the critical deadlock, yet one with the ability to make decisions with authority.

Marquis Kido, Lord Privy Seal, and an intimate advisor of the emperor, took it upon himself to find just such a man. On the same day that the cabinet resigned, he summoned Tojo to his private residence and asked him some pertinent questions. Tojo made an excellent impression. He respected the Imperial wishes and, as far as Kido was concerned, that was most important. As a soldier and subject of His Majesty, Tojo would comply if the emperor himself changed the decision reached at the September 6, Imperial conference. Kido felt this to be an important prerequisite for any candidate for prime minister.

Personally he did not care for Tojo and other people were more qualified for the position. Prince Higashikuni, an uncle of the emperor, was unquestionably suited to fill the vacancy. Even Tojo favored him. Kido, however, did not wish to involve a member of the Imperial family at such a critical time. If Japan did go to war and lost, it might topple the monarchy if it were concluded that the emperor was responsible for the catastrophe. Therefore, he recommended Tojo, whom he knew to be loyal to the throne, in addition to being a hard-working and dedicated subject. At such a time, on the brink of war, Tojo seemed the logical choice.

Thus, for better or worse, the army was given its opportunity to run the country. If the nation went under, it would be the army's responsibility.

After the council of elder statesmen (the Jushin) accepted Kido's recommendation, Tojo was summoned to the palace on October 17. There, to his great surprise, the bemedalled general was personally given the Imperial mandate to form a cabinet by the emperor himself. After a brief period in which to ponder this mandate, the fifty-seven-year-old Tojo accepted the post with great humility.

The foreign press quickly judged Tojo's appointment a sure sign that war was imminent. Throughout Japan newspapers responded in a positive vein:

> Tojo's aim was to build Japan into a high degree defense state. . . . Japan was imperiled by the encirclement of hostile powers and General Tojo, the soldier-premier, was a logical

choice at such a time.[7]

Tojo was not an adventurer. Many people had numerous adjectives to describe the new prime minister. Americans equated him with Hitler. Yet he was not the founder of a political party. As a soldier he was authoritarian and believed in his country's divine mission. He accepted the use of force if necessary in order to fulfill that mission. But he was not a political tyrant in the same vein as his Axis allies. Yes, Tojo did have control, but that control could only be exercised as far as the emperor allowed. The best description of Tojo would be that of a nationalist who believed in his sense of duty to his emperor and country.

After leaving the imperial residence, he first went to the shrine dedicated to Emperor Meiji where he offered homage, then to the Admiral Togo memorial before winding up at the Yasukuni Shrine dedicated to Japan's war dead.

On October 18 he was promoted to full general, a rank befitting his exalted political position. On the same day he began to staff his cabinet, choosing people whom he felt would provide the backbone for the times ahead. However, he took over the Home and War Ministries himself in order to ensure direct control of internal security and military affairs.

That same afternoon Tojo went on the radio and outlined his "determination to contribute to world peace by settling the China affair and establishing the Greater East Asia Co-Prosperity Sphere."[8]

The emperor then acted to rescind the September 6 Imperial Decree. No emperor had ever before rescinded a decision reached at an Imperial conference.

Tojo was ordered to "go to a blank paper."⁹

In America, the State Department viewed the new Japanese cabinet as possibly being workable. Even the Catholic Maryknoll Missionary, Bishop James Walsh, the superior general of the Maryknoll Order and later a prisoner in communist China until his release in 1970, reinforced the evaluation in a specially prepared memorandum for Hull, the American secretary of state, dated October 18, 1941.

Bishop Walsh considered the cabinet to be a product of the peace faction in the Japanese government. The American ambassador to Japan, Joseph Grew, noted to Washington that because Tojo was a general he could exert a far greater influence and control over the extremists and the ultranationalists within the army itself. U.S. Army intelligence, however, differed from the State Department view and concluded that the Tojo government was anti-foreign and highly nationalistic and would probably reflect Axis leanings.

Tojo was now faced with the decision as to which way to go. The two military services pressured him for an early decision. The Navy chief of staff, Admiral Nagano, said that the situation was urgent for the navy was consuming four hundred tons of oil per hour.

The army chief of staff added that at the present time the army had enough strength to seize Southeast Asia, but if Japan hesitated, her offensive ability would wane until gradually, by mid-1942, the United States would possess too much strength. This would deny Japan the ability to strike. Japan would then be completely at the mercy of the United States.

During the trials following the war, one of the crimes attributed to Tojo was the deliberate planning for war from the moment he became prime minister. The evidence, however, does not support this charge. War came not because it was desired, it came because there was no other option. On October 30, a staff study was presented to Tojo showing that the cost of proceeding without war was prohibitive in terms of Japan's longterm power position. Though desiring the success of the negotiations, Tojo would not compromise on any point detrimental to Japan.

On the last day of October the new prime minister called his cabinet together and discussed three options that the government could take. The first was to suspend all war preparations. The second was to decide on going to war at once. The last was to continue preparations with a firm decision to embark on war in early December while still conducting diplomatic negotiations.

The cabinet meetings were characterized by heated debates. Tojo recommended acceptance of the third option. Although it sparked heated exchanges Tojo said, "We are going to undertake both diplomacy and military operations simultaneously; so you must give your word that if diplomacy is successful, we will give up going to war."[10] As a compromise, however, November 30 was established as the deadline for the negotiations. If by that time no breakthrough had occurred, Japan would go to war.

On November 1 another important Imperial conference was held. There Tojo reiterated to the emperor that negotiations were getting nowhere and it appeared that war would begin soon. The emperor told him to use all means to break the stalemate in Washington. In response to that, Saburo Kurusu, an experienced foreign officer, was flown to Washington to assist Ambassador Nomura with the negotiations. Tojo told the emperor during another audience that he felt that Japan would be going to war shortly after the thirtieth of that month. It was after this conference that Admiral Yamamoto ordered the navy to take up battle stations for a surprise attack on the American fleet at Pearl Harbor.

Most evidence points to the fact that Tojo knew nothing of the Pearl Harbor plan until just about that very time. Two weeks later at a session of the Diet, Tojo broadcast a short but poignant speech to the nation. In it he said that Japan was at the crossroads of her long existence. She was not to be frustrated by other powers, he went on, in the successful conclusion of the China incident via an economic blockade.

Meanwhile the negotiations in Washington continued. Tojo's foreign minister, Togo, attempted to convince the United States that Japan was negotiating in good faith. But the Japanese diplomatic code, the Purple Code, had been broken, thanks to the genius of Col. William Friedman. This code showed the Americans that the Japanese were, in fact, negotiating in bad faith. Outwardly the Americans might see the Japanese attempting to negotiate but by reading the broken code, they were able to see the Japanese making preparations for war.

When Kurusu and Nomura presented Japan's final offer to Cordell Hull on November 20, the American secretary of state looked upon it with cynicism. The Japanese offered to withdraw from southern Indochina but in return wanted Hull's assurances of free access to the raw materials and oil of the Dutch East Indies along with the elimination of the United States embargo. The proposal stated that troops would remain in north Indochina and in China itself until the successful conclusion of the China incident.

The United States reply to the offer was received six days later. It reiterated America's insistence that Japan should not only withdraw from Indochina, but from all of China as well including Manchuria. If Japan would consent to these conditions, then the embargo would be lifted. To the Japanese this represented nothing more than an ultimatum. It appeared to them as if America was out for one thing, the strangulation of Japan, nothing less. They felt that the Americans were unwilling to bargain in good faith. The fact that Manchuria was even mentioned particularly irritated them since they considered that they had strong claims to that area.

Tojo claimed that Hull's note showed that the Americans were insincere and not willing to seek reconciliation.

On that same day an extraordinary session of the Diet was held. The emperor, dressed in full regalia, was seated upon his raised dais. Respectfully Tojo approached the throne whereupon the emperor read him a brief message which formally empowered the prime minister with the right to pass whatever laws were necessary to meet the crisis. The emperor had sanctioned Tojo's dictatorship. Tojo then spoke out angrily accusing the Americans, British, Dutch and the Chinese.

As far as the Japanese were concerned they were

fighting in China to secure their own future. From that vantage point the United States and others were viewed as adversaries. It was therefore a matter of life and death. The Americans were not sympathetic to the needs of the Japanese. Unquestionably, America, with its harsh exclusion policies,* looked upon the Japanese as an inferior race. Thus, from the Japanese perspective, war was not only necessary, it was mandatory.

For over a year Adm. Isoruku Yamamoto, the commander-in-chief of the Combined Fleet, had nurtured a plan for a surprise attack against the United States naval base at Pearl Harbor in Hawaii. Yamamoto had watched the turbulent world situation and lamented the progression of events. He harbored great misgivings when Tojo was appointed war minister in the second Konoye cabinet. The admiral believed Tojo to be a volatile man and a champion of the Tripartite Pact. The perceptive Yamamoto sensed what was in the making and was convinced that, "A war between Japan and the United States would be a major calamity for the world, and for Japan it would mean, after several years of war already, acquiring yet another powerful enemy—an extremely perilous matter for the nation."[11]

Fearing the prospect of war, Konoye invited Yamamoto to a meeting in order to discuss the navy's prospects in the event Japan became embroiled in a

---

*The United States placed harsh restrictions on Japanese immigration to America.

war with the United States and Great Britain. Yamamoto informed Konoye that, "If we are told to fight regardless of consequences, we can run wild for six months or a year but after that I have utterly no confidence. I hope you will try to avoid war with America."[12] Unfortunately, not all of the naval leaders shared this view. Yamamoto attempted to sway them by telling them what he had told Konoye.

Yamamoto thus found himself on the horns of a dilemma. He disagreed with the direction his country was taking and lamented watching it rush forward into a war he was certain could not be won. But, as commander-in-chief of the Combined Fleet he was not in a position to disassociate himself from any war that might break out. The political stance of his country was not his responsibility since he held firmly to the old navy tradition that only those in the Naval Ministry should become involved in politics. The balance of the navy should submit to the naval minister's authority. Thus, while outwardly gearing the navy for war, inwardly he grieved over the situation.

Tirelessly, Yamamoto began to prepare. Keenly aware of Japan's unique position he knew that he had to formulate a plan through which Japan could hope for ultimate victory. The United States was simply too great a country with a vast economic base and enormous industrial potential. After all, he had been there as naval attache and had viewed the industrial capacity. Japan's only hope, he reasoned, was some extraordinary measure which might end the war quickly. It was in this frame of mind that the Pearl Harbor operation was conceived.

If the navy could destroy the American warships as quickly as possible, if the Japanese fleet could strike a severe blow against the American Pacific Fleet and cripple its strength, perhaps Japan could achieve a negotiated peace.

When the plan was first presented for review, almost all ranking naval commanders disapproved of it. Most naval strategists over the years had accepted what came to be known as the orthodox plan. This called for a Japanese attack on the Philippines. The attack would prompt a response from America and cause her to dispatch its fleet to aid the besieged islands. Meanwhile, from positions of strength in the Marianas, the Japanese fleet could whittle the American fleet down in a campaign of attrition so that when the decisive sea battle (a la Tsushima Bay) occurred, the Japanese fleet could apply the coup de grâce on the remnants of the enemy. Of course this plan was hypothetical but over the years, during the course of war games, became the time-honored program for victory. Therefore, any deviation from this plan was considered unwise.

The Hawaiian operation, however, had been germinating in Yamamoto's fertile mind since sometime in 1940. He harbored grave doubts about the orthodox plan, concluding that an attritional battle was too risky. Japan could ill afford to lose too much, not with the American potential. However, an attack by aircraft against the American fleet would be less costly.

Early in 1941, around the time he was putting the Pearl Harbor plan into definite shape, Yamamoto began to give serious thought to retirement. After all, most commanders-in-chief only served for two years and in August that period would be up. Though he frequently stated that he looked forward to retirement, he knew that if he were called on to remain at the helm he would gladly do so.

The Pearl Harbor plan was officially drawn up and submitted on January 7, 1941 in a nine-page document. Yamamoto opened the document with the following statement:

> No one can make any definite predictions concerning the international situation, but it seems obvious that the time has come for the navy, and the Combined Fleet in particular, to go ahead with arming and training itself, and possibly drawing up a plan of operations on the assumption that war with America and England cannot be avoided.[13]

The formulated plan was based on Yamamoto's realization that victory had to be achieved the first day.

Ironically, just around this time, the American ambassador to Japan, Joseph Grew, cabled the State Department stating that the Peruvian minister had managed to find out from various sources that if trouble developed between the United States and Japan, the latter would make a surprise attack against the naval base at Pearl Harbor. Grew went on to say that his informant considered the rumors fantastic yet considered it important enough to inform his American colleague. This message was transmitted on January 20, 1941 but was disregarded in America. However, an interesting point is that the plan to attack

Pearl Harbor had not been accepted by anyone in Japan at that early date. In fact, Yamamoto was a voice crying out in the wilderness. The United States State Department seems to have accepted the news of the strike in the same frame of mind as most Japanese who had heard of it from Yamamoto. Impossible! Can never be! and numerous other statements of similar quality.

On the other hand, Yamamoto was convinced that the plan would succeed. As proof of this he pointed to the November 1940 attack by the Royal Navy against the Italian Fleet at Taranto. Of this attack he said, "If the British could sink ships at such a depth,* why not repeat this type of attack on a much bigger scale."[14]

Yamamoto's proposal now made the rounds of those naval units that would have to implement it in the event of hostilities. Furious debates commenced for and against the plan. The opposition included some very powerful personalities. Rear Admiral Fukodome, head of the First Division of the Naval General Staff, Captain Tomioko, head of the First Section, and Commander Miyo, air staff officer, were among the most vocal. One of the prime reasons for their opposition was the belief that the plan constituted simply too much of a gamble. What guarantee was there that the American Fleet would even be in Pearl Harbor at the time of the attack? they asked.

Those favoring the plan clung to Yamamoto's main

---

*Taranto harbor was forty-two feet deep, Pearl Harbor forty-five feet. It was considered too shallow for the use of torpedo bombs. Admiral Cunningham's Mediterranean Fleet proved otherwise.

argument that if war was indeed unavoidable, the only possible method of attack would be to destroy the enemy's predominance at the outset, thereby placing him at a disadvantage. Foremost among the champions of the plan was Commander Genda, head of the air units aboard the carriers.

Meanwhile, as the debate between the naval commanders continued, the Japanese army cast fate to the wind and took advantage of the situation in Europe by announcing in July that it had negotiated an agreement with the Vichy French government to form a joint protectorate of Indochina. This proved to be the straw that broke the camel's back as far as the United States was concerned. They countered the move by freezing all Japanese assets in the United States and halting all shipments of oil. Great Britain and Holland soon followed suit. The oil embargo was critical since Japan was entirely dependent on imports of this vital resource. It was an ultimatum. Japan's oil reserve was good for at least eighteen months, but after that, there would be nothing. Japan therefore had to agree to humiliate itself by kowtowing to the United States or it had to fight.

The navy was taken aback by the army's action in Indochina since not once did the two branches of the service consult regarding the potential consequences of the move.

In August, the navy began to prepare itself for the inevitable. War games were conducted concentrating on dry runs of the proposed Hawaiian operation. The air unit from the carrier *Akagi* travelled to Kagoshima Bay for training exercises. The interesting point about this harbor was its close resemblance to Pearl Harbor.

A fiery young aviator, Lt. Commander Mitsuo Fuchida, was posted to the carrier as its flight commander at the time. It was Fuchida whom Yamamoto had selected to lead the attack force against the American naval base.

Various problems had to be overcome before the operation could in fact be performed. Foremost among them was the monumental opposition to the plan. This negativism had to be surmounted.

Of a more technical nature was the problem of the depth of Pearl Harbor. Could torpedoes be used similar to the ones utilized by the British at Taranto? Torpedoes that could not sink beyond the forty-five-foot depth of Pearl Harbor. Yamamoto discovered that fitting them with wooden fins would keep the torpedoes from sinking too deep. That, he knew, would become one of the keys to success. The other would be whether or not the operation could be conducted in secrecy. Again Yamamoto was sure it could be and, despite all opposition, stuck to his guns.

Two strong voices against the Pearl Harbor strike were Admirals Kusaka and Onishi, chiefs-of-staff of the First and Eleventh Air Fleets respectively. During fleet war games that simulated a mock attack on the United States, the Japanese fleet suffered (on paper) a great deal of damage. Kusaka, who greatly respected Yamamoto, felt that the plan was too risky. Seeing the results of the war games he concluded that the Hawaiian attack was like "putting one's head in the lion's mouth."[15]

Another voice added to the opposition was that of Adm. Chiuchi Nagumo, commander of the Aircraft Carrier Fleet itself. The opposition decided to write to

Yamamoto requesting that the entire concept be abandoned. After reading the document in silence Yamamoto remarked that as long as he was commander-in-chief, the operation would proceed. Emphasizing that the action was vital, he resented having it called a gamble.

Through careful persuasion both Onishi's and Kusaka's resistance was broken. Yamamoto personally placed his hand on Kusaka's shoulder and explained that the Pearl Harbor raid had become an article of faith to him and that he would be most grateful if Kusaka would stop resisting. The latter finally came around and, along with Onishi, pledged to help prepare for the operation.

At an Imperial conference on September 6, the decision to go to war with the United States was reached. Exactly a month later, five days of map maneuvers were held on board Yamamoto's flagship, the aim being to acquaint various levels of commanders with the Hawaiian operation. Yamamoto reiterated his absolute intent on carrying it through if war became inevitable. He was so optimistic regarding the plan's success that even the chief of the Naval General Staff, Admiral Nagano, dropped his opposition. After that most of the others followed suit, following a dramatic scene during which Yamamoto threatened to resign if the plan were not adopted.

Outwardly Yamamoto gave the impression of a man chomping at the bit for action and intent on proving his plan feasible. Inwardly, however, he was deeply depressed over the whole turn in political affairs. More now than ever he did not want war. It was ironic that the man who, through the sheer power of his will, overcame all opposition to the Hawaiian plan was in fact the most reluctant of all.

Yamamoto was an enigma. He prepared for a war he did not want. He preached restraint while preparing one of the most infamous acts in history. He cautioned against underestimating his opponents yet his future plans were based on the premise that once beaten by a surprise attack, the enemy would simply turn over and give up. On September 18, during a speech in Tokyo to some old Nagaoka schoolmates, Yamamoto gave numerous reasons why Japan should avoid war with the United States:

> It is a mistake to regard Americans as luxury loving and weak. I can tell you that they are full of spirit, adventure, fight and justice. Their thinking is scientific and well advanced. Lindbergh's solo flight across the Atlantic was an act characteristic of Americans—adventuresome but scientifically based. Remember that American industry is much more developed than ours, and unlike us—they have the oil they want. Japan cannot vanquish the United States. Therefore we should not fight the United States.[16]

Prime Minister Konoye immediately branded Yamamoto as pro-American and pro-British upon hearing these words.

Yet Yamamoto continued to plan. A major question was the best route for the fleet to travel in order to ensure the vital secrecy of the operation. There were three possibilities: a northern route, a central Pacific route or a southern one. Yamamoto felt that the northern route held the greatest prospect for success because the warships could then travel the little-used waters of the northern Pacific. However, there were problems with that route. The seas would be rougher, making refuelling next to impossible. But even with that problem the chance of success would be better since the prospect of the fleet's detection would be greatly lessened.

Meanwhile, information regarding the disposition of the American fleet was being received from spies. Yamamoto wanted every scrap of information regarding the enemy's habits. U.S. intelligence units were able to monitor the transmissions of these secret agents but paid little attention to them because, as part of Yamamoto's cover plan, Japanese spies were relaying information from Portland, Oregon, San Francisco, Manila, Panama and San Diego. Pearl Harbor was but one of the many areas the Japanese were watching.

On October 17, the winds of war were blowing stormier as Japan once again underwent a change in government. Army Gen. Hideki Tojo became the new prime minister.

During the first week in November the Hawaiian operation finally became a fully accepted plan. Flight Commander Genda, who was supervising the flight training, could not inform his pilots that the target was Pearl Harbor. Genda unrolled a large map of Oahu containing a detail of Pearl Harbor. A cold chill was felt among the pilots as they heard the outline of the plan for the first time. On the fifth Yamamoto issued Operation Order No. 1, the Hawaiian operation. Eight days later he held a conference at Iwakuni

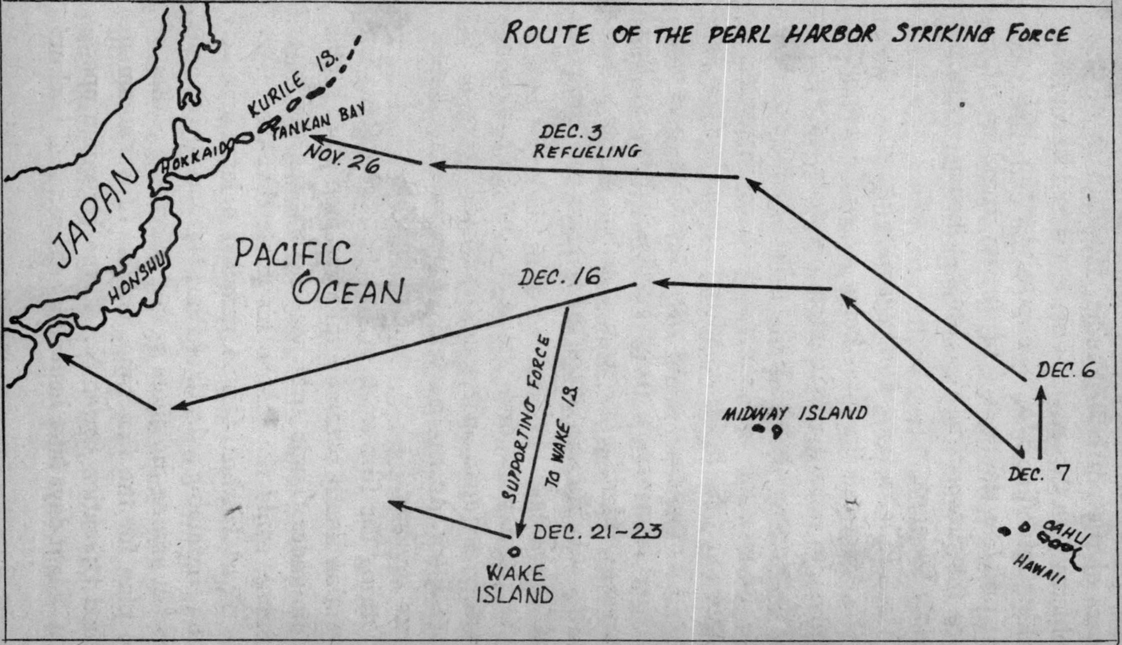

ROUTE OF THE PEARL HARBOR STRIKING FORCE

Naval Air Base to which all commanders-in-chief, chiefs-of-staff and senior staff officers were summoned for a detailed explanation and discussion of the operational order.

There, Yamamoto informed the gathering that it had been formally decided that December 8 (December 7 Hawaiian time) would be the official date for the opening of hostilities. He then went on to describe the route to be taken by the attacking force and to announce that the fleet would assemble by November 22 at Tankan Bay (Hitokappu Bay) in the Kuriles. The striking power of the fleet was invested in six carriers, *Kaga*, *Akagi*, *Hiryu*, *Soryu*, *Zuikaku* and *Shokaku*. Between them the carriers carried 423 planes. The fleet would sortie on November 26 and take the northern route to the vicinity of the Hawaiian Islands. He further announced that a force of 27 submarines were to be part of the force. This force would be largely composed of the large I-Class submarines but would also include a number of midget submarines as well. The latter were to slip into Pearl Harbor just before dawn and remain submerged while the aircraft attacked. They would then make a surprise attack after sunrise when the Americans thought they were safe. That portion of the plan was later modified to allow the midget submarines to attack at will.

The commander-in-chief then cautioned everyone that negotiations were still in progress and if an agreement were reached, the fleet, upon receipt of appropriate orders, would return to base. At this, Admiral Nagumo, commander of the task force, responded that it would be demoralizing to turn back a force already in motion. Yamamoto retorted that if there was anyone present unable to obey an order when given, he should resign then and there. All remained silent.

Feverish days of activity now engulfed the fleet. All inflammables, personal possessions and unnecessary items were taken ashore to be replaced by weapons, ammunition and food supplies. The planes too were prepared. Rudders and flaps on aircraft were treated with a special antifreeze grease to protect them from the anticipated cold of the northern Pacific.

On November 17, Admiral Yamamoto sailed into Ariake Bay aboard the *Nagato*. As soon as the anchor was dropped, the commander-in-chief headed for the *Akagi* where he wished Nagumo well and addressed the assembled officers and crew:

> Although we hope to achieve surprise, everyone should be prepared for terrific American resistance in this operation. Japan has faced many worthy opponents in her glorious history—Mongols, Chinese, Russians—but in this operation we will meet the strongest and most resourceful opponent of all.
>
> You may have to fight your way in to the target.
>
> It is the custom of Bushido to select an equal or stronger opponent. On this score you have nothing to complain about—the American Navy is a good match for the Japanese Navy.[17]

After the traditional meal, the parties toasted the success of the mission and parted company.

On November 22, the last ship in the fleet dropped anchor at the rendezvous point. Besides the carriers, Nagumo's fleet was supported by the battleships *Hiei* and *Kirishima*, heavy cruisers *Tone* and *Chikuma*, light cruiser *Abukuma* and nine of the navy's newest and most modern destroyers. A force of submarines would precede the fleet to Hawaii and take station there to act as watchdogs and report any unusual American activity. Some of these submarines carried midget submarines affixed to their decks. These two-man units would be launched prior to Nagumo's attack and make their way to Pearl Harbor where it was hoped their presence during the air raid would add to the confusion.

When all the ships were assembled at the rendezvous point, Nagumo called a meeting of his entire staff to review the latest intelligence reports and discuss the operation. The Japanese were relying on the fact that the American fleet routinely returned to Pearl Harbor to spend the weekend. Over a period of months, Japanese spies in Hawaii had been monitoring the American anchorage and reporting this fact. Since the date fixed for the attack, December 7, was a Sunday, the Japanese expected to catch the Americans napping.

However, the American carriers held to no such routine and tracking them was much more difficult. Since one of the primary objectives of the entire plan was the destruction of the American carriers, most of the discussion at the staff meeting centered around these ships.

In November of 1941 the Americans had a total of six fleet carriers available. Commitments to the protection of the Atlantic seaways demanded the attention of *Wasp*, *Hornet* and *Yorktown*. Consequently, the Pacific fleet was left with the *Enterprise*, *Saratoga* and *Lexington*. These three ships were the prize the Japanese sought. Unbeknownst to them, however, even as they made their final preparations, *Saratoga* was on the West Coast of the United States undergoing a refit. Therefore, the Pacific fleet was reduced to just the *Enterprise* and *Lexington*.

The lack of hard intelligence regarding the whereabouts of these two ships caused Nagumo a great deal of concern. It was entirely possible that the Japanese strike force could run into one or both of the American carriers en route to Hawaii. In addition, what if the *Lexington* and *Enterprise* were not present at Pearl Harbor at the time of the attack? Should Nagumo proceed anyway? Genda and Fuchida argued that yes, the attack should go ahead just as planned. Nagumo agreed. Had he any way of knowing it, he might have been consoled by the fact that the American intelligence community had lost track of all six Japanese carriers.

The following day, November 23, the captains of all the ships involved were summoned to a meeting aboard the *Akagi*. Heretofore, only the captains of the carriers were privy to the objective of the last few months of frantic training. When the other captains were informed of their operational plan, their reactions ranged from enthusiasm to outright glee.

Nagumo then announced that as soon as each wave returned to the carriers, it would be rearmed for another attack. This was the desire of Genda and Fuchida. In addition, he ordered each captain to institute tight security measures. There was to be no shore leave and no garbage was to be thrown overboard from that moment on. Finally, the operational plan itself was revealed.

The attack would go forth in two waves. The first, consisting of fifty horizontal bombers, forty torpedo bombers, fifty-four dive bombers and forty-five fighters would be launched one half hour before the second. After the fighters secured the air lanes over Hawaii and strafed the airfields, the dive bombers would concentrate on the airfields at Hickham, Wheeler, Kaneohe and Ford Island leaving the high-level and torpedo bombers free to deal with the American fleet. Thirty minutes later, the second wave, minus torpedo bombers since these should have achieved their goal during the first wave, would send its fifty-four horizontal bombers and thirty-six fighters against the airfields while eighty-one dive bombers concentrated on finishing off what was left of the American fleet. The heavy emphasis on the airfields indicates that the Japanese feared American retaliation and were taking no chances.

On November 26, in the middle of a driving snowstorm, the First Air Fleet weighed anchor and sailed off on its historic voyage.

Meanwhile, at Pearl Harbor, all was serene. The military forces had received word that war might come at any time and to prepare accordingly. However, this merely constituted a warning, not an alert since negotiations in Washington were still underway. Furthermore, the United States had concluded that any potential Japanese attack would be aimed at the Philippines. Few thought the Japanese navy capable of carrying out a full-scale attack on Pearl Harbor.

In one sense, the Americans were correct. Even as Nagumo sailed toward Hawaii, another strong Japanese fleet was moving steadily toward the Philippines intent on launching its own attack in that area immediately upon receipt of word that the Pearl Harbor attack was a success.

Nagumo's fears sailed with him. The night before sailing was a sleepless one as he attempted to come to grips with the awesome magnitude of his undertaking. Then there were the ever-present dangers. Would the American fleet, including the carriers, be present at the time of attack? Or could it be lying in ambush waiting for Nagumo to sail into a trap. One of his ships might be torpedoed by a lurking submarine. Then of course, there was the danger of discovery. It had already been decided to sink any ship they might run across, but what if that ship managed to get off a radio warning before it could be sunk? Based on the earlier war games, the Japanese navy expected to lose half of Nagumo's fleet. Which of the ships were now on their final voyage? Nagumo's fears would not abate until he was en route home.

Fortunately for the Japanese, the weather was with them. Overcast skies reduced the possibility of discovery to a minimum while the selected route itself, normally buffeted by storms during that time of year, remained relatively calm. A good omen. The selection of the northern route had been the proper one.

On December 2, Yamamoto sent the signal "Climb Mt. Niitaka." The brief message told Nagumo that any hope of reaching a negotiated settlement with the United States was past. The attack could proceed on schedule. Two days later, the First Air Fleet left the cold water of the north Pacific and began the final run in toward Pearl Harbor.

On the morning of December 7, 1941, Admiral Kimmel's United States Pacific Fleet swung peacefully at anchor under a warm, sunny sky. Present that morning at Pearl Harbor were eight battleships, the pride of the fleet. Seven of them were moored on the east side of Ford Island, rocking lazily at anchor. Two heavy cruisers, six light cruisers, twenty-nine destroyers, five submarines and a host of other shipping cluttered the harbor. *Lexington* and *Enterprise*, the two aircraft carriers, were absent from their berths. The former was off ferrying a squadron of planes for Midway while *Enterprise* performed a similar service for the Marine detachment on Wake Island.

If Kimmel was not anticipating trouble, neither was his army counterpart, General Short. The general's primary concern was, since the time of the war warning, sabotage. To guard against this the planes at Hickham and Wheeler Fields had been bunched together making it easier for sentries to protect them. There they sat like ducks on a pond.

That Sunday morning, Honolulu went about its business just as if nothing was amiss. Ship's crews prepared to embark for liberty, sailors and citizens alike prepared to attend church services and the radio stations played many of the popular tunes of the day. On board Nagumo's ships these radio transmissions were monitored. The Japanese knew that the Americans suspected nothing.

Fuchida and Nagumo had risen early. At 5:00 a.m. the flight commander reported to the admiral's cabin.

Nagumo wished him well and went on to say that he was confident of the mission's success. The two then proceeded to the briefing room where the *Akagi*'s pilots eagerly awaited the final briefing. Nagumo addressed them briefly and wished them all well.

The minesweeper *Condor* was the first American ship to make contact with the Japanese forces that fateful Sunday. At 0342 the ship's lookouts sighted the periscope of a midget submarine a few miles from the harbor entrance. The *Condor* immediately notified the destroyer *Ward* which was on patrol nearby. A two-hour search by the destroyer proved fruitless.

At 0633 another sighting was made by a patrolling aircraft. A periscope was seen in the wake of the repair ship *Antares* which was approaching the entrance to the harbor. In anticipation of *Antares*' arrival the anti-submarine net across the mouth of the harbor had been left open. The captain of the midget submarine was hoping to sneak into the harbor in *Antares*' wake before the net could be swung closed again.

Ward attacked with gunfire and depth charges. All evidence indicated that the midget submarine had been sunk. *Ward* dutifully notified Pearl Harbor of the attack on the submarine and proceeded to search for others. Thanks to an inexcusable series of delays, however, Admiral Kimmel did not receive the *Ward*'s report for over half an hour.

At 5:30, the cruisers *Chikuma* and *Tone* launched their scout planes. It had been decided that these planes would fly over the target area to determine if the American fleet was actually present. Naturally this increased the risk of compromising secrecy but

Nagumo was prepared to accept the risk.

Then the "Z" flag flown by Admiral Togo at Tsushima broke out at *Akagi*'s masthead to the shouts of banzai from those members of the fleet within viewing range.

Twenty minutes later, at a point approximately 220 miles north of Oahu, the six mighty carriers turned into the wind and prepared to launch their planes. Rough seas delayed the launching for almost half an hour but shortly thereafter, the entire strike was airborne. Then the fleet turned south once more to hover 180 miles north of the target area.

Meanwhile, thanks to their ability to read the Japanese code, American codebreakers in Washington had intercepted a diplomatic message whose wording could only mean that war was imminent. General Marshall, the American chief of staff, immediately sent off a telegram to Honolulu suggesting that a Japanese attack against American installations could be expected at any time. Unfortunately, the message went out over regular Western Union channels instead of the military one. The telegram was received in Hawaii at approximately 7:30 that morning but, since it was not marked urgent, the Western Union operator simply pigeon-holed it for routine delivery.

On the west side of Ford Island the American battleships were moored like sitting ducks. *California* was berthed alone, a few hundred yards ahead of the remaining ships on "Battleship Row." The oiler *Neosho* was stationed between the *California* and the remaining battleships. *Oklahoma* and *Maryland* were side by side next in line, the latter between *Oklahoma* and the shore. *Tennessee* was directly astern of the

Maryland with *West Virginia* alongside. Next in line was the *Arizona*, directly behind *Tennessee*. The supply ship *Vestal* was tied up alongside the battleship. At the rear of the line sat the *Nevada*, all alone. The eighth battleship, *Pennsylvania*, was in drydock undergoing refit. Groups of cruisers, destroyers and support ships littered the rest of the anchorage in small flotillas or individually.

At 0745 Fuchida, flying with the high level bombers, entered the air space above Oahu and gave the message "To-To-To" over his transmitter. This was the signal for attack. As the Japanese squadrons dove on their respective targets, Fuchida grabbed his microphone and shouted the words "Tora, Tora, Tora," the signal indicating the enemy had been surprised.

Aboard *Akagi*, Nagumo waited nervously on the bridge with his staff in total silence. The die had been cast. There was no turning back. All sorts of fears coursed through his brain, and the staff could see that their commander was deeply troubled. Then came the signal from Fuchida. Surprise was complete. The American fleet was present. Nagumo and Kusaka turned toward each other, smiled and wordlessly shook hands.

At Pearl Harbor itself the arrival of the Japanese air armada attracted little notice initially. American radar had discovered the flight but since a flight of American B-17s from the mainland was due to arrive that very same morning, the radar reports were ignored. Others felt that the planes were simply Army planes out for maneuvers. Once the bombs began to fall and the rising sun insignia on the wings was noted, reality struck home. The call went out: Air Raid—Pearl Harbor. This is no drill.

Over the airfields the Zeros peeled off and began their strafing runs. At Wheeler and Hickham the Japanese pilots could hardly believe their eyes as the American planes sat idly in bunches waiting to be destroyed. The Japanese fighter pilots had a field day with the sitting ducks. American aircraft were quickly destroyed where they sat and not one rose in opposition. Dive bombers followed the Zeros in and quickly destroyed hangars, runways and installations. The American Air Forces were wiped out in the space of a few minutes.

Thanks to a misinterpretation of Fuchida's attack signal, the torpedo planes and high-level bombers attacked simultaneously. Many of the ship's crews were already ashore enjoying their weekend. Others lolled in their bunks. Some of the ships were undergoing repairs. Only a handful were ready to raise steam at short notice. The Japanese attack had indeed taken everyone by surprise. Those few anti-aircraft batteries that were quickly manned found no shortage of targets as the enemy planes attacked from all angles. Unfortunately, because of the total lack of readiness of the fleet, the initial response to the attack was feeble at best.

One of the first ships hit was the *West Virginia*. Moored outboard of the *Tennessee*, two torpedoes slammed into her side within a few moments of the opening of the attack. Five more torpedoes followed and the ship took on a heavy list. For good measure enemy planes dropped two bombs on the crippled battleship. Thanks to the initiative of a handful of the ship's officers, counterflooding was quickly begun and, instead of capsizing, the *West Virginia* settled slowly to the bottom on an even keel. In contrast to some of her sister ships, *West Virginia*'s casualties were relatively light. Two officers and 103 men perished in the attack. Among the fatalities was the ship's skipper, Capt. Mervin Bennion, who was killed by shrapnel from a bomb that exploded on the *Tennessee*.

The *West Virginia* protected *Tennessee* from being struck by torpedoes but not from bombs. Two hit the battleship early in the battle causing some damage, but not enough to place the ship in jeopardy. Most of the *Tennessee*'s damage resulted from debris falling on board or from burning oil on the surface of the water. *Tennessee* listed five men killed in the action.

Directly astern of the *Tennessee*, the *Arizona* suffered the most. A torpedo missed the *Vestal* and blasted a hole in the ship's port side. Then the first bomb hit. The missile penetrated the main deck and exploded in the forward magazine. In seconds the entire forward part of the ship was an inferno with flames shooting over five hundred feet in the air. Throughout the fleet and ashore, horrified spectators watched. Adm. Isaac Kidd and Capt. Van Valkenburgh were killed instantly. Seven more bombs hit in rapid succession. The first of these went right down the stack.

Poor *Arizona* was overwhelmed so quickly that her crew never had a chance. Forty-seven officers and 1,056 men perished in a few horrible moments. With her back broken and on fire throughout, *Arizona* settled quickly to the bottom of the harbor.

Oklahoma took three torpedoes quickly. With her port side torn open, the battleship took on a heavy list. As the ship began to roll, two more torpedoes smashed into her, hastening the rate of list. In less than twenty minutes the battleship had turned turtle, trapping many of her crew below decks. Twenty officers and 395 men perished on the *Oklahoma*.

The *Oklahoma*'s position protected the *Maryland* from torpedoes. But it did not make the latter immune from bombs. Nevertheless, *Maryland* got off relatively light. Two bombs managed to hit her, but one of these was a relatively light one. Two officers and two men died on the *Maryland*.

At the head of "Battleship Row" the *California* was alone and vulnerable. For some reason the battleship's crew was slow to react to the attack. Watertight doors were left open and guns were not manned quickly. Consequently, when two torpedoes slammed into her side, the *California* began to flood quickly. A quick recovery by her shocked crew prevented the ship from capsizing. All efforts to get underway proved futile. *California*'s casualties were six officers and ninety-two men dead.

At the opposite end of the row the *Nevada* took a torpedo that tore a forty-five-foot gash in her bow. The battleship's crew managed to put up such a hail of anti-aircraft fire that the Japanese pilots began to give her a wide berth. Despite two bomb hits and the torpedo damage, *Nevada* began to get underway just before 0830. Bravely the huge ship began to slowly move down the channel amidst cheers from shore and the rest of the ships in the harbor. The *Nevada* moving out past all the carnage was a morale-raising sight.

The *Nevada* gave a respite to other ships in the fleet. Japanese pilots, intent on sinking the lumbering Goliath in midchannel, turned their attention from other targets and concentrated on the *Nevada*. The ship's sortie was short-lived, however. Fearing that the *Nevada* might be sunk in the harbor mouth, thereby bottling up the rest of the fleet, Admiral Furlong, senior officer in the area, ordered the battleship to beach herself and avoid being sunk.

Although "Battleship Row" attracted the bulk of the Japanese attention, other ships in the harbor came in for their share. The old battleship, *Utah*, which had been converted to a target ship, was hit by two torpedoes and capsized in short order. The Japanese flight commanders had been cautioned to avoid this all but worthless target, but the *Utah* proved too large and tempting for some of the pilots to resist.

Cruisers *Raleigh* and *Helena* were also hit by torpedoes. Quick action by both crews prevented the ships from sinking. Minelayer *Oglala*, moored alongside *Helena*, was not as fortunate. Her side was caved in by the explosion of the torpedo that hit the cruiser and the *Oglala* capsized almost immediately.

In the dry dock area damage was heavy. *Pennsylvania*, flagship of the Pacific Fleet, occupied the dock with the destroyers *Cassin* and *Downes*. All Japanese bombs missed the *Pennsylvania* but the luckless *Cassin* was blasted. The destroyer rolled over onto the *Downes*. Destroyer *Shaw* nearly had her bow blown off in a spectacular explosion that could be seen all over Oahu.

One by one the smaller ships began leaving the

harbor. Destroyers, as soon as they could raise enough steam, moved individually or in pairs out of the harbor. Cruiser *St. Louis* was one of the earliest ships to leave.

By 1000 the attack was over and the last Japanese plane was winging its way toward the carriers. In their wake they left a shattered American fleet and over twenty-two hundred Americans dead, not to mention the hundreds more wounded. *Arizona* and *Oklahoma* were total losses. The explosion of the *Arizona* seemed to take the heart out of the American command. The rest of the battleships were laid up for months undergoing refit and modernization. Eventually, the six survivors exacted retribution from the Japanese: at Leyte Gulf, throughout the Pacific Islands, and elsewhere.

In addition to the damage to the fleet, 98 American planes had been destroyed and another 106 damaged. The cost to the Japanese was incredibly low: 5 torpedo bombers, 15 dive bombers and 9 fighters failed to return to their mother ships. Most of these were from the second wave.

Even as the first wave began to arrive back aboard the carriers, the reports of widespread destruction were received with elation. Nagumo, however, could not get the American carriers out of his mind. Where were they? Surely by that time they must know of the attack. Were they poised to retaliate? It was a threat that could not be ignored.

Nevertheless, Fuchida and Genda urged another attack. They were sure that Pearl Harbor's defenses were shattered. Even though the U.S. fleet was battered, the installations at Pearl Harbor remained relatively unharmed. Genda and Fuchida insisted that a second attack be directed against the oil-storage tanks, repair facilities and other vital installations. The American fleet was certainly in no position to resist, they argued. The two aviators were, of course, entirely correct.

Nagumo was torn between the prospect of inflicting more damage or withdrawing with his fleet intact. Surely he had achieved his goal. The American fleet was critically wounded. Why risk the fleet?

Back in Japan, aboard the *Nagato*, Yamamoto was hearing those very same arguments. As the reports filtered in from the Pearl Harbor strike force, he listened in silence. In his heart he knew that Nagumo would elect to withdraw and admitted as much to his staff. However, he refused to interfere, preferring instead to leave the decision to the man on the spot.

Nagumo has been severely criticized for not sanctioning a follow-up attack. Had the port facilities at Pearl Harbor been destroyed, the American fleet would have had to retreat all the way to the West Coast of America. However, it must be remembered too that Nagumo felt out of his realm as regards aviation. Until the enormity of what he had accomplished sunk in, he remained uncomfortable. Consequently, he was vulnerable to outside influence. His chief of staff, Kusaka, whose opinion Nagumo valued, turned a deaf ear to Fuchida's and Genda's pleas. After listening to their arguments, he suggested that the fleet set a course for home. Relieved that someone else had eased the burden for him, Nagumo simply said, "Please do."

During the first two waves the Japanese had concentrated on the airfields and the ships in the harbors. The naval air station on Ford Island was also heavily damaged. In their zeal to sink the American ships, Japanese pilots at left Pearl Harbor's repair facilities relatively unscathed. Even more important, the huge fuel-storage tanks so vital to the fleet had been left undamaged. It was these targets that Genda and Fuchida had in mind when they urged another strike.

The attack on Pearl Harbor gave Yamamoto just what he was seeking, an early edge. Victory upon victory followed and in a few months the Japanese had conquered an area far greater than even they expected. But Yamamoto had said that an attack on the Americans would awaken a sleeping giant. How prophetic were those words.

With newer, more modern ships, and from a secure and relatively undamaged base at Pearl Harbor, the Americans began the slow, steady advance toward Japan.

NOTES

1. Courtney Browne, *Tojo: The Last Banzai*, p. 64
2. Alvin Coox, *Tojo*, p. 72
3. John Toland, *The Rising Sun*, p. 96
4. *Ibid*, p. 99
5. David Bergamini, *Japan's Imperial Conspiracy*, p. 735
6. Coox, *op. cit.*, p. 91
7. Browne, *op. cit.*, p. 101
8. *Ibid*, p. 104
9. Toland, *op. cit.*, p. 118
10. Coox, *op. cit.*, p. 147
11. Hiroyuki Agawa, *The Reluctant Admiral*, p. 186
12. Sir Michael Carver, ed., *The War Lords*, p. 397
13. Agawa, *op. cit.*, p. 220
14. Potter, *op. cit.*, p. 53
15. Agawa, *op. cit.*, p. 229
16. Carver, *op. cit.*, p. 397
17. Gordon Prange, *At Dawn We Slept*, p. 344

BIBLIOGRAPHY

1. Agawa, Hiroyuki. *The Reluctant Admiral.*
   Kodasha International Ltd., Tokyo, 1979.
2. Barker, A. J. *Pearl Harbor.*
   Ballantine Books, New York, 1969.
3. Bergamini, David. *Japan's Imperial Conspiracy.*
   Pocket Books, New York, 1971.
4. Browne, Courtney. *Tojo: The Last Banzai.*
   Holt, Rinehart & Winston, New York, 1967.
5. Carver, Sir Michael, ed. *The War Lords.*
   Little, Brown & Co., Boston, 1976.
6. Coox, Alvin. *Tojo.*
   Ballantine Books, New York, 1975.
7. Costello, John. *The Pacific War.*
   Rawson, Wade Publishers, New York, 1981.
8. Dull, Paul. *The Imperial Japanese Navy.*
   Naval Inst. Press, Annapolis, 1978.
9. Kimmel, Husband E. *Admiral Kimmel's Story.*
   Henry Regnery Co., Chicago, 1955.
10. Lewin, Ronald. *The American Magic.*
    Farrar Straus Giroux, New York, 1982.
11. Lord, Walter. *Day of Infamy.*
    Henry Holt & Co., New York, 1957.

12. Morgenstern, George. *Pearl Harbor.*
    Devin-Adair Co., New York, 1947.
13. Morison, Samuel E. *History of U.S. Naval Operations in World War II*
    Vol. III: The Rising Sun in the Pacific.
    Little Brown & Co., Boston, 1975.
14. Okumiya, Masatake and Horikoshi, Jiro. *Zero.*
    Ballantine Books, New York, 1956.
15. Pfannes, Charles and Salamone, Victor. *The Great Commanders of World War II*
    Volume IV: The Japanese.
    Zebra Books, New York, 1982.
16. Potter, John D. *Yamamoto.*
    Viking Press, New York, 1965.
17. Prange, Gordon. *At Dawn We Slept.*
    McGraw-Hill, New York, 1981.
18. Theobold, Robert. *The Final Secret of Pearl Harbor.* Devin-Adair Co., New York, 1954.
19. Toland, John. *The Rising Sun.*
    Random House, New York, 1970.
20. Toland, John. *Infamy.*
    Doubleday & Co., New York, 1982.
21. Willmott, H. P. *Empires in the Balance.*
    Naval Inst. Press, Annapolis, 1982.

CHAPTER TWO

THE BATTLE OF THE CORAL SEA

The Battle of the Coral Sea marked the halt to the vast unbroken string of Japanese victories. It also introduced a new type of naval warfare, one where the ships of both sides did not visually confront one another. To the Americans the Coral Sea was a shot in the arm, a badly needed victory when all other war news was bad. Actually, the effect of the battle on the Japanese was minimal, a minor setback from which they could easily recover. In fact, the Japanese left the Coral Sea having inflicted more damage on the Americans than they suffered. Both sides, however, considered the battle a victory, the Japanese a tactical one, the Americans a strategic success.

From the time of Pearl Harbor the Japanese series of victories had caused great dismay to the military leaders in Washington. The tidal wave seemed unstoppable. In southeast Asia, the Central and South Pacific, the story was the same. With the lone exception of Lt. Colonel "Jimmy" Doolittle's bombing raid on Tokyo on April 18, 1942, the news contained stories of one Allied disaster after another.

By April, 1942, the long-dreamed-of empire coveted by the Japanese finally seemed within reach. The ferocity and almost superhuman power of the Japanese onslaught took the world completely by surprise.

Like an octopus, Japanese tentacles extended over thousands of miles of former British, French, Dutch and American possessions. The Greater East Asia Co-Prosperity Sphere had become a reality. Even more remarkable was the relatively low cost of these conquests. The largest ship sunk thus far had been a destroyer, a mere hundred planes were lost, and the loss of troops was light.

Where the Japanese were euphoric, the same could not be said of the Allies. The great losses had punctured the notion of white supremacy forever. Asia would never be the same again. Her rapid victories gave the Japanese a feeling of invincibility. So sure were they of victory that they were convinced that whatever venture the military planned, ultimate victory was a foregone conclusion.

Even though success followed success, Admiral Yamamoto nevertheless remained troubled. Japan held the Dutch East Indies with its oil and natural resources. What should her next move be? The lightning conquests left his planners agog. Without any long-range strategic goals, a difference of opinion divided the naval leaders. Should Japan remain on the offensive or should she hold fast and consolidate her conquests? If she remained on the offensive, where would she go? India? Australia? Hawaii?

Yamamoto realized that the fleet had to prepare for future operations. His chief of staff had suggested consideration of any of the aforementioned objectives with special emphasis on Hawaii. Again the same reasons for the initial attack on these islands surfaced. The natural resources of the United States were so numerous that if Japan did not engage the American fleet in a decisive battle near Hawaii once and for all, the enemy would recover quickly and counterattack the Imperial Navy.

Other officers, however, were studying the possibility of an assault against the British aimed at achieving supremacy in the Indian ocean with the possibility of an eventual link-up with the advancing German army in the Middle East.

While Yamamoto's staff debated over India or Hawaii, the Naval General Staff planners in Tokyo were thinking along the lines of an operation toward Australia. They rightly observed that Australia would probably be used as the springboard of any future Allied counteroffensive. Australia, they felt, must either be conquered or cut off and neutralized. The army, however, vetoed any invasion of Australia since there were not enough troops available, thanks to the demands of the war in China. Actually, the army preferred an attack on Russia who at that time was embroiled in a life and death struggle with Nazi Germany. The Japanese anticipated a German victory and were eager to participate in it by stabbing their ancient foe in the back.

Yamamoto's primary concern, though, was to bring the war to a successful conclusion as swiftly as possible. He knew that the amazing string of victories could not continue for more than a year. Which then, of the three areas under consideration, would have the best chance of ensuring peace?

While the debate continued, Yamamoto decided to send Nagumo's carriers into the Indian Ocean to deal a decisive blow against the Royal Navy. Though this action proved to be another victorious campaign for the Imperial Navy, it was, like Pearl Harbor, a hit-and-run operation. There was no follow-up attack. In fact, this was the last time the Japanese navy ranged west of Singapore.

Finally, after two months of debate, Yamamoto made his decision. He resolved to seize Midway Island, believing it useful as an advance base for air and submarine patrols. More important, it would, he felt, draw out the American fleet for a decisive naval battle. The admiral was convinced that this operation would accomplish what Pearl Harbor had left undone. With a conclusive victory, the American will to fight would be undermined and they would be forced to sue for a negotiated peace on Japanese terms.

On April 2, Yamamoto's planning officer, Commander Watanable, travelled to Tokyo to represent Plan AF, a joint Midway and Aleutian operation, to the Naval General Staff. The plan was overwhelmingly rejected as too risky. The General Staff's view was that Midway was much too far away and would prove difficult to keep supplied. As an alternative, they proposed an attack on New Caledonia, Fiji and Samoa in order to isolate Australia from the United States. That, they claimed, would serve to draw out the American fleet even more so than a Midway operation.

Watanable telephoned Yamamoto informing him of the Naval General Staff's opinion. Yamamoto replied that Watanable should tell them that it would be Midway or nothing. The Naval General Staff quickly gave their consent, basing their decision on the fact that Yamamoto was considered the greatest admiral since the great Togo. If he felt that strongly about

Midway, the plan should proceed.

The commander-in-chief wanted the assault to take place during the first week of June when the moon was full. The Naval General Staff, however, requested more time to prepare and suggested instead that the operation take place at the end of the month. Yamamoto would not hear of this delay, reasoning that the longer it was delayed, the more chance of success was reduced. Though they gave in, the Naval General Staff did not have complete confidence in the plan.

During the debate, neither of the two key admirals slated to command the operation, Nagumo and Kondo, were asked their opinion. The primary reason for this was that they were busy elsewhere with other operations. Unfortunately, this was a great mistake since both of these commanders could have added their own insights, particularly about the readiness of the fleet. After all, the fleet had seen nonstop action since late November and it was exhausted and in urgent need of a rest. When this was presented to Yamamoto as a reason for delaying the Midway operation, again he would not hear of it. The commander-in-chief seemed obsessed by the fear that the United States would soon counterattack.

At this point Doolittle's bombers raided Tokyo. The daring attack caused Yamamoto's Midway plan to be accepted quickly and with little opposition.

Meanwhile, as the preparations for the Midway attack proceeded, Yamamoto initiated plans for an operation aimed at advancing the Japanese position in the South Pacific via the seizure of the southern New Guinean port of Port Moresby. Three Japanese carriers, the small *Shoho* and the big fleet carriers

Zuikaku and *Shokaku*, were dispatched to the Coral Sea as protection for the Port Moresby invasion fleet.

The American commander-in-chief in the Pacific, Adm. Chester Nimitz, meanwhile received information from his intelligence officers, Rochefort and Layton, that if the Japanese desired to control eastern New Guinea, they would have to seize Port Moresby which sat on the Coral Sea.

By the middle of the month additional radio intercepts convinced Nimitz that Port Moresby was the next Japanese target. Intelligence reports indicated that the Japanese transports would enter the Coral Sea escorted by the *Shoho* and that two large carriers would be included in the strike force. It was further learned that Tulagi and Guadalcanal in the Solomon Islands would be taken at the same time. Nimitz knew that the Japanese had to be stopped.

Nimitz ordered Rear Adm. Frank Jack Fletcher's *Yorktown* force, then operating in the South Pacific, to retire to Tongatabu for replenishment and then rendezvous with Rear Adm. Aubrey Fitch's force, centered around the carrier *Lexington*. The combined force would then move into the Coral Sea and attempt to foil the Japanese advance.

The Japanese considered the isolation of Australia essential. They knew that that country could serve as the springboard for an Allied counteroffensive. Recognizing this, the Japanese navy proposed an invasion plan for the northern part of Australia, the conquest of New Caledonia, the Fiji Islands and Samoa. These conquests, they believed, would give them mastery of the Coral Sea and successfully isolate Australia from the United States. The Japanese army did not care for the navy plan; they saw it as an overextension of their forces. The army was already overburdened, particularly since the war in China was consuming much of their resources. An invasion of Australia was, for the time being, totally out of the question. A compromise was finally reached but it entailed a scaling down of the naval objectives.

Meanwhile, as the army-navy debate continued, the Japanese extended their control to northern New Guinea and immediately began construction of air bases from which they could attack Port Moresby by air. In the interim, on March 11, Premier Tojo delivered a threatening message to Australia. He said:

> Australia must learn that defense against our invincible forces is impossible in view of her sparse population, the vastness of her territories and her geographical position which makes her so distant from both the United States and Britain.[1]

The following day Tojo reiterated the message to a special meeting of the Japanese parliament. At this point Australian Prime Minister Curtin made a special appeal for help:

> This is a warning. Australia is the last Allied bastion between the West Coast of America and Japan. If she succumbs, the entire American continent will be wide open to invasion. Some people think that the Japanese will bypass Australia and that they will be intercepted and destroyed in the Indies. But, I tell you that

saving Australia will be the same as saving the western side of the United States. However that may be, Australia will, if invaded, fight to the last man and will apply the scorched earth policy.[2]

Curtin's appeal was not necessary for the United States already recognized the importance of Australia. It would not be abandoned. Adm. Ernest King, chief of Naval Operations, had already ordered Nimitz to keep open the lines of communication between Hawaii and Australia. To ensure this King called for continued action in the Pacific. He wanted the carriers to hit the Japanese with nuisance raids. Hit them, run and hit them again. Though intended to keep the Japanese off balance, in reality the effort hardly bothered the enemy. In fact, the raids had been likened to a flea on a dog's back, annoying but hardly lethal.

The Allies did fear for Australia. The Japanese were convinced that the Americans would use Australia for a jumping-off point from which to launch a counteroffensive. That fear was reinforced when Gen. Douglas MacArthur escaped from the encirclement of the Philippines and reached Australia on the seventeenth of March.

This new fear compelled the Japanese naval leaders to push forward a plan for dealing with Australia. Since the army refused to support an invasion, the only hope of eliminating the threat was by blockading any possible attempt to reinforce the Land Down Under. In order to accomplish this blockade, the capture of Port Moresby, New Caledonia, Fiji and Samoa was deemed vital.

After the psychological impact of the Doolittle raid, the Japanese formulated their next moves. The first step would be the occupation of Tulagi in the southern Solomons, where a naval air base would be established from which the northern part of the Coral Sea could be controlled. Following this would be an invasion of Port Moresby in order to bring northern Australia within range of Japanese aircraft. This operation was known as Operation MO. Next the Japanese would attack Midway and occupy strong points in the Aleutian Islands with the objective of precipitating a decisive naval battle. Finally, once these operations were complete, Fiji and Samoa would be taken, thereby severing the life line between Australia and America.

There was no doubt on the Japanese part that victory was certain. Puffed up by their recent conquests they were supremely confident that victory would come easily. This confidence, however, caused them to underestimate the potential of enemy reaction and resulted in them trimming to a minimum the number of ships available for Operation MO and allocate them to the more elaborate and vital attack on Midway scheduled for June.

The final plan for MO was as follows. One landing group made up of the Twenty-second Destroyer Division, one troop ship, one seaplane transport and a handful of support vessels were assigned to seize Tulagi. Another group of two light cruisers, three gunboats and a minelayer would proceed to the Louisade Archipelago and establish an air base there. A landing group comprising eleven troop ships supported by a light cruiser and sixth Destroyer Flotilla was responsible for seizing the airstrips in the area around Port Moresby. Covering this invasion force was the light carrier *Shoho*, four battle cruisers, a destroyer and one tanker. To guard the approaches to Port Moresby a striking force of two large carriers, six destroyers and one tanker was assembled. This force would intervene if the enemy appeared on the scene. Finally, a force of seven submarines was assigned to patrol the area while the Twenty-fifth Air Group from Rabaul provided long-range reconnaissance and bombing patrols.

Each force had its own separate commander. Rear Admiral Shima had the Tulagi group; the Louisade operation force was commanded by Rear Admiral Marushige. The Port Moresby force was led by Rear Admiral Kajioka and the covering force was commanded by Rear Admiral Goto. The commander of the all important striking force was Rear Admiral Takagi. The entire operation was the responsibility of Vice Admiral Inoue.

Though each arm seemed separate, they all had one ultimate objective; the capture of Port Moresby. The striking force was ordered to move east of the Solomons and from that point approach Port Moresby through the Coral Sea, while Goto's force sailed south through the Jomard Passage. Thus, if an American fleet appeared in the Coral Sea it would find itself caught between the converging Japanese forces and easily be destroyed. Since the Japanese anticipated the presence of only one American carrier, they remained highly optimistic.

On April 16, the *Lexington* and her escorts sailed from Pearl Harbor and headed for the South Pacific.

Five days later, Admiral Fitch received instructions to rendezvous with Fletcher's force 250 miles southwest of Espiritu Santo in the New Hebrides. On May 4, British Adm. J.G. Crace's cruiser force consisting of the *Australia* (flagship), *Hobart* and the American *Chicago* was ordered into the Coral Sea.

Crace's force was designated Task Force 44. Although he had the ability to read the Japanese transmissions, the big question facing Nimitz was whether or not his forces were strong enough to defeat the Japanese.

On May 1, Admiral Inoue sat aboard his flagship, the cruiser *Kashima*, and proudly reviewed his plan, supremely confident that his superior forces could readily destroy any opposition put forth by the Americans. Each of his scattered formations was by now moving toward its destination from Truk and Rabaul. Inoue was certain of victory.

After fueling from the tanker *Neosho*, Fletcher's Task Force 17 moved toward the Coral Sea. The American commander sailed westward knowing full well that any Japanese move toward Port Moresby would have to traverse the Jomard Passage.

On the evening of the third, Fletcher was handed a report from General MacArthur's headquarters stating that a reconnaissance plane from Australia had sighted two Japanese transports landing troops on Tulagi Island. Fletcher was shocked into immediate action. The presence of enemy forces in that area could not be ignored. He therefore decided to mount an attack against Tulagi. Bad weather, however,

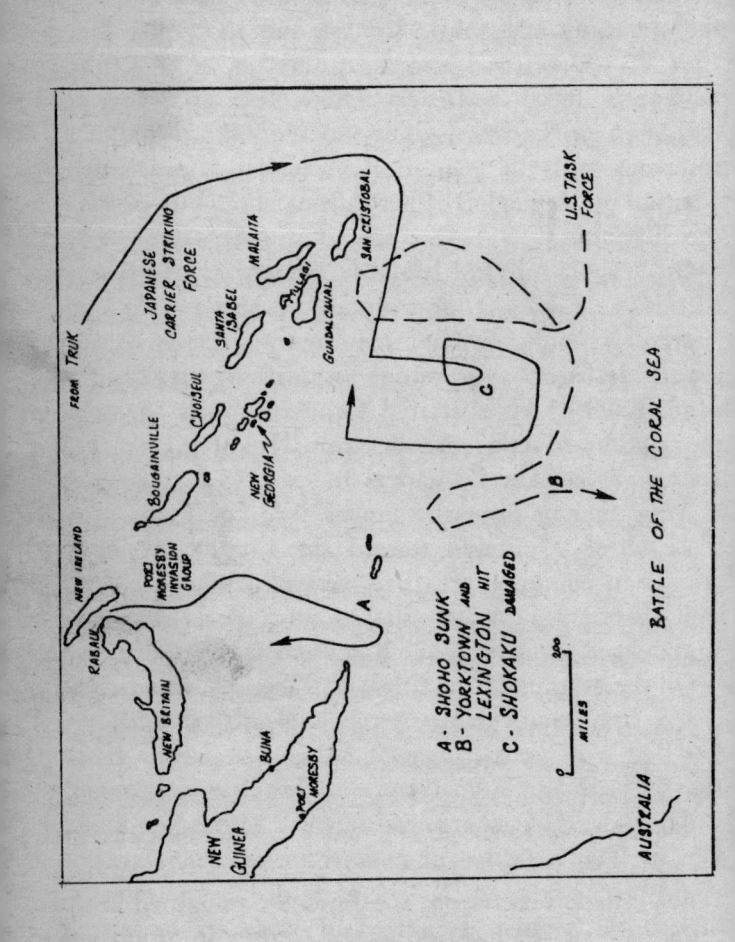

BATTLE OF THE CORAL SEA

hindered the American force as it approached the Solomons. Fletcher needed to be within one hundred miles of Tulagi before his planes could be launched.

Since it was absolutely essential that each American task force maintain radio silence, Fitch, in Task Force 11, was not apprised of Fletcher's plan. Not until the morning of the fourth did he find out what Fletcher was up to, but since he was too far away there was nothing the *Lexington* group could do to support Task Force 17.

At 0630 on the fourth the *Yorktown* turned into the wind and launched her first wave of aircraft. At 0815 the Japanese on Tulagi were surprised by bombs dropped by the American planes. By 0930 all aircraft had landed safely back aboard the *Yorktown*. Though the attack accomplished very little, the overenthusiastic pilots exaggerated the raid into a great triumph. Fletcher wisely discounted the extravagant claims of his pilots and decided to send another wave against the target. The Americans made the same approach but when they arrived over the target they found the Japanese waiting for them. Nevertheless, the attack was a success, but once more the returning pilots exaggerated their claims. Fletcher decided to launch one final attack. This too resulted in negligible damage to the Japanese positions.

The primary result of Fletcher's attack was to alert the Japanese to the presence of an American aircraft carrier operating in the Coral Sea. Very little damage was inflicted. However, the Japanese remained in the dark about the location of the *Lexington* group and assumed that only the *Yorktown* was in the vicinity.

Fletcher dutifully informed Nimitz of his action

and the results. Nimitz said, "The Tulagi Operation was certainly disappointing in terms of ammunition expended to results obtained."[3] After a day of action Fletcher proceeded southeast for a time, then altered course to the south in accordance with the original plan for the rendezvous with Task Force 11.

On May 5, at 0815 the two American groups linked up. For the rest of the day, as both forces marked time, Fletcher took the opportunity to refuel his ships from the *Neosho*. By early evening, having completed the refueling operation, Fletcher, who by virtue of his seniority had assumed overall command, ordered a change in course to the northwest. He remained convinced that the Japanese would enter the Coral Sea via the Jomard Passage.

Having left Rabaul already, the Japanese fleet was approaching the Louisades while the striking force maneuvered east of the Solomons. The jaws of the gigantic pincer were closing.

On the morning of the sixth there was a general feeling of expectation aboard the American ships. Fletcher decided to form a single task force with himself in overall command and Fitch responsible for air operations. Unfortunately, it was some time before Fletcher informed Fitch of this. Meanwhile the Japanese striking force was by now west of Rennell Island, northwest of the American position. Takagi had decided to head south in search of his opponent.

The Americans also spent the morning of the sixth searching for the Japanese. All efforts were unsuccessful but at 1100 a Japanese reconnaissance float plane spotted the American force and reported its coordinates to Rabaul. Due to an incredible delay in transmission, Takagi did not become aware of the sighting until the next day. This spared the Americans a potential disaster.

At noon of the same day Fletcher received a message from MacArthur's command stating that the latter's reconnaissance planes had located a light carrier approximately sixty miles south of Bougainville and had made an unsuccessful attack. This enemy carrier was, of course, the *Shoho*.

Admiral Inoue was apprehensive. He knew now that two of his forces had been discovered and that an American naval force was in the Coral Sea. Yet he remained confident of success and issued order for the MO operation to proceed as scheduled.

Later in the afternoon Fletcher received a more specific picture of the disposition of the Japanese forces. The exact location of the striking force, however, remained a mystery. At the same time, Takagi was experiencing difficulty. Unable to locate his adversary, he ordered his forces to alter course and refuel. Ironically, at that very time he was a mere seventy miles from Fletcher's ships.

In ignorance of just how close the Japanese striking force was, Fletcher decided to move further southeastward in order to be in a more favorable position to strike at the landing force the next morning. The day ended in anticipation. One historian of the battle described May 6 as one "spent in a game of blind man's bluff based on information supplied by third parties."[4]

As darkness descended on the Coral Sea both forces rested fitfully knowing that the events of the next day would be crucial.

At 0200 the following morning the Japanese striking force commander altered course southward. At 0600 reconnaissance planes took off in search of the American fleet. Then, at 0736 the *Zuikaku*'s radio received an electrifying message reporting the presence of one carrier and one cruiser. What the errant pilot had discovered, however, was the *Neosho* and the destroyer *Sims*. Nevertheless, the Japanese immediately began to prepare an attack.

By 0810 the Japanese planes were in the air and winging their way toward the hapless American ships. When the planes reached the area they immediately recognized the error in the sighting report but it was too late to do anything about it. The two ships put up a gallant defense but the result was a foregone conclusion. Both were simply overwhelmed. *Sims* was sent to the bottom and *Neosho* was left a blazing wreck. She drifted helplessly for four days until located by the destroyer *Henley*. After rescuing what remained of the crew, *Henley* sank the tanker.

The sacrifice of the *Neosho* and *Sims* had not been in vain. Their death provided a diversion which allowed Fletcher to operate unopposed.

At 0625 the American ships were 115 miles south of Rossel Island, the most eastern point of the Louisades. Fletcher was now ideally situated to inflict damage on any ships moving through the Jomard Passage. At 0645 he decided to split his forces, directing Crace of Task Force 44 to move westward and block the southern exit of the passage. Fletcher himself would take the carriers in search of the Japanese carriers.

At 0810 a Japanese reconnaissance plane sighted

Crace's small force. The British admiral knew what to expect. It wasn't, however, until 1400 that his radar picked up Japanese aircraft heading his way. These planes were land-based aircraft from Rabaul.

Crace's cruisers put up a wall of anti-aircraft fire, so thick that the enemy planes experienced enormous difficulty when they attempted to press home the attack. More planes arrived and dropped torpedoes which the cruisers managed to evade, albeit with difficulty. Further waves followed and each time Crace's ships avoided the bombs and torpedoes. Crace's handling of his ships was magnificent. Not only had the force avoided being hit but it remained in an ideal position astride the Jomard Passage. In addition, because the Japanese elected to concentrate on Crace's force, Fletcher was left undisturbed in his search for the Japanese carriers.

Fletcher was not idle. Task Force 17 launched continual searches for the enemy fleet. Fletcher waited impatiently for a sighting report. At 0815 the message he wanted to hear was received: Two aircraft carriers and four heavy cruisers 10 degrees 3 minutes N, 152 degrees 27 minutes E. Anxious to hit the enemy before his own force was sighted, Fletcher wasted no time in issuing the order to launch planes.

At 0925 the *Lexington* started launching aircraft, followed a few minutes later by the *Yorktown*. Then the bad news was received. A later sighting confirmed that the target was not two aircraft carriers but two cruisers and two destroyers. It was not the main Japanese force after all. Ironically, Fletcher's force made the same mistakes in identification as the Japanese, who were precisely at that time attacking the

Neosho and *Sims*.

Admiral Inoue, however, was distressed by the turn of events. The presence of Crace's force caused him to temporarily reverse the course of the landing force until the threat could be eliminated.

Meanwhile, a reconnaissance plane from the *Lexington* located Goto's fleet containing the light carrier *Shoho*. Acting on that report, Task Force 17's planes altered course toward the position of this latest sighting. When they arrived on the scene the Americans wasted no time in attacking. The *Shoho* was overwhelmed in a few minutes. At least thirteen bombs and seven torpedoes slammed into the helpless flattop. Fletcher rejoiced when he monitored the radio message, "Scrub one flattop." Nevertheless he continued to harbor a fear since the larger enemy carriers had still not been located. In addition, by that time the report of the attack on the *Sims* and *Neosho* had come in and dampened the admiral's momentary elation.

Inoue was shaken by the loss of the *Shoho* and the continued presence of Crace's ships in the Jomard Passage. The American success was something he had not anticipated and it rattled him. As far as he was concerned the entire MO operation was in jeopardy unless the American threat could be eliminated. That task would be up to Takagi.

Admiral Takagi too was rankled over the news of the *Shoho*'s demise. He knew now that his adversary had more than the reported one carrier. The time lost attacking the *Neosho* and *Sims* distressed him immensely. When his planes returned, Takagi ordered them immediately refuelled and prepared for another attack. There was a distinct hazard in this, however, for the hour was late and meant night flying.

The Japanese pilots took off a short while later and headed toward the last known position of the American force. Meanwhile, the weather began to deteriorate and the sky began to darken. By the time the Japanese planes reached the calculated point of attack, their prey was not to be found. Although the flight leader ordered a search, the poor visibility and weather conditions made the task virtually impossible. Consequently, the despondent Japanese turned back to their ships.

In the fading light the Japanese pilots searched for their ships but many of them ran into problems. One attempted to land on what he thought to be his own carrier but was in fact the *Yorktown*. One can only imagine the amazement of the pilot, who had recently jettisoned his torpedoes and bombs to conserve fuel, when he found himself about to land on the very ship he had set out to destroy. At the last instant he realized his mistake, quickly opened the plane's throttle to maximum and made a hasty retreat. Twenty minutes later the scenario was repeated by other Japanese planes. By the time the Japanese pilots did locate their own fleet, losses were heavy. Of the twenty-seven planes that had taken off before nightfall, only six landed intact. The balance had either been lost at sea or damaged to one degree or another.

As the seventh closed, Fletcher and Takagi remained eager for battle, but both remained unaware of each other's position. The fog of war was at its thickest. Both commanders, however, looked forward to the next day when each felt the climax of the battle would be reached.

During the night the Japanese striking force moved north. Before sunrise reconnaissance aircraft were sent off to search a broad area. At 0833 the first contact with Task Force 17 was made. The battle was on.

Fletcher had also sent off reconnaissance flights. At 0833 the *Lexington*'s radio operators intercepted the Japanese sighting report. Fletcher now knew that he had been located. Five minutes later came word from one of the American search planes giving the location of the Japanese fleet. Fletcher ordered his carriers to turn into the wind and launch planes.

Though the Japanese had launched their planes first it was the Americans who got in the first blow. Sighting the *Shokaku* the U.S. pilots went to work. The enemy combat air patrol intercepted the attackers and a wild dogfight ensued. Nevertheless, two American bombs struck home on the *Shokaku*, one on the starboard side, the other on the stern. A few miles away was the *Zuikaku* but at the time of the attack this carrier was sheltering under the safety of a convenient rain squall and remained undiscovered. By the time the American attack was over, the *Shokaku* had taken three bomb hits, 180 members of the crew were killed and a further 40 badly injured. But the *Zuikaku* remained unscathed.

While the Americans were hitting the Japanese, the latter's pilots were approaching Task Force 17. At 1100 they arrived over the American carriers. Both the *Lexington* and *Yorktown* were easily visible since the sky was clear over the American position.

The Japanese dove on the American carriers. A

heavy screen of anti-aircraft fire caused many of the attackers to take notice. One of the Japanese flight leaders commented:

> Never in all my years in combat have I even imagined a battle like that! When we attacked the enemy carriers we ran into a virtual wall of anti-aircraft fire, the carriers and their supporting ships blackened the sky with exploding shells and tracers. It seemed impossible that we could survive our bombing and torpedo runs through such incredible defenses. Our Zeros and enemy Wildcats spun, dove and climbed in the midst of our formations. Burning and shattered planes of both sides plunged from the skies. Amidst this fantastic "rainfall" of anti-aircraft and spinning planes I dove almost to the water's surface and sent my torpedoes into the *Saratoga*-type carrier. I had to fly directly above the waves to escape the enemy shells and tracers. In fact, when I turned away from the carrier, I was so low that I almost struck the bow of the ship, for I was flying below the level of the flight deck. I could see the crewmen on the ship staring at my plane as it rushed by. I don't know that I could ever go through such horrible moments again.[5]

Capt. Frederick Sherman maneuvered the *Lexington* skillfully, avoiding the bombs and combing the torpedo wakes. But there were simply too many of the enemy, pressing home their attack tenaciously. At 1120 the "Lady Lex's" luck ran out. A torpedo slammed into the port side forward. A few seconds later another one struck the same side near the bridge. The huge ship was seriously hurt. The *Yorktown* managed to avoid the torpedoes aimed at her, thanks to the brilliant efforts of her captain.

The American fighter planes were so preoccupied with chasing the torpedo planes away and were thus close to sea level that they failed to notice the flight of enemy dive bombers circling overhead. Even if they had noticed them there were too few American planes and they were too low to make any difference.

The Japanese dive bombers dove for the attack. At 1120, just as the *Lexington* was reeling from her twin torpedo hits, the *Yorktown* took a bomb that penetrated four decks and started fires below decks. Fortunately none of her vital areas were affected and the ship's maneuverability and speed were unharmed. Once more Captain Buckmaster's brilliant seamanship paid off. The *Yorktown* sustained no further damage.

It was not the same story with the *Lexington*. The great ship seemed to be a magnet drawing the bulk of the Japanese attackers in her direction. At 1125 a bomb struck the carrier on the port bow. This was followed immediately by another on the superstructure. Three more near misses caved in the ship's side and she began to take water. The *Lexington* was seriously hurt. Nevertheless, she continued to make twenty-five knots and her maneuverability seemed unimpaired. By 1140 the Japanese attack was over and the Americans began to lick their wounds.

At 1200 the fires on board the *Yorktown* were declared out and she was able to launch planes. Half an hour later, the *Lexington*'s fires were also declared extinguished and she too was able to resume aerial operations. Then, at 1247, a tremendous explosion shook the *Lexington*. The Japanese bombs had ruptured the ship's aviation fuel lines and fumes from the leaking petrol had penetrated many areas of the ship. These fumes were ignited by a spark from a generator and the resulting explosion racked the ship stem to stern.

As the *Lexington* burned with a great pall of smoke over her, Captain Sherman was eventually forced to call a halt to air operations, an hour after the explosion. Any planes in the air would have to use the *Yorktown*. Despite her damage, however, the *Lexington* continued to maintain speed.

Lexington's fire and damage control parties fought valiantly against the fires raging throughout the ship but it was an uphill battle. Two hours after the first explosion, another one destroyed the ship's boiler room vent system. This forced Captain Sherman to order an abandonment of that section as thick black smoke penetrated the boiler rooms, choking everyone there. Consequently, the mighty ship's speed began to drop as no one remained to man the boilers.

The *Lexington* was clearly in her death throes. Despite all efforts on the part of her crew, the fires continued to rage. At 1515 Captain Sherman ordered all wounded evacuated via lifeboat but the balance of the crew continued to struggle against the fires.

At 1630, the *Lexington* came to a stop. Half an hour later Admiral Fitch managed to convince Captain Sherman that the struggle was useless and that he should abandon ship. At 1707 the order was given. Fletcher ordered Admiral Kinkaid's escort force to move in and rescue the survivors.

Kinkaid quickly ordered the cruisers *Minneapolis* and *New Orleans* and the destroyers *Anderson*, *Hammann* and *Morris* to begin rescue operations. Not one of the crew members who were forced to abandon the *Lexington* were lost after hitting the water. Kinkaid's rescue operation was a brilliant feat of seamanship.

Meanwhile, after a final tour during which continued explosions kept tearing the *Lexington* apart, Captain Sherman and his executive officer, reassured that they were the only remaining men alive on the carrier, abandoned ship.

At 1830 the fires reached the area where the *Lexington*'s torpedo warheads were stored. A huge explosion blasted a great hole in the flight deck. Admiral Fletcher ordered the destroyer *Phelps* to close the carrier and sink her with torpedoes. At 2000 the Phelps fired four torpedoes at point-blank range and the "Lady Lex" plunged to the bottom of the Coral Sea, taking 216 members of her crew with her. However, Kinkaid's ships had managed to rescue over 2700 men.

Faced with the loss of the *Lexington*, Admiral Nimitz ordered Fletcher to break off the battle and withdraw. He could ill afford to risk the loss of another carrier with the defense of Midway at stake. Task Force 17 turned around and headed for Pearl Harbor.

What of the Japanese losses? The *Shoho* of course had been lost early in the battle. The large fleet carrier *Shokaku* was seriously damaged and although her fires were quickly brought under control, she was incapable of conducting flying operations. At 1300 on the eighth the ship was ordered to return to Japan for extensive repairs that would take more than two months.

As for the *Zuikaku*, although she was not attacked by the Americans, many of her air crews had been lost during the fight and the debacle of the night preceding the battle. Thus, although the lost aircraft could be easily replaced, the air crews could not and she too would be forced to sit the Battle of Midway out, thereby reducing the Japanese fleet carrier force by one third.

Though Inoue had cancelled the landings at Port Moresby, he felt that he had won a great battle. The admiral mistakenly believed that both American carriers had been sunk. One can easily see how he could have made this mistake since it was reported to him that both enemy carriers were on fire, as indeed they were initially. But as we have already seen, the *Yorktown*'s fires were brought under control in quick fashion. Therefore, since he believed that no enemy carriers remained to thwart the landings, why didn't Inoue follow up this victory with an immediate landing on Port Moresby? Perhaps his over cautiousness stemmed from his fear of not having enough air support thanks to the loss of the *Shoho* and the departure of Admiral Takagi's striking force. The loss of ninety-seven aircraft must have had more than a slight influence on his final decision.

Just how vital was the Battle of the Coral Sea and whose victory was it really? In America the press heralded the battle as a brilliant victory. In bold print the New York Times trumpeted:

The Japanese have been beaten back after a long battle in the Pacific in which between seventeen and twenty-two of their ships were either sunk or damaged. The enemy is in flight pursued by the Allied forces.[6]

Hanson Baldwin went so far as to say, "that the course of the war both in the Pacific and the world as a whole may well have been entirely changed. This battle bids fair to being one of the greatest in the history of the United States Navy."[7]

On the other side of the world the Japanese also claimed a smashing victory. Even Hitler sent a congratulatory message.

> After this fresh defeat, the warships of the American Navy will hardly dare to oppose the Imperial Navy, since any vessels with presumption enough to join battle with the Japanese fleet may be regarded as already lost.[8]

But who actually won? The Japanese had earned a tactical victory but had suffered a strategic setback. The loss of the *Lexington* was a high price for the Americans to pay for the sinking of the *Shoho*. On the other hand, the relatively light damage to the *Yorktown* more than outweighed the losses suffered by the *Shokaku* and *Zuikaku*, both of which would have to sit the next campaign out. Furthermore, the Americans had foiled the Japanese in their primary objective, the invasion of Port Moresby. Thus, when all facts were balanced, it can probably be stated that the Coral Sea was an American victory.

There were many lessons to be learned from the battle, lessons that would prove invaluable later in the war. Mistakes were made on both sides but from those mistakes the Americans learned; the Japanese did not.

The Battle of the Coral Sea was also an historic milestone. It was the first time ever that the ships of either side did not see or fire on each other. Instead, the air groups assumed the role of long-range guns.

The battle also marked the first halt in the Japanese string of victories. It was the first in which aircraft carriers played the major role. The battle thus became the prototype of a long series of naval air battles which eventually saw the Americans gain the upper hand in the Pacific war.

One postscript to the battle was the plight of the tanker *Neosho*. When the Japanese, in their zeal to get at the enemy, mistook her and the destroyer *Sims* for a carrier and cruiser, they left both ships sinking. The Sims eventually succumbed to her mortal wounds but the blazing *Neosho* continued to float. Eventually her fires burned themselves out leaving the ship a burnt-out hulk drifting helplessly and unable to get under way. Some of her crew abandoned ship and attempted to make land in lifeboats. This effort ended unsuccessfully with tragic consequences. Those that did remain with the ship were finally rescued after four days. The destroyer *Henley*, which had been dispatched to search for the *Neosho*, found her on the eleventh. After taking the survivors aboard, the *Henley* sunk the hapless *Neosho* with torpedoes.

NOTES

1. Bernard Millot, *The Battle of the Coral Sea*, p. 20
2. *Ibid*, p. 20
3. Samuel Elliott Morison, *History of United States Naval Operations in World War II, Vol. IV: Coral Sea, Midway and Submarine Actions*, p. 27
4. Millot, *op. cit.*, p. 56
5. Masatake Okumiya and Jiro Hurikoshi, *Zero*, pp. 104–105
6. Millot, *op cit.*, p. 109
7. *Ibid*, p. 109
8. *Ibid*, p. 110

BIBLIOGRAPHY

1. Adams, Henry. *1942: The Year That Doomed the Axis*.
   David McKay Co., New York, 1967.
2. Costello, John. *The Pacific War*.
   Rawson Wade Publishers, New York, 1981.
3. Frank, Pat and Harrington, Joseph. *Rendezvous at Midway*.
   The John Day Co., New York, 1967.
4. Hoehling, A.D. *The Lexington Goes Down*.
   Prentice-Hall, New Jersey, 1971.
5. Hoyt, Edwin. *Blue Skies and Blood*.
   Paul S. Eriksson, New York, 1975.
6. Lundstrom, John. *The First South Pacific Campaign*.
   Naval Institute Press, Annapolis, 1976.
7. Millot, Bernard. *The Battle of the Coral Sea*.
   Naval Institute Press, Annapolis, 1974.
8. Morison, Samuel E. *History of U.S. Naval Operations in World War II, Vol. IV: Coral Sea, Midway and Submarine Actions*.
   Little Brown & Co., Boston, 1949.
9. Okumiya, Masatake and Harikoshi, Jiro. *Zero*.
   Ballantine Books, New York, 1956.

10. Pfannes, Charles and Salamone, Victor. *The Great Commanders of World War II, Vol IV: The Japanese.*
    Zebra Books, New York, 1982.
11. Pfannes, Charles and Salamone, Victor. *The Great Admirals of World War II, Vol. I: The Americans.*
12. Potter, E.B. *Nimitz.*
    Naval Institute Press, Annapolis, 1976.
13. Toland, John. *The Rising Sun.*
    Random House, New York, 1970.

CHAPTER THREE

THE BATTLE OF MIDWAY

The first few months of WW II in the Pacific bore witness to one of the most incredible strings of conquests in modern military history. When Japan decided to go to war against the United States the commander-in-chief of the Japanese fleet, Admiral Yamamoto, was dismayed. Reluctantly he prepared the fleet for war but predicted that unless the U.S. was dealt a crushing blow immediately, the cause was futile. If, however, America could be hit hard at the outset, then Japan would run wild for six months, Yamamoto said.

Yamamoto proved to be partially correct. From December through May the forces of Japan went on a rampage in the Pacific. Thousands of square miles of territory fell to their all-conquering army and navy. The American Pacific Fleet was destroyed at Pearl Harbor. Indochina, the Philippines, Malaya, Singapore and the Dutch East Indies were conquered in quick succession. The *Prince of Wales* and *Repulse* were sunk, the British fleet driven from the Indian Ocean to sanctuary on the west coast of Africa, India was threatened and large chunks of China occupied.

As the successes continued to mount, Yamamoto remained troubled. Even more than his anxiety over an American counterthrust was the fear that Tokyo, or even worse, the Imperial Palace, would be bombed. So obsessed was he that daily he asked for the weather forecast for the Tokyo area and would be happy the rest of the day when he heard that it was cloudy near the capital. Then he could rest secure that no bombing raids would take place on that particular day. To many this was an ungrounded fear. Where could American bombers come from? Any enemy carrier would have to come within two hundred miles of Japan and by that time they could easily be destroyed by the air force.

Then the impossible happened. On April 18, two American carriers were detected 720 miles from Tokyo. When he received the warning, Yamamoto did not demonstrate undue alarm. The carriers would not be in position to launch their aircraft until the following morning. That would give the Japanese defenders ample time to deal with them. Kondo's Second Fleet was immediately dispatched to intercept and deal with the enemy.

Suddenly, as the defensive dispositions were being made, Yamamoto's worst fears became a reality. Tokyo was bombed. How could this be? Reports quickly followed that American B-25 bombers were also attacking Nagoya, Yokohama and Kobe. Where had these army planes come from? Midway?

Actually, the B-25s were lead by Lt. Col. James Doolittle who flew the planes (after many weeks of practice) from the decks of the aircraft carrier *Hornet*, part of Adm. William Halsey's task force. These planes were capable of flying much further than the conventional carrier aircraft, thus the attack was launched from a position approximately six hundred miles from Japan. Since these large planes could not land aboard the carriers, they were ordered to fly onto China and land behind friendly lines. Therefore, as soon as the launch was complete, the American task force reversed course and hightailed it for home, completely eluding the pursuing Japanese.

Only sixteen planes were used in the American attack and, in reality, did little damage. The Japanese punned the commander's name and called it the dolittle raid. As far as Yamamoto was concerned, however, the raid was a disgrace and served to confirm his conviction that the United States' fleet had to be brought to battle and destroyed.

On April 22, the First Air Fleet reached home minus the carriers *Zuikaku* and *Shokaku*. These two ships were left behind to support the Japanese operations against Port Moresby in New Guinea. Kondo's Second Fleet had reached home a week earlier only to be hastily sent back to sea to search for the American task force that had carried Doolittle's raiders on their bombing mission against Japan. This attack was the final straw as far as Yamamoto was concerned. Midway had to be captured.

Both Nagumo and Kondo pleaded for a delay of the Midway operation. Their crews were worn out and their ships badly in need of overhaul. Both fleets had been in constant action since early January, Kondo in the East Indies and Philippines, Nagumo conducting raids in the Solomons, Darwin and the East Indies. Both fleets had then joined hands to drive the British from the Indian Ocean.

But Doolittle's raid made Yamamoto determined that such an event would never occur again. He took it as a personal insult. Although Nagumo too felt that the conquest of Midway was necessary, surely, he said, it could wait until the fleet had rested and the ships were in shape to go to sea again. Kondo opposed the operation completely. Yamamoto would not be swayed. The Midway operation would proceed on schedule. Nagumo and Kondo were ordered to have their respective fleets ready for sea by the end of May.

Aboard the Second Destroyer Flotilla anchored at Kure, rumors began to circulate of an ambitious operation aimed at the capture of Midway. Admiral Tanaka harbored reservations regarding the feasibility of such an ambitious adventure. After six months of war Japan had achieved every one of her projected goals. Just as Yamamoto had predicted, she had run wild. To bite off more than she could chew was to court disaster.

Tanaka expressed his reservations during a conference with his captains. When Captain Hara of the *Amatsukaze* asked if the Midway plan was a fact, Tanaka replied, "As a matter of fact I am not sure of it. I hope it's untrue."[1] But the plan was indeed a fact. On May 21, Tanaka's flagship, the light cruiser *Jintsu*, led six destroyers out of the harbor for the four-day voyage to Saipan. Tanaka had been selected to command the escort for the troop convoy assembling at Saipan. These troops were the assault forces for the operation.

While preparations for Midway proceeded, Yamamoto initiated an operation aimed at advancing the Japanese position in the South Pacific via the seizure of Port Moresby. Three carriers were dispatched to protect the invasion fleet moving through the Coral Sea.*

The setback in the Coral Sea failed to deter Yamamoto. He still had the four large carriers of the First and Second Air Divisions. In addition, there was no assurance that the Americans would even oppose the Midway operation.

Unlike the Pearl Harbor attack, the security of which had been relatively loose, a tight veil of secrecy cloaked the plans for Midway. On the other hand, even if Nimitz did oppose the Japanese moves he could do so with only two carriers since it was assumed that the damage to the *Yorktown* would lay that ship up for many months.

Since the Americans had broken the Japanese naval code it was no trouble for them to determine that the enemy was planning another major move. Every wireless transmission between the various Japanese headquarters and fleets were quickly read and carefully scrutinized by American codebreakers. Only the eventual target remained a mystery since the Japanese did not refer to Midway by name.

Thanks to the efforts of his codebreakers, Nimitz was convinced that Midway was the Japanese target. His suspicions merely confirmed what his instincts had already told him. The problem was how to convince others who had reached different conclusions.

MacArthur and King felt that the next Japanese move would be in the New Guinea-Solomon Islands area. Nimitz told Comm. Joseph Rochefort, his chief

---

*See Chapter 2.

codebreaker, that concrete evidence was required. Evidence that would prove without a shadow of a doubt that Midway was on the Japanese agenda.

Rochefort's staff had been picking up repeated Japanese references to something called AF. The cryptologists were certain that AF was actually Midway. If the skeptics were to be silenced they would have to prove it beyond a shadow of a doubt. Accordingly, Rochefort suggested to Nimitz that he order Midway to send a radio message in the clear stating that its water distillation system had broken down. Nimitz agreed to the ruse. Two days later a Japanese message was intercepted and decrypted. The message stated that AF had an acute shortage of fresh water. At last, hard evidence.

Yamamoto's plan was an elaborate one calling for the various fleets involved to set out from dispersed locations, yet he expected them all to arrive in their designated positions precisely on schedule. At the same time as he attacked Midway, Yamamoto planned to assault the Aleutian Islands hoping that this attack would decoy the American forces north.

The Japanese plan of attack for Midway called for Nagumo's carriers to bombard the island prior to the invasion. Yamamoto would support Nagumo from a distance with the Main Body, a portion* of which would be detached while at sea and take up a position from where it could support either the Aleutian or Midway operation. Kondo's fleet had an even more complicated role. After leaving Japan it would link

---

*Guard Force.

MIDWAY

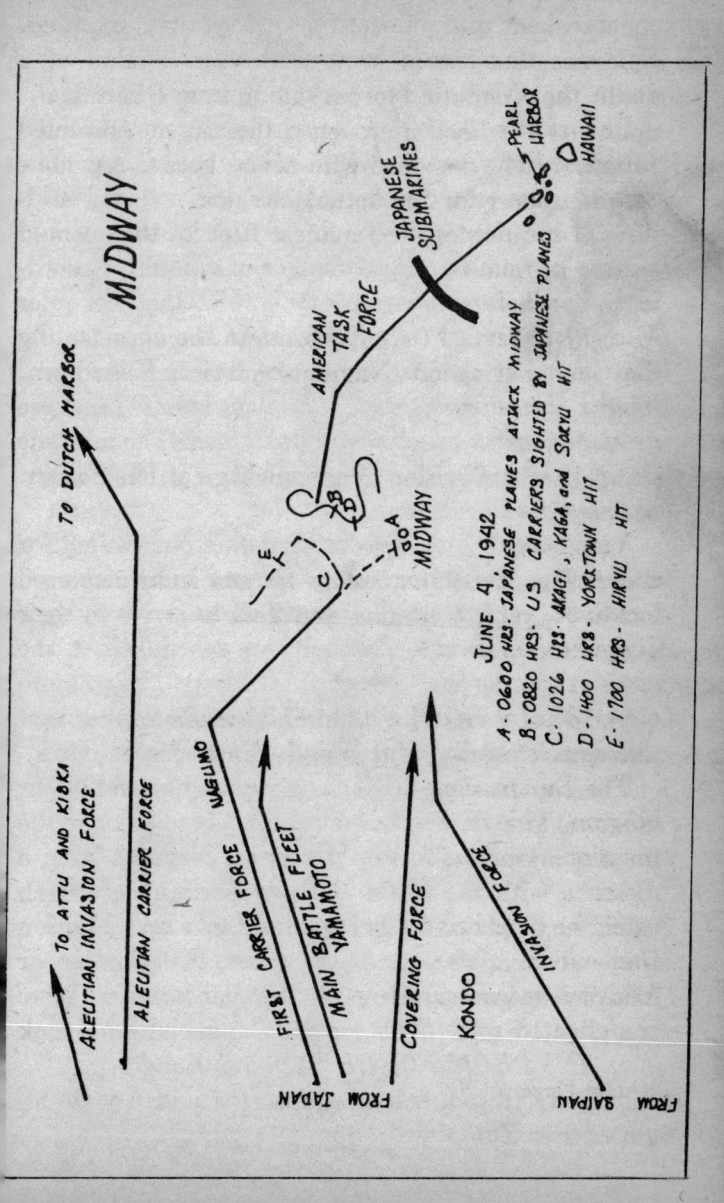

JUNE 4, 1942

- A - 0600 HRS. JAPANESE PLANES ATTACK MIDWAY
- B - 0820 HRS. US CARRIERS SIGHTED BY JAPANESE PLANES
- C - 1026 HRS. AKAGI, KAGA, and SORYU HIT
- D - 1400 HRS. YORKTOWN HIT
- E - 1700 HRS. HIRYU HIT

TO ATTU AND KISKA
ALEUTIAN INVASION FORCE
ALEUTIAN CARRIER FORCE
TO DUTCH HARBOR

FROM JAPAN
FIRST CARRIER FORCE NAGUMO
MAIN BATTLE FLEET YAMAMOTO
COVERING FORCE
KONDO INVASION FORCE
FROM SAIPAN

MIDWAY
AMERICAN TASK FORCE
JAPANESE SUBMARINES
PEARL HARBOR
HAWAII

up with the occupation forces sailing from Guam and Saipan. As the fleet approached the target, Admiral Kurita would be detached with his cruisers to provide close-in support for the actual invasion.

The disposition of the Japanese fleet for the operation was as follows:

STRIKING FORCE (Admiral Nagumo)
First Carrier Division (Nagumo): carriers *Kaga* and *Akagi**

Second Carrier Division (Yamaguchi): carriers *Soryu* and *Hiryu**

Support Force (Abe): battleships *Haruna* and *Kirishima*
cruisers *Nagara*, *Chikuma* and *Tone**
eleven destroyers

MAIN BODY (Admiral Yamamoto)
battleships *Nagato*, *Mutsu* and *Yamato**
light carrier *Hosho*
cruiser *Sendai*
nine destroyers

Guard Force (Takasu): battleships *Ise*, *Fuso*, *Yamashiro* and *Hyuga**
cruisers *Kitakami* and *Oi*

INVASION FORCE (Admiral Kondo)
Main Body (Kondo): battleships *Hiei* and *Kongo*
light carrier *Zuiho*

seaplane carrier *Chitose*
cruisers *Atago*,* *Chokai*, *Myoko*, *Haguro* and *Yara*
eight destroyers

Close Support (Kurita): cruisers *Kumano*,* *Suzuya*, *Mikuma* and *Mogami*
two destroyers

Transport (Tanaka): cruiser *Jintsu**
ten destroyers and fifteen transports

   ALEUTIANS FORCE (Admiral Hosogaya)
light carriers *Ryujo* and *Junyo*
cruisers *Nachi*,* *Maya*, *Takao*, *Abukuma*, *Kiso* and *Tama*
twelve destroyers

Hard evidence notwithstanding, there were some Americans who remained unconvinced. There was always a possibility that the Japanese were practicing a deception game of their own. Despite the critics, however, Nimitz knew that he had to act with speed. Aware that he would be confronted by a superior force he would nevertheless have to make do with whatever forces were available.

There was no margin for error. If the American forces were scattered to cover all potential targets there would be no single force left sufficiently strong to halt

*Flagship.

a Japanese attack. Nimitz would have to gamble on Midway.

At that time the backbone of the American forces were the three fleet carriers, *Enterprise*, *Yorktown* and *Hornet*. But the *Yorktown* was in urgent need of at least three months worth of repairs thanks to the damage incurred in the Coral Sea.

Meanwhile, the cryptographers also discovered that the Japanese planned to assault the Aleutians as well. Originally, Nimitz had not planned to defend these islands but later had second thoughts since the Aleutians were U.S. territory. To allow the Japanese to conquer the islands by default would constitute a severe blow to American morale. Consequently, Nimitz formed a North Pacific force under Admiral Theobold to deal with the potential threat.

The cryptographers continued to feed Nimitz every bit of intelligence gathered. From this information Nimitz was able to form an excellent picture of just what he was up against. The data was uncannily accurate. Thanks to it, Nimitz was able to develop a defensive plan. The brilliant codebreakers even managed to pinpoint the actual dates of the Japanese attacks: June 3 for the Aleutians and June 4 for Midway.

In developing this strategy, Nimitz concentrated on what he considered the key Japanese forces, Admiral Nagumo's four large carriers. Eliminate them and the Japanese plan would fall apart.

On May 26, Halsey's task force returned to Pearl Harbor. When Nimitz met face to face with Halsey he was shocked at the latter's haggard and sickly appearance. In addition, the fire-breathing admiral was suffering from a severe skin disorder. There was no question that the nervous strain of the previous weeks was causing Halsey to suffer and that he required immediate hospitalization. Unfortunately, this would make him unavailable for the forthcoming battle. After a brief argument, Halsey conceded he was too ill for command. He did, however, recommend that Rear Adm. Raymond Spruance be given his command. Nimitz concurred readily for he knew Spruance was a deep thinker who reacted coolly in combat. Nevertheless, the loss of Halsey continued to nag at Nimitz.

The choice of Spruance caused many brows to furrow. Granted, he could draw from the experience of Halsey's staff. Still, he was not an aviator. Halsey, however, had recommended him because after years of close friendship he knew Spruance to be an officer of great ability. In fact, he wrote:

> I consider him fully and superbly qualified to take command of a force comprising mixed types and to conduct protracted independent operations in the combat theater in wartime.[2]

Nevertheless, the aviators were skeptical.

Before leaving Pearl Harbor Spruance received his orders from Nimitz who added this warning before finishing his conversation:

> You will be governed by the principle of calculated risk, which you will interpret to mean avoidance of exposure of your force to attack by

superior enemy forces without good prospect of inflicting, as a result of such exposure, greater damage on the enemy.[3]

Spruance and Nimitz quickly set to the urgent task at hand. The former added some of his own theories to the plan that was already in place. Together, the two admirals forged the plan which would ultimately bring victory to the American forces.

On May 27, Fletcher's Task Force 17 arrived back at Pearl. Immediately the battered *Yorktown* was sent into dry dock. Nimitz met with the dockyard workers and told them that the ninety-day estimate for repairs to the ship was unrealistic. He then proceeded to shock them with the pronouncement that he wanted the *Yorktown* ready for sea within three days. Work commenced around the clock and the impossible was achieved. The repair teams rose to the occasion magnificently and three days after the *Yorktown* was docked, the huge carrier was ready to raise steam. Nimitz's judgment had proved correct.

In the interim, Nimitz briefed the exhausted Fletcher on the plans for the Midway operation even though he was under pressure from King to relieve Fletcher due to the latter's apparent lack of aggressiveness. Nevertheless, Nimitz elected to make the decision on his own. Accordingly, he requested Fletcher to commit his conduct of operations at the Coral Sea to writing. Nimitz would then use that document to determine if indeed Fletcher was fit to remain in command.

The following day Fletcher submitted a superbly written report. After reading it, there was little doubt in Nimitz's mind that Fletcher simply was not suited to command an offensive operation. Nevertheless, with Halsey on the sidelines this was no time to relieve his only other senior commander. Fletcher would have to remain on until the conclusion of the forthcoming battle at Midway.

During the planning sessions, the Americans emphasized that surprise would be their greatest weapon.

> The guiding principles were that the Americans, with inferior forces but presumably better information concerning the opposition, must get the jump on the enemy and must catch the enemy carriers in a vulnerable state.[4]

Accordingly, the American planners hoped that they could catch Nagumo's carriers while they were in the process of recovering the Midway attack force.

On May 28, Spruance, in command of Task Force 16, comprising the *Enterprise* and *Hornet*, steamed out of Pearl Harbor escorted by the cruisers *Atlanta*, *Pensacola*, *Minneapolis*, *New Orleans*, *Northampton* and *Vincennes* and nine destroyers. Two tankers and two more destroyers followed.

The following day, the temporarily reprieved Fletcher sailed aboard the miraculously repaired *Yorktown*. Task Force 17 also contained the cruisers *Astoria* and *Portland* and six destroyers. Spruance wanted to hit the Japanese before they hit him. He wisely considered the enemy carriers to be the primary target, followed by the battleships and cruisers. An ironic turn of events for one who held the battleship in deep respect. Now he considered them a secondary target.

The greatest weapon in Spruance's arsenal was, of course, surprise. In order to ensure that surprise was thorough he ordered complete radio silence. On the thirty-first he took station about 325 miles northeast of Midway at a spot designated Point Luck. On June 2, Fletcher with the hastily repaired *Yorktown* arrived on station and assumed tactical command. However, he was wise enough to inform Spruance that during the heat of the battle he could feel free to operate independently.

Meanwhile, on May 27, Admirals Nagumo, Kondo, Hosogaya and Tanaka put to sea with their respective fleets. Yamamoto would personally lead his own force to sea early the next day and maintain station approximately six hundred miles to the rear of Nagumo's carriers. From that point forward all the various elements would be out of touch with each other since Yamamoto demanded that absolute radio silence be maintained at all times.

Just as at Pearl Harbor, Nagumo would exercise tactical command of the First Carrier Division as well as overall command of the entire First Air Fleet. Admiral Yamaguchi would have tactical command of the Second Carrier Division.

In order to alert himself to the movements of the American fleet, Yamamoto had designed two plans. One called for a seaplane to lay at French Frigate Shoals and conduct daily reconnaissance flights over Pearl Harbor. The second called for two submarine picket lines to be established, one near the area that the seaplane was operating from and the other between Midway and Hawaii, directly astride the route any American fleet would have to travel en route to Midway. Thus assured of accurate intelligence, with his flag flying from the monstrous battleship *Yamato*, the commander-in-chief of the Combined Fleet took his force to sea.

As the old saying goes, the best laid plans of mice and men often go astray. When the Japanese submarine scouting unit arrived at French Frigate Shoals it found the area patrolled by an American seaplane tender. After watching the area for a few days in the vain hope that the American ship would leave, the commander of the submarines radioed Kwajelein and told them not to dispatch the seaplanes. Operation K, as the plan was known, would have to be scrapped.

Thanks to the herculean effort on the part of Pearl Harbor's dockyard workers, the *Yorktown* was ready for sea far sooner than anyone dreamed possible. The proposed course of Fletcher's force would take it directly over the anticipated position of the second Japanese submarine picket line. But the picket line failed to materialize. The sailing of the submarines had been delayed. Consequently, by the time they arrived in position on June 2, Fletcher and *Yorktown* had long since passed through the position.

The next day, however, radio operators aboard the *Yamato* began to intercept numerous American transmissions. Although they were unable to decipher the messages, Yamamoto was notified of the activity. His staff accurately concluded that the American fleet was at sea. Yamamoto concurred with his staff's conclusion but refused to break radio silence and notify Nagumo. The commander-in-chief incorrectly assumed that Nagumo's force had monitored the same enemy transmissions and could draw their own conclusions. Unfortunately, the receivers on *Akagi* were nowhere as strong as those on the *Yamato*. Therefore the First Air Fleet was unable to intercept the American transmissions. Prior to sailing, Nagumo's chief of staff had urged that Yamamoto forward all messages but the latter was so intent on maintaining radio silence he flatly refused. Yamamoto seemed obsessed with secrecy.

With all the preparations final and the wheels in motion, all Nimitz could do now was sit idly by and wait for the Japanese to make their move. Control of events now passed to Spruance and Fletcher. However, Nimitz could retain tactical control of all land, sea and air forces from his headquarters at Pearl Harbor. This was in contrast to the course adopted by his opponent, Yamamoto, who elected to sail with the fleet. Reduced to impotence by the necessity of maintaining radio silence while at sea, the great Japanese admiral was forced to rely on subordinates to make the crucial life and death decisions.

Late in the afternoon of June 2, the First Air Fleet ran into heavy overcast weather. All through the night the fleet steamed through dense fog. It was Nagumo's intention to hover out of range of land-based planes until the night preceding the actual attack. Under cover of darkness he would then run in toward the target. Since the fleet was approaching Midway, this necessitated a temporary change of course.

When dawn arrived on June 3, Nagumo's ships found themselves still shrouded in dense fog. Consequently the order to change course could not be given by signal lamps or flags. Nagumo therefore ordered a low-frequency message sent to all ships informing them of the intention to change course. He was lucky. Yamamoto's flagship picked up *Akagi*'s weak signal; the American fleet, even closer than Yamamoto, did not.

Later that same day Fletcher and Spruance linked up northeast of Midway. Unlike his opponent, Fletcher knew that the enemy fleet was at sea. Admiral Fletcher was the senior of the two American commanders and was thus in overall command. However, since Spruance was totally familiar with the operation of his own Task Force 16, Fletcher decided that during the battle his own Task Force 17 and Spruance's would operate independently. He then moved both groups to a position approximately two hundred miles north of Midway. Fletcher suspected that the Japanese carriers would approach Midway either from the west or northwest. Thus the American carriers were ideally positioned to intercept the Japanese fleet.

Around 0600 on June 3, a patrolling American float plane discovered Tanaka's invasion force about 600 miles south of Midway plodding slowly eastward. Tanaka immediately radioed Yamamoto on the *Yamato*, informing the commander-in-chief that the cat was out of the bag; he had been sighted. Unfortunately, Yamamoto failed to inform Nagumo that the invasion convoy had been detected. It was assumed that Nagumo's force could monitor Tanaka's transmission. But Nagumo had not intercepted the transmission. Consequently he sailed blindly into the battle totally unaware that the Americans were waiting.

Now that the occupation force was discovered Tanaka knew that it was only a matter of time before the Americans made him the object of their attention. Late in the afternoon a formation of B-17s arrived over the convoy. As soon as the American planes were sighted Tanaka ordered the fleet to begin a predetermined series of evasive maneuvers aimed at throwing off the aim of the American bombardiers. The skillful evasive tactics were successful as the bombs fell harmlessly into the sea. Conversely, despite a heavy barrage of anti-aircraft fire, no hits were obtained on the bombers.

Tanaka knew now that the Americans would contest the invasion with everything they had. He never did have confidence in the venture and during the lull of the preceding weeks was able to think of even more reasons why the venture might fail. Now, with his own presence discovered, those reservations deepened. Admiral Tanaka spent a very restless night aboard the *Jintsu*.

The two fleets groped for each other unaware of the other's exact location. Nagumo seemed in high spirits as the fleet sailed serenely toward the target. Seemingly he had little to fear. No messages had been received from the patrol planes at French Frigate Shoals or the submarine pickets. The American fleet was probably still in Hawaii.

On the other hand, Fletcher knew that the Japanese were approaching. Thanks to the American intelligence reports he even knew the order of battle and the ships involved. What he did not know was the whereabouts of the Japanese fleet.

At 0400 on June 4 the four Japanese carriers burst

into activity. Pilots were awakened and given breakfast before being briefed on their assignments. Half an hour later seven search planes were launched by the escorting battleships and cruisers. There should have been eight but the *Tone* encountered problems with one of its catapults. The search planes were to fan out and look for any enemy ships that might be lurking in the vicinity of Midway. The missing *Tone* plane left a gap in the fan.

At 0445 Nagumo's carriers, having turned into the wind, launched their first strike against Midway Island. Yamaguchi's two carriers launched 36 level bombers, Nagumo's 36 dive bombers and each of the carriers added 9 Zero fighters as escort, a total of 108 planes. As soon as the launching was complete the ships' crews began to arm another equally strong strike with bombs and torpedos. Thus, in the event enemy ships were located, the Japanese would be ready to strike at a moment's notice. In addition to those already airborne and the one waiting on the carrier decks, a formation of fighters hovered over the fleet as a combat air patrol.

Standing on the bridge observing the launch, Nagumo exuded confidence. Thanks to the lack of intelligence reports there was no reason for him to feel otherwise. No enemy fleet had been reported in the region. This meant that there would be no fleet action until at least after the invasion. At that point he would be ready to meet any threat. In the meantime he stood confidently watching the activity. The Japanese strike winged its way toward Midway. It would be an hour or more before they arrived over the target.

At 0500 the *Tone* finally ironed out its catapult

problems and launched its remaining scout plane. That half hour delay proved fatal since the American fleet was positioned precisely in the area that the *Tone*'s second plane was to search.

As they approached Midway, the Japanese planes were discovered by a patrolling American aircraft who immediately sounded the warning. Almost immediately all American planes on the island began to scramble and were airborne before the enemy arrived over the target. A few minutes before 0630, American fighters located the flight of Japanese bombers and maneuvered to intercept. The Zeros managed to beat back the American attack without loss to the bombers who arrived over Midway exactly on schedule.

The Japanese planes peeled off and began to hit the American installations. To their misfortune all the American planes had managed to get airborne but hangars, runways and installations were subjected to a severe pounding.

In thirty minutes, the attack was over. Midway was a shambles. However, the Japanese flight commander was disappointed with the results of the raid. It was fine to destroy installations, but the striking arm of the island's defenses, the aircraft, remained intact. Accordingly, at 0700 he radioed the fleet suggesting that another strike was needed. Since losses were relative light—three level bombers and one dive bomber to anti-aircraft fire and two Zeros to the enemy fighters—the flight commander was sure that one more strike would finish the job.

Nagumo hesitated. Was another strike warranted? As he stood contemplating his next move, bombers from Midway arrived over the fleet and began to drop their lethal loads. Thanks to skillful maneuvering on the part of the ship's captains, none of the bombs found their target but the attack convinced Nagumo that another strike was called for. He therefore ordered that the planes carrying torpedos be re-armed with bombs. Those planes being held in reserve to attack any American naval forces would be used to deliver a second strike against Midway. Of course, it would take time to re-arm these planes.

At 0730 while the re-arming proceeded, *Tone*'s plane made contact with the American fleet but reported that no carriers were present.

Based on *Tone*'s sighting report, Nagumo began to second guess himself. If *Tone*'s plane had only been launched on time he would not now be faced with this dilemma. Nagumo's primary objective was of course the American fleet so once again he changed his mind. The order went out, cancel re-arming the planes for another attack on Midway. Replace the bombs with torpedos. Aboard the *Hiryu*, Yamaguchi raged. Why not attack with those aircraft which were already waiting? However, Nagumo knew that his fighters, both those en route back from Midway and those flying combat air patrol, were low on fuel. He refused to consider sending off an attack without the proper escort and decided instead to refuel the Zeros while the re-arming proceeded.

While the activity proceeded furiously, another American attack by planes from Midway took place. Again no hits were achieved on the Japanese fleet but half an hour later, just as the Midway flight was returning to the carriers, a force of B-17s flew high over the fleet and dropped their loads. Once more violent evasive maneuvers succeeded in throwing off the aim of the American bombardiers and no hits were made, but the furious maneuvering caused additional delays. In the midst of all this confusion, another message was received from *Tone*'s scout plane repeating that no carriers were with the American fleet.

Now Nagumo had another choice to make. Should he recover the planes returning from Midway or should he launch the strike first? Since the first strike was dangerously low on fuel he chose to recover it.

That morning Spruance and Fletcher watched in anticipation as the sun rose over a gentle sea. The sky was clear. It was a perfect day for war. American scout planes were up early searching for the enemy. At 0534 a search plane from Midway Island located the Japanese carriers but failed to give their position. Eleven minutes later the same plane reported a flight of enemy aircraft heading for Midway. Still there was no report of the exact location of the enemy fleet. The men aboard the American carriers were uneasy. Spruance wanted desperately to strike the Japanese carriers before they could launch a second attack against the island but first they had to be found. Finally, a few minutes after 0600, came the electrifying word that two enemy carriers and battleships heading for Midway were approximately 180 miles northwest of the island.

After studying the report, Spruance ordered his planes readied for launching. He did not care to wait; he was going for the enemy's jugular. Halsey's chief of staff, Capt. Miles Browning, was responsible for coordinating the launch. He recommended that it take place at 0700. Spruance concurred.

Spruance's plan called for a coordinated attack by both the *Enterprise* and *Hornet* air groups flying in company. Then, when the enemy carriers were located, each group would attack independently. As current doctrine dictated, the dive bombers were to coordinate their attack with the torpedo planes skimming the surface of the waves. Both groups would be protected by a fighter escort.

In the midst of launching planes, Spruance was handed a message indicating a Japanese scout plane was on the horizon. Now more than ever Spruance knew that the enemy carriers had to be attacked. The launching of his own planes seemed to take an eternity. As the minutes ticked away, Spruance decided to send the dive bombers, already airborne, ahead of the torpedo planes. At 0745 he gave Lt. Comm. Wade McClusky the green light to attack. So much for plans for a coordinated attack. Nevertheless, Spruance felt that to delay any longer would be too dangerous.

The American were still unaware of the exact location of the enemy ships. Consequently, once the two torpedo squadrons from Spruance's ships were airborne, they flew slightly divergent courses which gradually drew them apart.

An hour after Spruance's initial launch, Fletcher launched a full strike from *Yorktown* consisting of torpedo and dive bombers with a handful of fighters for escort.

As the American planes winged their way toward the Japanese, both carrier formations remained alert to the possibility of an enemy attack. For the commanders, Fletcher and Spruance, the radio silence was maddening. For over two hours no reports were received from their aircraft.

Around 0830 the recovery of the Japanese planes returning from Midway commenced. Below decks the re-arming of the next strike continued for the second time. Because of the urgency of the situation and the succeeding conflicting orders, there had not been enough time to properly stow the removed armaments. Torpedos and bombs were stacked loosely around the decks and in hangars as the furious pace of the crews took priority.

By 0915 the recovery was complete. If no further problems were encountered, Nagumo felt that the entire complement of planes could be refuelled, rearmed and ready to launch in a little over an hour.

While the sailors aboard the Japanese carriers continued their frantic pace, the *Hornet*'s Torpedo Squadron 8 located the Japanese fleet and dove to sea-top level to attack. The slow, lumbering torpedo planes were easy targets for the circling Zeros. The next few minutes witnessed a slaughter. All fifteen of Lieutenant Waldron's planes were destroyed by the tenacious Japanese pilots before they could even draw into range. Out of forty-five pilots and crewmen, only one man survived.

Right behind Torpedo 8 came the *Enterprise*'s Torpedo 6. Selecting as their targets the *Kaga* and *Akagi*, Torpedo 6 suffered almost the same fate as had the planes from the *Hornet*. Nine of the fourteen attackers fell victim to the experienced Zero pilots. For the terrible price they paid, the American torpedo squadrons had nothing to show. No hits were obtained on the Japanese ships.

By now Nagumo was deeply concerned. His staff

and the carrier captains exhorted their crews to a greater effort in completing the task of readying the planes. At 1000 the third American torpedo squadron, Torpedo 3 from the *Yorktown*, arrived on the scene. Again the American squadron paid a heavy price. The swarming Japanese fighters made short work of the vulnerable torpedo planes and their attack on the *Soryu* went for naught; the Japanese carrier emerged unscathed. But this time the sacrifice of the American pilots was not in vain.

Unlike the torpedo squadrons from the *Hornet* and *Enterprise*, the squadron from the *Yorktown* was accompanied by a full strike of fighters and dive bombers. Arriving over the Japanese fleet the torpedo planes skimmed the waves and launched their attack first.

Meanwhile, Nagumo's spirits were lifting. It was obvious that this latest American attack was doomed to suffer the same fate as its predecessors. In addition, his original estimate that his own planes would not be ready until 1030 had proved erroneous. Fifteen minutes ahead of schedule all planes were ready for launching. At 1020, therefore, Nagumo ordered all carriers to turn into the wind and begin launching planes. In the midst of this maneuver all hell broke loose.

The sacrifice of the American torpedo planes had not been in vain. Their attack had lured the Japanese combat air patrol down to the surface in defense of their ships. Consequently, when the American dive bombers arrived overhead, there were no fighters present to contest their attack. The Zeros were still down on the deck searching for any American torpedo planes that might have eluded them. In that position they never saw the American dive bombers forming up for the attack.

Screaming out of the sky came Lt. Comm. Wade McClusky's thirty-seven Dauntless dive bombers from the *Enterprise*. McClusky's formation had been searching without success for the Japanese fleet and, low on fuel, were returning to their ship when they stumbled across Nagumo's formation by accident. Splitting his formation, McClusky gave the order to nose over and attack *Kaga* and *Akagi*.

At the same time, *Yorktown*'s eighteen dive bombers, which had accompanied the torpedo planes, focused their sights on the *Soryu*. Their leader, Lt. Comm. Max Leslie, soon had his squadron in a steep dive with their fingers poised on their bomb releases.

The unsuccessful torpedo attacks had drawn the Japanese fighters down to sea level to meet the threat. After having turned back the torpedo bombers the Zeros were flying at wave-top level searching for any American planes that might have eluded them. In that position, they never saw the American dive bombers.

The Zeros did not have the capability of climbing quickly enough to intercept the American dive bombers. Consequently, except for the feeble anti-aircraft fire from the carriers, the Devastators found the field clear. Within minutes, three Japanese carriers lay blazing.

Kaga took four hits immediately. Fires and explosions erupted as the frantic crew attempted to clear the deck of the fuel lines still lying about. Almost immediately, the carrier's captain knew that his ship was doomed.

As the crew of the *Soryu* looked on in awed amazement at the fate of the ships of the First Carrier Division, their awe turned to terror as three hits, ideally placed along the length of the ship, turned the *Soryu* into a blazing inferno. From stem to stern the flight deck was one huge mass of flame.

Aboard *Akagi*, Nagumo's flagship, the story was the same. One bomb hit forward, another landed on the stern and destroyed the ship's rudder. The fatal blow, however, was the hit that plunged through the central elevator to explode among the torpedos on the hangar deck. As already seen, the Japanese sailors, in their haste to obey the order to re-arm the planes, had left them strewn about the deck. Fuchida recalls:

> I was horrified at the destruction that had been wrought in a matter of seconds. There was a huge hole in the flight deck just behind the midship elevator. The elevator itself, twisted like molten glass, was drooping into the hangar. Deck plates reeled in grotesque configurations. Planes stood tail-up belching livid flames and jet-black smoke. Reluctant tears streamed down my cheeks as I watched the fires spread.[5]

In the very brief span of a few minutes the once proud First Air Fleet was a wreck as crews struggled to contain the fires. Only the *Hiryu* managed to escape. When the American attack came in she was conveniently shielded by a nearby rain squall.

Aboard the flagship, Nagumo's chief of staff, Kusaka, urged the admiral to leave the ship and transfer to another. Nagumo refused. His depression was so deep by that time he seemed intent on sharing the fate of his fleet. *Akagi's* skipper, Captain Aoki, attempted to convince Nagumo that he was perfectly capable of handling the activity aboard ship without the admiral's assistance. Once again, Nagumo refused to listen. Finally Kusaka used the argument that the surviving portion of the fleet required direction and that it was Nagumo's duty to provide guidance. There was no disputing this argument. Nagumo gave in. The destroyer *Nowaki* came alongside and sent its launch to fetch Nagumo and other members of the staff. At 1045, the admiral boarded the launch for the trip to the cruiser *Nagara*, the facilities of which were more suited to that of a flagship than that of the destroyer. Forty-five minutes later, Nagumo climbed the *Nagara's* ladder, still shaken.

At the very moment Nagumo was leaving the *Akagi*, the entire crew was abandoning the *Soryu*. The fires aboard the ship could not be contained. Captain Yanagimoto therefore gave the order to abandon ship. There was no question but that the ship was doomed.

Back aboard the *Enterprise* Spruance waited agonizingly for results. He was able to monitor snatches of cryptic exchanges between pilots but nothing definite. He would have to wait for his pilots to return before getting the full story. Meanwhile, what remained of the torpedo planes limped homeward. Many of the surviving pilots were forced to ditch at sea. Some of the more fortunate ones managed to reach Midway. Spruance was disappointed with the early results.

Finally the dive bombers began to return. Little by little Spruance was able to piece together the facts of their attack. Three Japanese carriers were blazing. The brave attack of the torpedo planes had allowed the dive bombers to attack unimpeded even though they were low on fuel. Incredibly, the piecemeal American attack had carried the day.

But the Japanese still had teeth that had not been yanked. Admiral Yamaguchi's *Hiryu* remained undamaged. At 1055 he launched his long-delayed attack. An hour later this formation located the *Yorktown*.

Spruance was still assessing his pilots' information when he received a frantic message from the *Yorktown* stating that she was under attack. Unfortunately, the *Hornet* and *Enterprise* were in the midst of recovering aircraft and were unable to intercede. Sadly Spruance watched as a large column of black smoke rose from the stricken *Yorktown*.

Although most of the planes were either destroyed by American fighters or diverted from their target by heavy anti-aircraft fire, three pilots pressed home their attacks and dealt a crippling blow to the hastily repaired veteran of the Coral Sea.

Even as the attackers were winging their way home, Yamaguchi was preparing another strike with orders to find any undamaged American carriers, since by then it was obvious that the *Yorktown* was not alone. By 1330 that afternoon this second strike of torpedo planes was streaking for the American fleet.

Precisely one hour later, the second strike located the already crippled *Yorktown*. Admiral Fletcher had already transferred to the cruiser *Astoria* but

Yorktown's commander, Captain Buckmaster, remained aboard and maneuvered to avoid the enemy torpedos. Unfortunately, his efforts proved futile as the great ship's reduced speed made maneuvering difficult. Two torpedos slammed home and the *Yorktown* stopped dead in the water. She would take no further part in the battle. Ten minutes after the first torpedo hit, Captain Buckmaster ordered the ship abandoned.

Admiral Yamaguchi glimpsed a ray of hope on the horizon. The returning torpedo pilots reported that they had not attacked the same ship as the dive bombers had. Based on their reports, Yamaguchi concluded that the odds were now even, one Japanese carrier against one American. He erred of course since *Hornet* and *Enterprise* were both in full fighting trim. At 1600 Spruance ordered both his carriers to launch a strike and destroy the remaining Japanese carrier.

Admiral Tanaka listened incredulously to the radio reports of the systematic destruction of Nagumo's carrier force. Nevertheless, a message was received ordering him to proceed with the attack. An hour later, however, this order was cancelled and the transports were ordered to return to base. But Tanaka was directed to proceed with his destroyers and carry out a bombardment of Midway.

The admiral was furious. If the Americans possessed enough power to annihilate Nagumo's powerful force, what could his puny destroyers hope to accomplish?

Spruance, meanwhile, gathered his staff together and began to plan his next move. Obviously the remaining Japanese carrier had to be eliminated. But where was it? To avoid the pitfalls of the morning attack which saw his planes fly aimlessly in search of the enemy fleet, Spruance decided to wait before launching a new strike.

Browning urged Spruance to launch the planes immediately. The admiral, however, refused to be coerced into a wild goose chase. No, the planes would not be launched until confirmation was received of the location of that remaining carrier.

Even as the luckless *Yorktown* was undergoing her ordeal, that ship's scout planes were searching for their antagonist. In midafternoon they struck pay dirt. The location was passed to Spruance who was ready.

While Spruance's planes were revving their engines on the carrier decks in preparation for takeoff, Yamaguchi was passing the order for yet another attack. Thanks to the heavy losses incurred during the two attacks on the *Yorktown*, few Japanese planes answered the call. However, Yamaguchi was perfectly willing to sacrifice them to achieve victory. Refuelling and re-arming began. That remaining American carrier had to be found and put out of action.

Precious little time was available since, as we have already seen, the two fleets were by now only an hour's flying time apart. Before *Hiryu*'s planes were ready, the American planes arrived. The result was the same as the morning. Four bombs struck *Hiryu* in rapid succession. In minutes the ship was wrapped in a pall of smoke and flame. Its forward elevator was blown up against the bridge and leaned at an odd angle. *Hiryu* was doomed and, with it, Yamaguchi's hope for victory.

It was obvious that there would be no salvaging of the *Hiryu*. When the order went out to abandon ship, the valiant Yamaguchi decided to remain aboard and go down with his ship. He addressed those members of the crew still remaining:

> As commanding officer of this carrier division, I am fully and solely responsible for the loss of *Hiryu* and *Soryu*, I shall remain on board to the end. I command all of you to leave the ship and continue your loyal service to His Majesty, the Emperor.[6]

Even with the news of *Hiryu*'s loss Yamamoto continued to press on in the vain hope of bringing the American fleet to battle. Eventually though, he realized that it was hopeless so around 0300 the following morning, he ordered the entire operation scrapped and all ships to retire.

After abandoning the *Yorktown*, Fletcher had turned tactical command over to Spruance, since his new flagship lacked the facilities for conducting a full-scale battle.

Midway still had to be protected. The Japanese surface force of battleships and cruisers remained intact. These ships could conceivably press on toward Midway. Spruance was faced with a dilemma. Should he proceed westward and intercept the enemy surface force or should he move out of harm's way?

Recalling Nimitz's injunction, Spruance decided not to risk a fleet encounter at night. Instead of intercepting the enemy he would position himself so that by morning he would be ideally situated to either oppose a landing on Midway or launch a strike against the remaining Japanese ships. He issued orders to move eastward until midnight, turn north for an hour, then move westward so that at first light he would be ready to meet any contingency. After issuing these orders, Spruance retired for the night.

After breakfast the following morning an excited Browning urged Spruance to head full speed toward the enemy and attack them before they got away. The admiral hesitated. The weather was not ideal for flying and there was always the possibility that the Japanese still had one carrier left. (Actually they did have four small carriers which Yamamoto was recalling to join the main body of the fleet.) Before committing his own fleet, Spruance wanted to be sure. He did not launch any scout planes, preferring instead to rely on reports from submarines and Midway's patrol planes.

Nevertheless, by noon Spruance was on the move. He had finally decided to destroy the retreating enemy. In the interim Browning had developed an attack plan and circulated it among the squadron leaders. Upon receipt of the plan, Wade McClusky stormed onto the bridge and protested that Browning's plan was bad. He disputed the chief of staff's calculations.

McClusky claimed that the bombs his planes were to carry were much too heavy and the range was too far. His planes would not have enough fuel to accomplish the return trip to their carriers. A heated argument ensued during which Spruance sided with McClusky, to the dismay of Browning. Enraged, the chief of staff stormed from the bridge.

Despite the disagreement the American fleet continued to close the gap on Yamamoto's retreating force. At 1500 Spruance launched a strike toward the anticipated Japanese position. Unfortunately, the American planes were only able to locate two small ships which they attacked unsuccessfully. As the planes returned to their carriers darkness was beginning to settle over the fleet.

Fearing that many of the pilots would be lost due to lack of experience in landing on carrier decks in darkness, Spruance ordered the ships to illuminate their flight decks, a most controversial directive in light of the possibility that enemy submarines were lurking nearby. If this were true, the deck lights would make it easier for subs to discover the American carriers.

Another night of doubt as to the true Japanese intentions passed. On the sixth, search planes located the Japanese surface fleet approximately 130 miles southwest of the American position. Yamamoto was still retiring to the west. Spruance immediately ordered scout planes from his cruisers to maintain contact with the enemy.

At 0800 the *Hornet* began launching planes. *Enterprise*'s squadrons followed in short order. The American pilots quickly located a force of Japanese ships retreating to the west. Instead of the main body of Yamamoto's fleet, however, these ships proved to be the aforementioned cruisers of Admiral Kurita.

By evening Spruance began to realize that he would have to call off the pursuit. The decision was a painful one but his destroyers were dangerously low on fuel and the aviators exhausted after three days of combat. Spruance was also aware that he would soon be in range of enemy aircraft based on Wake Island. Accordingly, the admiral officially terminated the battle.

Though criticized for terminating the pursuit, Spruance's decision was a wise one. Yamamoto still held a trump card, a potential ambush by his surface force supported by Wake's aircraft. Spruance would not be lured into the trap. Instead, the American fleet headed back to Pearl Harbor.

For his performance during the battle Spruance was awarded the Distinguished Service Medal. The accompanying citation read:

> For exceptionally meritorious service in a position of great responsibility as Task Force Commander, United States Pacific Fleet. During the Midway engagement, which resulted in the defeat of and heavy losses to the enemy fleet, his seamanship, endurance and tenacity in handling his task force were of the highest quality.[7]

Magnanimously, Spruance remained silent about his reservations regarding Browning's performance. Ironically, the latter was also awarded the Distinguished Service Medal for his "brilliant execution and judicious planning."

Spruance was also unhappy with the performance of Rear Adm. Marc Mitscher who flew his flag in the *Hornet* during the battle. He blamed Mitscher for the carrier's uneven performance. "Spruance's judgment of Mitscher was unfortunate because he would harbor a built-in prejudice for the wizened aviator."[8]

Indirectly, he blamed Mitscher for the loss of the *Yorktown* because the *Hornet* had failed to locate the Japanese carriers on June 4. Most of the carrier's planes flew aimlessly about without making contact with the enemy. Had they located the enemy force, Spruance maintained, they could have destroyed the enemy ship that later attacked the *Yorktown*. Fortunately, Mitscher was able to redeem himself later in the war.

Two postscripts remained to the battle. Yamamoto had earlier ordered Vice Admiral Kurita of the Close Support Group to take his Cruiser Division 7 to carry out a night bombardment of Midway. Shortly after midnight these orders were cancelled and Kurita was directed to withdraw. Just as the ships were reversing direction, a report was received that one of the lookouts had sighted a submarine. In the resulting confusion the cruiser *Mogami* collided with the *Mikuma* causing extensive damage to both ships.

Kurita pondered this latest dilemma. Should he risk exposing the entire formation to attack? Unwilling to accept this risk, he ordered the two damaged ships to proceed to port on their own, escorted by the destroyers *Arashio* and *Asashio* while he set out for the rendezvous with the rest of the combined fleet with his two remaining ships, flagship *Kumano* and *Suzuya*.

The next morning, American carrier planes were out hunting any cripples. Discovering the oil slick from where the *Mikuma*'s fuel tanks had been holed by the collision with *Mogami*, the American planes followed the trail and found the retreating cruisers just before 1000. *Mogami* was the first to feel the wrath of the American aviators. Her rear turret was destroyed by bombs and many men were killed. Then attention shifted to the *Mikuma* which was pounded unmercifully. Two and a half hours later another attack arrived over the hapless ships. Heavy fires blazed out of control on the *Mogami* while *Mikuma* was pummeled into a blazing hulk. Badly on fire, her captain gave the order to abandon ship but so intense was the heat that the *Arashio* could not approach to take off the crew. Consequently, they were required to jump over the side where they were fished from the water by the escorting destroyers.

Two hours later, the final attack of the day set off *Mikuma*'s torpedos and the ship rolled over and sank. In this attack, *Mogami* lost an additional ninety men, making the total for the day over three hundred dead. Fortunately, after the third attack the Americans came no more. *Mogami* managed to reach Truk on the fourteenth but she was out of the war for thirteen months while her unrecognizable upper decks were replaced. *Mikuma* was the first heavy cruiser lost during the war.

The second postscript involves the *Yorktown*. Although heavily damaged, the ship remained afloat. Admiral Fletcher decided to attempt repairs in hopes of towing the carrier back to Pearl Harbor. Around 1330 on June 6, the Japanese submarine I-168 spotted the carrier and fired a spread of torpedos. The fish struck home. One of them also broke the back of the destroyer *Hammann* which was tied up alongside, giving aid to the stricken carrier. *Hammann* sunk immediately. A short while later, *Yorktown* herself rolled over on its side and plunged beneath the waves.

As Nagumo leaned out over the bridge of the retreating *Nagara* he watched in silence as his once-mighty carrier fleet burned before taking its final plunge. He was acutely aware of the ramifications. The back of the Japanese navy was broken. Not only had four valuable ships been lost, so too had many skilled pilots lost their lives. These were irreplaceable.

The experts have called Midway the turning point of the entire Pacific war, and rightly so. No more would the awesome Japanese carrier fleet roam the Pacific leaving death and destruction in its wake. The Japanese navy did not have the ability to recover from the blow.

Who was at fault for the debacle at Midway? Certainly Nagumo must shoulder a great deal of the burden. His indecisiveness at the crucial time was a major factor in the subsequent events of June 4, 1942. However, there were extenuating circumstances.

Nagumo approached Midway blind. No intelligence reports had been received by his fleet so there was no way he could know of the American presence. In fact, the lack of intelligence indicated to Nagumo that just the opposite was true. Yamamoto's assumption that the American fleet was at sea was not forwarded to Nagumo. Neither were the reports of American attacks on Tanaka's convoy. Therefore, there was no way Nagumo could know that the secrecy of the entire operation was compromised. Instead, he steamed serenely on toward the fate that awaited him.

Another major factor contributing to the outcome of the battle was the splitting of the Japanese fleet. Of course Nagumo had nothing to do with this. Yamamoto, with a powerful battle fleet, was six hundred miles to the rear of the carriers. One light carrier was with this force, another with Kondo's invasion force and two others with the Aleutians strike force. Had these four ships been assigned to Nagumo and combined in one powerful striking force, perhaps the scales of victory would have tipped the other way.

What did the Battle of Midway mean to the Americans? It meant the halt of Japanese expansion to the east and the restoration of the balance of naval power in the Pacific. At the same time it removed the threat to Hawaii and the West Coast of the United States. Therefore, it was truly a turning point in the war.

NOTES

1. Tamiechi Hara, *Japanese Destroyer Captain*, p. 97
2. Thomas Buell, *The Quiet Warrior*, p. 122
3. F. P. Forrestel, *Admiral Raymond A. Spruance U.S.N.*, pp. 38-39
4. E. B. Potter, *Nimitz*, pp. 49-50
5. John Costello, *The Pacific War*, p. 319
6. Mitsuo Fuchida and Masatake Okumiya, *Midway*, pp. 197-198
7. Forrestel, *op. cit.*, p. 56
8. Buell, *op. cit.*, p. 149

BIBLIOGRAPHY

1. Agawa, Hiroyuki. *The Reluctant Admiral*.
Kodansha International, Tokyo, 1979.
2. Buell, Thomas. *The Quiet Warrior*.
Little Brown & Co., Boston, 1974.
3. Costello, John. *The Pacific War*.
Rawson Wade Publishers, New York, 1981.
4. Dull, Paul. *A Battle History of the Imperial Japanese Navy*.
Naval Institute Press, Annapolis, 1978.
5. Forrestel, E.P. *Admiral Raymond A. Spruance U.S.N.*
U.S. Govt. Printing Office, Washington, 1966.
6. Fuchida, Mitsuo and Okumiya, Masatake. *Midway*.
Naval Institute Press, Annapolis, 1955.
7. Hara, Tamiechi. *Japanese Destroyer Captain*.
Ballantine Books, New York, 1961.
8. Lord, Walter. *Incredible Victory*.
Harper & Row, New York, 1967.
9. Pfannes, Charles and Salamone, Victor. *The Great Commanders of World War II Vol. IV: The Japanese*.
Zebra Books, New York, 1982.

10. Pfannes, Charles and Salamone, Victor. *The Great Admirals of World War II Vol. I: The Americans*.
    Zebra Books, New York, 1983.
11. Potter, John. *Yamamoto*.
    Viking Press, New York, 1965.
12. Potter, E.B. *Nimitz*.
    Naval Institute Press, Annapolis, 1976.
13. Smith, S.E. *The U.S. Navy in World War II*.
    William Morrow & Co., New York, 1966.

CHAPTER FOUR

THE NAVAL BATTLES IN THE SOLOMONS

Following the victories at Coral Sea and Midway, the American chiefs of staff felt it was high time they went on the offensive. But where to strike? From his headquarters in Australia General MacArthur proposed the immediate seizure of Rabaul, the vital Japanese naval base on the island of New Britain. Admiral King considered MacArthur's plan to be far too ambitious. Rabaul was too heavily defended for a direct assault. In addition, an attack on Rabaul would have to be primarily a naval operation and King was vehemently opposed to MacArthur commanding naval forces.

On the other hand, General Marshall tended to side with MacArthur. Throughout the early summer of 1943 the debate between Marshall and King continued in a heated manner. The naval planners had proposed an assault on Rabaul through the eastern Solomons where it was felt the Japanese were weaker. The only drawback in this proposal was that the attack would have to be led by a naval commander and the Solomons were situated in MacArthur's Southwest Pacific area of responsibility.

Meanwhile, a few days prior to the Battle of the Coral Sea, the Japanese had seized the island of Tulagi in the southern Solomons. They quickly constructed a seaplane there from which they could easily conduct a surveillance of the line of communication between America and Australia. A few weeks later the Japanese occupied the neighboring island of Guadalcanal and began immediate construction of an airstrip. When the Americans learned of this development they knew what target to strike first. Enemy aircraft based on Guadalcanal would be a distinct threat.

As the debate between he and Marshall continued, Admiral King took the bull by the horns and ordered Admiral Nimitz to seize Guadalcanal and Tulagi even though they were west of the 159 degree line which divided Nimitz's and MacArthur's commands. On June 25 King presented the Joint Chiefs of Staff with a prepared plan. Having already promised MacArthur the command, MacArthur found himself in a bind. Ironically, MacArthur himself backed down from his direct approach to the Rabaul plan and accepted the indirect plan which the naval planners had drawn up.

But the question of command remained unresolved. This subject was debated for days. Finally, the conflict reached a climax on June 29, when King and Marshall agreed to meet face to face. The next day a compromise was reached. The Southwest Pacific boundary was shifted westward, thus placing the islands of Guadalcanal and Tulagi in Nimitz's sphere. MacArthur could no longer claim that he should command all naval forces in his area since the lower Solomons no longer lay there. Instead, Vice Adm. Robert Ghormley, Nimitz's deputy in the South

THE NAVAL BATTLES FOR GUADALCANAL

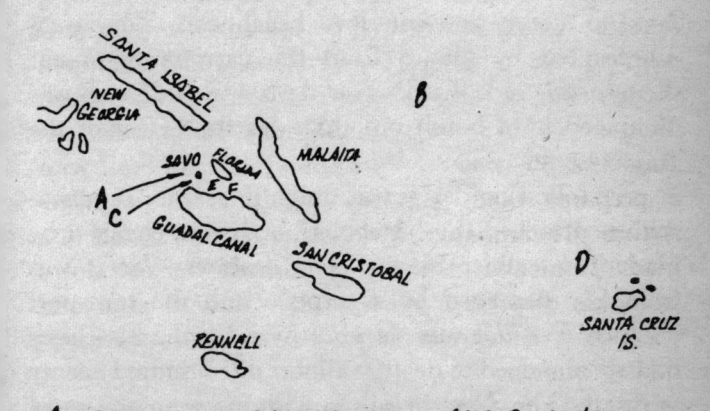

A. BATTLE OF SAVO ISLAND - AUG. 9 1942
B. BATTLE OF THE EASTERN SOLOMONS, AUG. 23-25
C. BATTLE OF CAPE ESPERANCE, OCT. 11-12, 1942
D. BATTLE OF THE SANTA CRUZ ISLANDS, OCT. 26
E. NAVAL BATTLE OF GUADALCANAL, NOV. 13-15, 1942
F. BATTLE OF TASSAFARONGA, NOV. 30. 1942

Pacific, would command the assault on Guadalcanal and Tulagi.

On August 7, 1942, Gen. Alexander Vandergrift led a force of U.S. Marines ashore on Tulagi and Guadalcanal. Tulagi fell in a few days. On Guadalcanal, the Marines encountered little initial opposition and quickly moved inland, took the incomplete airfield, and renamed it Henderson Field.

The Japanese wasted little time in striking back. A flight of bombers was quickly dispatched from Rabaul to attack the American beachhead. They were intercepted by planes from the carriers *Saratoga*, *Enterprise* and *Wasp*. The destroyer *Mugford* was damaged by a bomb but that was the extent of the Japanese success.

The following day it was much the same. Japanese planes attacked the beachhead and were engaged by American carrier planes. The destroyer *Jarvis* was critically damaged by a torpedo and the transport *George F. Elliot* was set afire by a bomb. Fletcher's planes managed to destroy almost one hundred enemy aircraft. The *Enterprise*'s squadrons were the most active of the three carriers and gave a good account of themselves. Nevertheless, by evening on August 8, twenty-one American planes had been lost.

At a pre-invasion conference of all key commanders of the assault, Admiral Fletcher had stunned everyone by announcing that he would protect the American beachhead for two days only. Having lost two carriers already—*Lexington* in the Coral Sea and *Yorktown* at Midway—and with these losses still fresh in his mind, he was not about to expose his precious ships to land-based air attacks. Thus, after dark on the eighth,

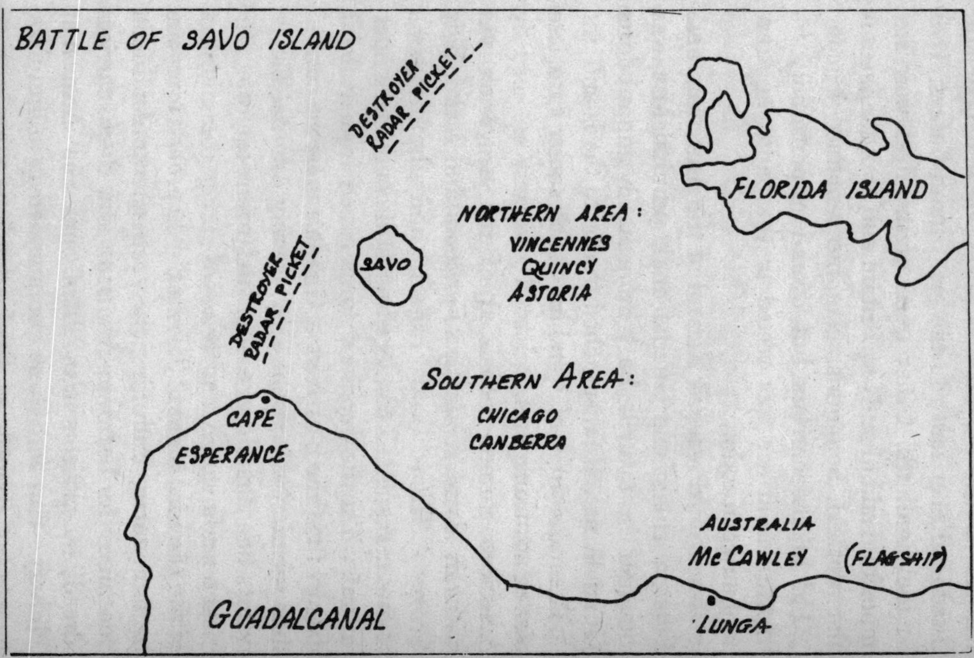
BATTLE OF SAVO ISLAND
DESTROYER
RADAR PICKET
FLORIDA ISLAND
NORTHERN AREA:
VINCENNES
QUINCY
ASTORIA
SAVO
DESTROYER
RADAR PICKET
SOUTHERN AREA:
CHICAGO
CANBERRA
CAPE
ESPERANCE
AUSTRALIA
McCAWLEY (FLAGSHIP)
GUADALCANAL
LUNGA

Fletcher ordered his force to draw out of range.

Admiral Yamamoto was determined to hold onto Guadalcanal. After having restructured the fleet after the horrendous defeat at Midway, he had taken the combined fleet south to the great naval base at Truk in the Carolines. Other units of the fleet were stationed at Rabaul on New Britain and at other bases in the northern Solomons. Nagumo remained in command of the carriers but overall responsibility for operations at sea was vested in the hands of Adm. Nobutake Kondo.

When word reached Rabaul of the American landings on Tulagi and Guadalcanal, Admiral Mikawa's reaction was to strike back immediately and reinforce Guadalcanal. He dispatched troops to the island and took a squadron of warships south to strike at the American transports.

Mikawa's force consisted of the heavy cruisers *Chokai*, *Aoba*, *Kinugasa*, *Furutaka* and *Kako*, light cruisers *Tenryu* and *Yubari*, and the destroyer *Yunagi*. Fletcher's carriers were still conducting operations when the Japanese force sailed from Rabaul, but by the time it arrived at Guadalcanal, the carriers had withdrawn from the area, leaving Admiral Turner with a handful of cruisers and destroyers to protect the beachhead.

On the fatal night of August 8–9, Turner's force was split in three. Patrolling the eastern entrance to the Slot were the destroyers *Monsenn* and *Buchanan* and the light cruisers *San Juan* and the Australian *Hobart*. This force was commanded by Adm. Norman Scott. North of Savo Island were the cruisers *Quincy*, *Astoria* and *Vincennes* and the destroyers

Helm and *Wilson*. South of Savo were the destroyers *Patterson* and *Bagley*, with the American cruiser *Chicago* and the Australian cruisers *Australia* and *Canberra*. Northwest of the northern force on the opposite side of Savo, Admiral Crutchley RAN,* who was in overall command of the latter two forces, stationed the destroyer *Ralph Talbot*. Directly south of this ship was the destroyer *Blue* guarding the remaining approach to the beachhead. The two picket destroyers were on guard to warn the cruiser forces of any approach by Japanese ships.

Mikawa's plan was relatively simple. He would enter the waters north of Guadalcanal (an area subsequently dubbed Ironbottom Sound because of the great number of ships that rested on its bottom) in the early morning of August 9 and strike the American ships protecting the landing force. Then, after the destruction of the covering force, the Japanese ships would attack the defenseless transports before retiring toward Rabaul.

A combination of Japanese luck and American mistakes allowed Mikawa to approach undetected. The Japanese force had been sighted by an Australian pilot, but the report of the sighting did not reach Turner until eight hours later. When he did receive the report he was misled by the pilot's mistaking two of Mikawa's cruisers for seaplane tenders. Because of the tardy and inaccurate report, Turner felt that the

---

*Royal Australian Navy.

Japanese would not attack that night but would first attempt to establish a seaplane base north of Guadalcanal and attack at a later date.

Late in the evening of the eighth, Turner, not expecting an attack and worried over Fletcher's decision to leave with his carriers, summoned Admiral Crutchley to a conference aboard his flagship which was moored off the beachhead, twenty miles from Savo. Taking the *Australia*, Crutchley left his remaining cruisers behind.

With Crutchley absent, all hell broke loose in the vicinity of Savo. Mikawa's force slipped undetected past the patrolling *Ralph Talbot* and *Blue*. After two days at general quarters and not anticipating hostile action, the Allied naval force was fatigued. At 2345 the *Ralph Talbot* did send off a sighting report stating that three planes were headed for the beachhead. The cruiser captains erroneously assumed that the planes were friendly. However, the aircraft had in fact been sent on ahead by Mikawa.

At 0020 on the ninth, Mikawa, by now in view of Savo Island, ordered his ships to battle stations. A few minutes later lookouts aboard the flagship, *Chokai*, sighted the *Blue*. Mikawa slowed the formation and allowed the *Blue* to pass serenely by. The American destroyer had not noticed a thing.

An unwilling participant in the battle was the destroyer *Jarvis*. The damaged destroyer was heading for Australia so that the bomb damage sustained the previous day could be repaired. The *Jarvis* was the first ship attacked by Mikawa's force. Around 0130 the *Yunagi* peeled off from the Japanese formation and attacked the American destroyer with torpedos but failed to score a hit.

Meanwhile, the Japanese had also sighted Crutchley's southern force at 0136. Torpedos were launched against the unsuspecting American force almost immediately. Five minutes later Mikawa ordered his ships to begin firing.

The ships of the southern force were ignorant of the approach of the enemy. Not until shells began to fall around them did they realize the peril facing them, but by then it was too late. The *Canberra* was smothered by a hail of shells in a few moments. Over two dozen shells pounded the hapless Australian cruiser. Burning and listing, she staggered out of the battle.

At the same time the *Chicago* came awake. Before she could retaliate, however, a torpedo slammed into her and blasted off the ship's bow. Although spared the hail of shells, the cruiser had all it could do to stay afloat, let alone retaliate. The two destroyers were spared.

Mikawa now turned his force toward the northern force. Incredibly, the southern force failed to report that it was under fire so the remaining three American cruisers had no knowledge that a hostile force was approaching them.

Following the easy victory over the southern force Mikawa split his force in order to trap the Americans between the two wings of his formation. At 0150 the left wing consisting of the *Yubari*, *Tenryu* and *Furutaka* opened fire on the *Astoria*, the last ship in the American line. On the fifth salvo the Japanese gunners struck pay dirt. The *Astoria* began to blaze, making her a relatively easy target to spot. Shell after shell landed on her decks. Nevertheless, before she was overwhelmed, the *Astoria* managed to hit the *Chokai* on her forward turret putting those guns out of commission.

The *Astoria* and *Vincennes* were overwhelmed quickly also. Countless shells and torpedos slammed into both cruisers and within minutes they were listing and burning, struggling to remain afloat. All efforts to save the stricken ships proved futile. *Quincy* was the first to sink, at 0235. Fifteen minutes later the *Vincennes* followed her to the bottom of Ironbottom Sound. The *Astoria* lasted until shortly after noon time before slipping beneath the waves. The burnt-out hulk of the drifting *Canberra* was scuttled at 0800 the next morning.

Following the destruction of the American ships guarding Guadalcanal, Mikawa paused briefly north of Savo contemplating his attack on the now-defenseless transports. Fortunately for the Americans the Japanese commander began to harbor reservations. He knew that he had earned a great naval victory at minimal cost but he also knew that a third American force was guarding the opposite approach to the beachhead and Mikawa did not know the strength of this force. Had he known that Scott's force was too far away and that its main strength was merely two light cruisers, perhaps he might have decided otherwise. Then of course he could not ignore the threat of the American carriers. Mikawa did not know that Fletcher had left the scene entirely and therefore he had no wish to expose his fleet to carrier-based air attack as it retired up the Slot. Consequently, Mikawa reversed course and headed back toward Rabaul.

Shortly after making his decision, the Japanese force was sighted by the northern American picket destroyer, *Ralph Talbot*. There was little the tiny destroyer could do to halt Mikawa's force. After firing starshells to identify the ships moving by, the Japanese ships fired on the destroyer. The *Ralph Talbot* was quickly put out of commission and she drifted south out of control until around noon the next day when she was able to get underway.

Flushed with success and feeling that he had earned a great naval victory in spite of the fact that the American transports were unscathed, Mikawa headed home. His failure to attack the beachhead was another in a long series of Japanese failures to follow up their victories. Had he gotten loose among the transports the entire story of Guadalcanal might have had a different outcome.

A postscript to the Battle of Savo was the fate of the destroyer *Jarvis*. Around 0200 the *Yunagi*, which had left the main Japanese force to deal with her, further damaged the American destroyer with gunfire. Although she remained afloat and under control, the *Jarvis'* speed was greatly reduced. Around 1300 the following day, a flight of Japanese torpedo planes discovered her north of Guadalcanal and quickly sent the little ship to the bottom.

The Japanese did not make it back to Rabaul unscathed. As it retired up the Slot, Mikawa's force, which had been split, was sighted by the American submarine S-44. The S-44 fired four torpedos at a cruiser. At least one, perhaps two, struck the *Kako*. The huge hole in her side caused the cruiser to roll over and sink quickly. It was the final victim of the Battle of Savo Island.

Yamamoto was determined to hold onto Guadalcanal. After restructuring the fleet following the horrendous defeat at Midway, he had taken the combined fleet south to the naval base at Truk in the Carolines. Other units of the fleet were based at Rabaul on New Britain and at bases in the northern Solomons. Admiral Nagumo continued to command the aircraft carriers but overall responsibility for operations at sea was vested in the hands of Adm. Nobutake Kondo.

Faced with the problem of reinforcing Guadalcanal, Yamamoto created the Guadalcanal Reinforcement Group. The question of a commander for this force was an easy one. Since the primary role would be born by destroyers, a top-notch destroyer commander was called for. In Yamamoto's eyes, Adm. Raizo Tanaka was one of the finest, if not the very best, in the entire navy. His exploits to date attested to this fact and he had already proven his ability for escorting convoys. Furthermore, not only was Tanaka's brilliance recognized throughout the fleet, he was highly popular. Thus, no one but Tanaka was surprised when he was summoned to Yamamoto's headquarters and entrusted with the heavy burden of reinforcing Guadalcanal.

When confronted with the facts of this latest venture, Tanaka called the effort "Bamboo Spear Tactics," and made no secret of his opposition to the methods—piecemeal reinforcement of Guadalcanal. Tanaka argued that the entire concept would serve no other purpose but to keep feeding men and material into a meat grinder. In addition, unlike his superiors, Tanaka was a bit more respectful of his opponents. After the war he stated:

> We were flushed with victories and we never imagined we could lose. We had victory disease, a blind arrogance, supreme confidence and utter contempt for the enemy. My superiors were certain that single battalions and a few guns would easily dislodge the enemy from Guadalcanal. In the end, this tactic of piecemeal reinforcements led to tragic consequences.[1]

Nevertheless, on the evening of August 15, Tanaka loaded almost one thousand troops of the Ichiki Detachment* aboard his destroyers and set off for Guadalcanal. Thus began a series of exploits that would earn Tanaka the grudging respect and admiration of his opponents and the nickname "Tenacious Tanaka."

Covered by the darkness of night, Tanaka's destroyers crept up to the coast of Guadalcanal on the evening of August 18 and landed the troops without incident. It all seemed so easy that Tanaka decided to press his luck further and took his ships down the coast of the island to carry out a bombardment of the American positions near Henderson Field and on Tulagi. But he lingered too long at the well.

The only thing the bombardment accomplished was a precious waste of darkness. Consequently, daylight

---

*After the commander of the formation, Colonel Ichiki

found Tanaka steaming back up the Slot. Since the operation had gone off without a hitch, the pace was unhurried. Suddenly, U.S. Army B-17s arrived over the formation and dropped their bombs. One hit was made on the destroyer *Hagikaze*. Tanaka ordered full speed ahead and drew out of range, the damaged *Hagikaze* limping along.

Precisely as Tanaka had cautioned, the effort was in vain. Armed with faulty intelligence reports that vastly underestimated American strength on Guadalcanal, Colonel Ichiki launched an attack on August 24. At the Battle of the Tenaru River his force was annihilated. Those that survived the battle were fair game for the American fighter planes that strafed their positions. The proud Colonel Ichiki wrapped himself in his colors and committed hara-kiri.

Another effort to reinforce Guadalcanal was hastily prepared. The remainder of Ichiki's command would be delivered to the island. This time Tanaka would have the support of not one, but two powerful fleets. Intent on bringing the American fleet to battle, Admiral Kondo with the cruisers *Tone*, *Atago*, *Takao*, *Maya*, *Myoko*, *Haguro* and *Yura*, battleship *Mutsu*, seaplane carrier *Chitose*, light carrier *Ryujo* and six destroyers moved east of the Solomons. Kondo planned to detach the *Ryujo* and her escorts when he was in range of Guadalcanal so that the carrier could perform a dual role. Its planes would attack American positions on the island while the carrier itself served as a decoy for the American fleet.

Following Kondo's advance force was a second, more powerful striking force under Nagumo. In addition to the large carriers *Shokaku* and *Zuikaku*, the force contained the battleships *Hiei* and *Kirishima*, cruisers *Kumano*, *Suzuya*, *Chikuma* and *Nagara* and six destroyers. Once the American fleet was located, planes from the two carriers would attack. At the same time, Kondo hoped to get in a blow with his surface ships.

American codebreakers had concluded that the Japanese were preparing a major operation and that the fleet was ready to move south. Admiral Nimitz ordered Admiral Fletcher to take his task force, containing the carriers *Wasp*, *Enterprise* and *Saratoga*, to the east of the Solomons and intercept the Japanese fleet moving south from Truk. In addition to the three carriers, Fletcher's force contained the cruisers *Australia*, *Hobart* (both RAN), *Minneapolis*, *New Orleans*, *Portland*, *Atlanta*, *San Juan*, *San Francisco* and *Salt Lake City*, battleship *North Carolina*, and eighteen destroyers. The screening ships were evenly distributed among three task groups centered on each of the carriers.

The morning of August 23 found both the American and Japanese forces approaching each other. Fletcher was due east of Malaita Island while Tanaka and the transport group was approximately 250 miles to the northwest. Steaming parallel to Tanaka, but about 80 miles further east was Kondo's main body. Nagumo's strike force followed over 100 miles to the rear.

At 0950 a patrolling PBY aircraft sighted Tanaka's force moving south. Both Fletcher and Henderson Field put up search planes to confirm the sighting but none of the planes were successful because forty minutes after reporting that he had been sighted,

Tanaka was ordered to reverse course. Then at 1430, he was ordered to reverse course once more so that he could reach Guadalcanal and unload his precious cargo under cover of darkness. For the remainder of the day both sides probed for each other to no avail.

At 1800 Fletcher made a calculated error which more than likely cost him the battle. Since there had been no further sighting reports, Fletcher could not be sure that the Japanese fleet was at sea and, even if it were, when battle would be joined. He therefore ordered the *Wasp* and her escorts south to refuel, thereby reducing the size of his task force by one third.

Like Tanaka, Kondo too had reversed course late in the day. Around 0040 the following morning he ordered the *Ryujo* to leave the main body and proceed on her mission of striking Henderson Field and serving as a decoy. Then, at 0530, Kondo with the main body doubled back on its original course.

The *Ryujo* was sighted shortly after 0900 by another patrolling PBY. An hour later the sighting was confirmed by a second sighting. It was some time, however, before the confirmation reached Fletcher on the *Saratoga*. When it did, he immediately ordered Admiral Kinkaid on the *Enterprise* to launch a multiplane search. At the same time, the *Saratoga* began to prepare a strike against the lone Japanese carrier.

At 1345 nearly forty planes began to roar off the flight deck of the *Saratoga* and headed toward the *Ryujo*'s reported position. The latter, meanwhile, had launched an attack against Henderson Field.

Forty-five minutes after the *Saratoga*'s flight was launched, one of the *Enterprise*'s scout planes located

Nagumo's force with the *Zuikaku* and *Shokaku*. Fletcher immediately attempted to divert the *Saratoga*'s attack to meet the more serious threat, but communications were bad and the flight leader failed to receive the message.

The *Saratoga*'s planes arrived over the *Ryujo* around 1545. The small carrier was overwhelmed. No one knows for sure just how many bombs landed on the carrier—accounts vary between four and ten—but at least one torpedo plowed into her side and within minutes the *Ryujo* was turned into a drifting, blazing inferno. All efforts to save her were in vain and four hours later the ship rolled over and sank.

Meanwhile, the Japanese had located Fletcher's force. At 1507 Nagumo launched a full strike from his two carriers. As the Japanese planes headed off toward the Americans two daring scout planes from the *Enterprise* arrived on the scene. Braving the heavy anti-aircraft fire the pilots dove on the *Shokaku* and succeeded in inflicting mild damage.

The American force had a combat air patrol of some fifty planes in the air when the Japanese planes arrived on the scene around 1640. *Saratoga* was separated from the *Enterprise* by ten miles of sea and it was the latter that took the brunt of the Japanese attack.

Admiral Kinkaid was on the bridge of the *Enterprise* with Capt. Arthur Davis when the first Japanese strike arrived overhead. He watched in awe as the combined combat air patrol and heavy anti-aircraft fire of the escorting warships beat the first wave back without mishap to the carrier.

Before the Americans could catch their breath,

however, a flight of enemy dive bombers arrived over the fleet. Once again it appeared as if the legendary luck of the "Big E" would hold. The first wave of attackers were destroyed or driven off just like the torpedo planes a few moments earlier. But there were simply too many of the attackers. At 1714 a bomb plunged through three decks and exploded. Thirty seconds later another rammed through to the ship's innards. A third bomb tore a gaping hole in the flight deck. Badly damaged, the *Enterprise* limped out of the battle.

Brilliant efforts by her damage-control teams stemmed the blazing fires and saved the ship. Hasty repairs to the flight deck allowed Kinkaid to recover his planes but half an hour after the first bomb struck the carrier's rudder jammed and she went dead in the water with another Japanese strike headed her way.

Luckily, the next Japanese flight miscalculated the American's position and failed to locate either of Fletcher's carriers. That night, her rudder repaired, Kinkaid took the *Enterprise* back to Noumea.

Meanwhile, the *Saratoga*'s planes failed to locate Nagumo's force. Two of the planes did, however, stumble across Kondo's force. Their attack was rewarded with slight damage to the *Chitose*.

The main objective of the entire Japanese operation, Tanaka's landing at Guadalcanal, was thwarted. By the morning of the twenty-fifth his force was still almost one hundred miles north of their objective. At 0935 that morning the force was attacked by planes from Henderson Field. The *Jintsu*, Tanaka's flagship, was hit by a bomb and seriously damaged. Tanaka was knocked unconscious for a brief period and upon recovering, shifted his flag to the destroyer *Kagero* and ordered the *Jintsu* back to Truk. In the same attack, the transport *Kinryu Maru* was set ablaze by American bombs.

Tanaka ordered the destroyer *Mutsuki* to close the stricken transport and take off survivors. While this operation was in progress a flight of B-17s arrived and sent both ships to the bottom. The rest of the transports turned back.

The Battle of the Eastern Solomons was technically an American victory. The reinforcement attempt was turned back and the Japanese lost the *Ryujo*. Nevertheless, the *Enterprise* had been seriously mauled and would be out of action for some time. This left the Americans with just three carriers remaining in the South Pacific.

For some time Admiral Nimitz had been unhappy with the unspectacular performance of Fletcher. The carrier commander was a tired man and he lacked the aggressive spirit that Nimitz was seeking. The Battle of the Eastern Solomons gave Nimitz the excuse he needed. Fletcher was relieved.

On Guadalcanal, the Tokyo Express continued to run troops and supplies ashore. Meanwhile, the beleaguered Marines held off every attempt to throw them back into the sea but they were running short of essentials and casualties mounted daily.

On October 9, ten American transports, loaded with troops and supplies, sailed from Noumea for Guadalcanal. Covering the operation was TF 17 comprising the carrier *Hornet*, four cruisers and six destroyers hovering just under two hundred miles east of Guadalcanal. A second force, under Admiral Lee, built around the battleship *Washington*, patrolled east of Malaita Island. Adm. Norman Scott's TF64, with the cruisers *San Francisco*, *Salt Lake City*, *Boise* and *Helena* and destroyers *Farenholt*, *Laffey*, *Buchanan*, *Duncan* and *McCalla*, waited near Rennell Island in case the Japanese decided to attack the supply ships.

Meanwhile, the Japanese were also preparing for a major reinforcement run to Guadalcanal. The leading elements of the vaunted Sendai Division were loaded on six destroyers and dispatched down the Slot protected by the seaplane carriers *Chitose* and *Nisshin*. A close covering force under Admiral Goto would protect the landings and, under cover of darkness, bombard the U.S. positions. Goto's force contained the cruisers *Aoba*, *Furutaka* and *Kinugasa* and the destroyers *Fubuki* and *Hatsuyuki*. A third Japanese force with the light carriers *Junyo*, *Hiyo*, and *Zuiho* sailed from Truk to provide long-range cover from a position northeast of the Solomons.

In midafternoon of the eleventh, a wandering B-17 sighted the Japanese relief operation approaching Guadalcanal. Scott was quickly notified and within a hour was racing at full speed for Ironbottom Sound. Around 2200 the American admiral ordered his cruisers to launch their float planes. The planes were ordered to scout the area and, when they ran short of fuel, to land at Tulagi instead of back aboard the cruisers.

Scott felt that the Japanese would repeat their tactic of covering the off-loading of troops and supplies by sending an advance force into Ironbottom Sound as a bombardment force. If this occurred they would use the shortest route, between Savo Island and Cape

Esperance. It was there that Scott decided to patrol. As the American force came abreast of the patrol area Scott placed his task force in line ahead, three destroyers in lead followed by the cruisers and the two remaining destroyers *Buchanan* and *McCalla*.

At 2250 the *Salt Lake City*'s scout plane sighted the enemy transport group. Scott altered course to the northeast and lay in wait for the approaching enemy.

Unaware of the presence of American warships, Goto headed straight for Ironbottom Sound. At 2325 *Helena*'s radar made contact with the enemy but her captain was unsure of the reading and failed to report the sighting to Scott who, five minutes later, ordered a reversal of course since the formation was getting too far away from Cape Esperance.

The American column had still not resumed position when, at 2342, *Helena*'s captain finally made a sighting report. At the same time gunners aboard the *San Francisco* sighted the enemy formation. After a confusing series of TBS* messages, the *Helena* opened fire, almost four minutes after sending off the sighting report. Within seconds the rest of the American column opened fire. But the destroyers were still out of position.

Scott had achieved what every naval commander dreams of in a surface battle: he had capped the enemy's T. Goto was sailing in line ahead at right angles to the U.S. battle line. As a result, the Americans were able to bring all their guns to bear while the Japanese could only fire their forward turrets. In

*Talk Between Ships.

addition, the Japanese had not sighted the American ships and were unaware of Scott's presence until shells began to fall on and around their ships. With everything going his way, Scott threw away the advantage.

Thinking that his cruisers were firing at their own destroyers (the destroyers did in fact come under friendly fire), Scott ordered a cease fire. A few more salvos were loosed before every ship acknowledged the order and some of these took their toll.

Meanwhile, immediately after the Americans opened fire, Goto ordered a turn to starboard. During the turn his flagship *Aoba* was smothered in a hail of shells that mortally wounded the Japanese admiral. On fire and seriously damaged, the cruiser completed a 180-degree turn. *Furutaka* was also hit by shells and at least one torpedo from the American destroyers. Although she also completed her turn it was clear that the *Furutaka* was doomed as her speed began to drop off and the fires raging the length of the ship illuminated the entire area.

Four minutes after ordering the cease fire, Scott directed his ships to resume firing. But the lull had given the Japanese breathing room. From somewhere in the American line a searchlight snapped on and picked out *Fubuki*. Virtually every U.S. ship turned their guns on the highly visible target and in less than five minutes the hapless destroyer was blasted to the bottom.

As already seen, when the confused action began the American destroyers had yet to resume their positions in line and as a result the *Laffey*, *Duncan* and *Farenholt* found themselves between their own forces and the enemy. When the battle erupted all three ships headed for the enemy immediately. *Duncan* was hit badly by fire from both sides and *Farenholt* took a few shell hits but her damage was minimal. In a sinking condition, *Duncan* steamed out of line. Nevertheless, all the destroyers had managed to launch their torpedos. At least one of these found the *Furutaka*.

Just before midnight, Scott altered course to parallel the Japanese line. Five minutes later he called for another cease fire so that he could take stock of the situation. Just then the *Kinugasa*, which along with *Hatsuyuki* had turned opposite the other Japanese ships, opened fire with guns and torpedos. The captain of the *Boise* ordered his ship's spotlight turned on to light up the stricken *Aoba*. This made the American cruiser a perfect target for the well-aimed guns of *Kinugasa*. The *Boise* took a direct hit in one of her powder rooms and staggered out of line on fire. Following this exchange the battle died down. By 0030 the action was over.

Furutaka succumbed to her damage at 0040 and rolled over and sank. The *Duncan* survived until noon before her fires got the best of her and she slipped beneath the waves. Destroyers from the Japanese transport force remained behind to search for survivors but broke off the operation just before daylight. As they retreated up the Slot they were pounced on by planes from Henderson Field. The Americans sent the destroyers *Murakumo* and *Natsugumo* to the bottom.

Although the Battle of Cape Esperance had been a tactical victory for the Americans, the Japanese still managed to carry out their relief operation. Nevertheless the cost was high: one cruiser and three destroyers sunk, *Aoba* badly damaged and Goto killed. Had it not been for a series of errors on the American side the battle might have been even more decisive.

Despite Scott's victory, the Tokyo Express continued to run. Japanese efforts were even intensified. Admiral Kurita took the battleships *Kongo* and *Haruna* into Ironbottom Sound on the night of October 13. Escorted by Tanaka's Second Destroyer Flotilla the Japanese heavies lobbed over nine hundred shells into the Henderson Field area. Tanaka's smaller ships sailed back and forth along the shore hurling smaller caliber shells into the American positions. After exhausting his ammunition, Kurita returned whence he had come. In his wake he left fifty aircraft destroyed.

Owing to Kurita's feat and the continuing bombing raids from Rabaul and the Shortlands, the Japanese felt that aerial supremacy over Guadalcanal had finally been achieved. Another supply run was sent down the Slot even as Kurita was steaming homeward. Six transports anchored at Tassafronga the following night and began to land over four thousand troops.

While the transports were discharging their passengers, Admiral Mikawa attempted a repeat of Kurita's effort. The cruisers *Chokai* and *Kinugasa* paraded up and down offshore heaving eight-inch shells into the Marine positions on the night of the fourteenth. A few hours after midnight Mikawa broke off the action and returned up the Slot leaving Tanaka and his destroyers to cover the unloading of the six transports.

Since they were confident that Henderson Field was

out of commission once and for all, the Japanese thought it safe to unload the transports in broad daylight with relative impunity. Unfortunately, they were unaware of the existence of an auxiliary airstrip behind the American lines.

Kurita and Mikawa's bombardment caused heavy damage not only to the American planes but also to the stocks of aviation fuel as well. Nonetheless, the Americans set to work salvaging whatever they could. Early in the morning after Mikawa's raid one plane managed to take off from the auxiliary airstrip. The pilot soon sighted the Japanese transports near Tassafronga and managed to hit one of them with a bomb. Tanaka felt that the attack of one lone plane was no cause for alarm. If this was all the enemy had to strike back with there was nothing to fear.

The Americans were far from beaten, however. A remarkable effort on the part of their ground crews succeeded in securing some aviation fuel. Others worked furiously to patch together some of the damaged planes. Around noon, a strike was ready for takeoff.

An hour later the small flight of planes roared over the Japanese transports. Within minutes three of the ships were on fire and in a sinking condition. A shocked Tanaka ordered the remaining ships to haul off at high speed until nightfall. There was no way he could have known that the American attack represented a maximum effort on their part.

Two nights later the Tokyo Express was back. While the transports unloaded under cover of darkness Tanaka's destroyers, accompanied by the cruisers *Myoko* and *Maya*, bombarded the American positions once more. This time the auxiliary airstrip came in for its share of attention.

The failure to halt the nightly runs of the Tokyo Express or to tip the scales in the battle for Guadalcanal troubled Admiral Nimitz deeply. Something had to be done and the most important change needed was to replace the commander of the South Pacific area, Admiral Ghormley. The latter had become pessimistic about the area and had even proposed evacuating the area. What the situation needed was an infusion of fresh blood, someone that was highly aggressive. Nimitz had just the man waiting in the wings, Adm. William F. Halsey, fresh from sick leave. Ghormley was replaced.

As a result of the losses incurred at Cape Esperance, Yamamoto delayed the beginning of an all-out offensive. Unless the army accomplished something, he said, he would take the Japanese fleet out of the area. Accordingly, the Sendai Division began an all-out attack on October 25 and quickly announced that Henderson Field had been captured. The report was totally false. For two days the Sendai battered themselves against the well-dug-in Marines. The bulk of the division's troops were left dead on the battlefield without having made any significant progress. Nevertheless, the premature announcement of the fall of Henderson Field stirred the Japanese fleet to action.

Yamamoto directed that the route from Rabaul to Guadalcanal be cleared at all costs. His latest elaborate plan called for a large convoy of reinforcements to head for Guadalcanal. At the same time, he hoped to lure the American fleet into the ever-elusive all-out battle. Admiral Tanaka with the cruiser *Yura* and eight destroyers would run the reinforcements into Guadalcanal. Covering Tanaka's sortie would be Admiral Abe's Vanguard force with the battleships *Hiei*, and *Kirishima*, cruisers *Tone*, *Chikuma*, *Suzuya* and *Nagara* and seven destroyers. Directly behind Abe's force would be Nagumo's Striking force of carriers *Shokaku*, *Zuikaku* and *Zuiho*, cruiser *Kumano* and eight destroyers. Kondo's Advance force was to remain northeast of Nagumo in the event it was needed. This force was escorted by ten destroyers and included the cruisers *Atago*, *Takeo*, *Myoko*, *Maya* and *Isuzu*, battleships *Haruna* and *Kongo* and the carriers *Junyo* and *Hiyo*. Shortly after setting out the latter developed engine trouble and was sent back to Truk escorted by two destroyers. As indicated, it was a typical Japanese operation with elaborate plans for precise timing by a divided force.

American intelligence reports indicated that the Japanese were preparing another major offensive. Unfortunately, Halsey was ill-equipped to offer a powerful resistance. The *Wasp* had been sunk by a Japanese submarine on September 15. Two weeks earlier the *Saratoga* had also been torpedoed by an enemy submarine. Although the carrier survived the attack, it would be some months before she was ready for action again.

Nevertheless, Halsey was determined to thwart the latest Japanese effort. The *Enterprise*, under Admiral Kinkaid, sailed from Noumea on October sixteenth after hasty repairs to the damage incurred at the Battle of the Eastern Solomons. Kinkaid's TF 61 also contained the battleship *South Dakota*, cruisers *Port-*

land and *San Juan* and seven destroyers. At sea Kinkaid was joined by Admiral Lee's TF 64 with the battleship *Washington*, cruisers *San Francisco*, *Atlanta* and *Helena* and six destroyers.

On October 24, Kinkaid's force linked up with TF 17 under Admiral Murray northeast of Espiritu Santo. Murray's force was centered around the carrier *Hornet* and included cruisers *Pensacola*, *Northampton*, *Juneau* and *San Diego* and six destroyers. As senior officer, Kinkaid assumed overall command and took the American fleet north of Santa Cruz Island to await word of the Japanese approach.

On October 23, a Catalina flying boat sighted the Japanese Vanguard force moving south. Kinkaid moved to intercept at once.

Around 1200 on the twenty-fifth, an American patrol plane from Espiritu Santo sighted Nagumo's Striking force also moving south. The American carriers were far to the south but as soon as he drew within range, Kinkaid launched search planes from his own force. An hour later a full strike from the *Enterprise* was in the air and headed toward the reported enemy position even though the Americans were at extreme range.

Nagumo, however, was taking no chances. His force had spotted the American reconnaissance plane. Just around the time the *Enterprise* was launching its strike he reversed course. Consequently, when the *Enterprise* pilots arrived over the spot where the Japanese fleet was reported, they found nothing but empty ocean. Throughout the rest of the day the two fleets probed for each other without success. After dark, Nagumo turned south once more.

Half an hour after midnight another American patrol plane reported that the Japanese fleet was approximately three hundred miles north of Kinkaid's position. Another sighting, three hours later, was reported via Noumea. This latter report, placing the enemy one hundred miles closer to the Americans, didn't reach Kinkaid until after 0500. By that time the admiral had already launched his own patrol planes. Accompanying the delayed sighting report from Noumea was one from Halsey, direct and to the point. ATTACK—REPEAT—ATTACK.

This report confused the issue by reporting the presence of one enemy carrier whereas the earlier report confirmed the presence of two or more carriers. The hundred-mile difference in the reported enemy position muddied the position even further. Therefore, Kinkaid decided to wait for verification from his own patrol planes before acting.

At 0415 that morning Nagumo's battleships and cruisers launched their scout planes with orders to locate the enemy fleet. Nagumo had bitter memories of what the lack of sufficient intelligence had meant to the Midway operation. Therefore, half an hour later, thirteen additional scout planes were launched from the carriers. The admiral was taking no chances.

Meanwhile, the *Enterprise* launched a flight of scouting planes, each one armed with a five-hundred-pound bomb. If any of the planes located the enemy they were to attack only after reporting the enemy's position.

Around 0630 two *Enterprise* planes located the Japanese force containing the *Junyo*. Twenty minutes later Nagumo's main force of three carriers was sighted. In the interim, however, the Japanese had also located Kinkaid's force.

At 0630 Nagumo was handed a radio dispatch informing him that the American fleet had been sighted. The message made no mention of the size or makeup of the American fleet. Half an hour later, however, one of *Shokaku*'s scout planes reported the presence of a large enemy fleet including a carrier. This was the message Nagumo was waiting for.

In anticipation of locating the U.S. carriers early, Nagumo had directed his carriers to have their planes armed, fueled and waiting on the flight decks. Fifteen minutes after receipt of the sighting report, a force of forty bombers escorted by twenty-seven fighters was winging its way south. Nagumo had struck first. Kinkaid's strike from the *Hornet* was not launched until a quarter of an hour later.

Both fleets were a beehive of activity. Second strikes were being readied by both sides when, at 0740, two of the *Enterprise*'s planes dove out of the clouds and unloaded their bombs on the *Zuiho*, tearing a fifty-foot hole in her flight deck. Although her speed was unimpaired, the carrier was unable to launch or recover planes. Nagumo ordered *Zuiho*'s captain to take his ship back to Truk. Although visibly upset, Nagumo pressed on. Precisely on schedule, at 0800, *Shokaku* and *Zuikaku* launched their second strikes.

During the next few hours events occurred in rapid succession. Shortly after the Japanese launched their second strike, *Hornet* and *Enterprise* launched theirs. Outward bound, *Enterprise*'s strike passed within sight of the Japanese planes heading in the opposite direction. The Japanese hit pay dirt first.

A few minutes after 0900 the Japanese located the American ships. At that particular moment the *Enterprise* was engulfed by a rainstorm so the Japanese concentrated on the only major target in sight: the *Hornet*. There were simply too many enemy planes for the American combat air patrol and anti-aircraft fire to contend with. The unfortunate *Hornet* was hit by four bombs and two torpedos. In addition, two dying Japanese pilots plunged their burning aircraft into the stricken carrier. Burning from stem to stern, the *Hornet* went dead in the water and took on a list.

While the *Hornet* was undergoing her ordeal, the carrier's own dive bombers were forming up to attack Nagumo's ships. The *Shokaku* was blasted open by four direct hits. Unfortunately, the American torpedo planes failed to locate the enemy.

Meanwhile, *Hornet*'s crew was struggling desperately to keep the ship afloat. Fires raged out of control and the carrier was unable to maneuver. A second enemy strike bypassed the *Hornet* and concentrated on the undamaged *Enterprise*.

Hatless and helmetless, Kinkaid was pacing the bridge in his shirt sleeves when the enemy planes arrived overhead. Disdaining efforts to make him seek shelter, the admiral directed the *South Dakota* and the anti-aircraft cruiser *San Juan* to form a tight circle around the carrier. For the past few hours Kinkaid had been busy monitoring reports, directing the battle and issuing orders for the salvation of the *Hornet*. Now he could only stare in awe as the Japanese pilots peeled off for the attack.

The combined firepower of the *San Juan* and *South Dakota* accounted for more than half of the attackers.

The *Enterprise*'s combat air patrol shot down others but there were simply too many attackers to contend with. Two determined enemy pilots managed to sneak through the hail of fire and steel to plant their bombs on the flagship. The forward elevator was jammed in the down position and fires broke out beneath decks.

Hard on the heels of the dive bombers came a formation of torpedo bombers. Fortunately the bomb hits had not affected the carrier's mobility. Her skipper, Capt. Osborne Hardison, skillfully maneuvered the huge ship and managed to elude the torpedos. Thanks to his brilliant efforts, the ship was spared further damage.

Kinkaid was now faced with a dilemma. *Hornet* was in dire straits and *Enterprise* was badly damaged. He ordered the *Northampton* to take the *Hornet* in tow, but these efforts ultimately proved futile as did all efforts to extinguish the raging fires. Even if the ship could be saved, she would obviously be out of the war for many months. Then there was also *Hornet*'s planes to consider. With the ship unable to recover aircraft and a mile-high cloud of smoke hanging over her, Kinkaid ordered the *Hornet*'s planes to land on the *Enterprise*.

Despite the gaping hole in her flight deck caused by the elevator being jammed, Kinkaid ordered Captain Hardison to begin recovering planes. As soon as the first group was landed, Kinkaid ordered them refuelled and flown to Espiritu Santo. In this way room was made for other returning planes. Although a number of the American planes were forced to ditch at sea, Kinkaid's decision undoubtedly saved a number of pilots' lives. After the recovery operation was complete, the admiral ordered the *Enterprise* to leave her present position so that additional enemy attacks would be unable to locate her. Then he turned his attention to the fate of the *Hornet* once more.

The *Hornet*'s planes had already exacted some measure of retribution. The four bomb hits had torn open the flight deck of the *Shokaku* as Nagumo looked on in horror. Fortunately for the Japanese most of the ship's planes were already aloft and so escaped the fate of the Japanese carriers at Midway.

As for the stricken *Hornet*, thanks to the effort of her crew, steam was raised and the great ship managed to get underway, but at a greatly reduced rate of speed.

Nagumo was still not satisfied. Thirsting for revenge he launched another strike in midafternoon as soon as the planes were re-armed and refuelled. Two hours out from their mother ships this flight pounced on the luckless *Hornet* again after failing to locate the still-seaworthy *Enterprise*.

The Japanese were aware of the *Hornet*'s plight. Kondo sent a squadron of destroyers racing to the scene. What a coup it would be if the *Hornet* could be towed triumphantly into Tokyo Bay and displayed for all to view. On the other hand, Kinkaid was just as determined to avoid having this happen. He ordered the destroyers *Mustin* and *Anderson* to sink the carrier after the ship had been abandoned. Several torpedo hits and numerous shells later the *Hornet* still refused to sink. Then reports of the enemy surface reports caused Kinkaid to order all American ships from the area.

When the leading Japanese ships arrived on the

scene the *Hornet* was almost white-hot from the intense fires raging throughout her. There were no signs of life anywhere. The destroyers were left with little choice but to sink the carrier with torpedos.

The American fleet was hard pressed. With the *Enterprise* badly damaged and the *Hornet* gone, Kinkaid withdrew. Kondo knew that the Japanese had won a significant victory and was not anxious to press his luck. Late that night after a halfhearted pursuit, he gave the order to withdraw.

Kinkaid was criticized for abandoning the *Hornet*. Halsey never forgave him for it but the latter's mind was clouded by his fierce fighting spirit that demanded a fight to the finish. Kinkaid had a cooler head. He was able to look ahead to the consequences. The *Enterprise*, damaged elevator and all, was the only American carrier left in the Pacific. He had no other choice but to take her out of harm's way and hope that she could be repaired speedily. Events ultimately proved his decision correct for the "Big E's" presence was felt a few weeks later at Guadalcanal.

The victory at Santa Cruz encouraged the Japanese to make one final all-out effort to drive the Americans from Guadalcanal. At the same time, Nimitz wanted to end the struggle once and for all. More troops and supplies, however, were required before this could be accomplished.

On November 8, Admiral Turner with four transports loaded with six thousand troops left Noumea accompanied by the cruisers *Portland* and *Pensacola* and two destroyers. The next day Admiral Scott with the *Atlanta* and four destroyers and three more transports carrying another one thousand troops followed. At the same time, Adm. Daniel Callaghan sailed from Espiritu Santo with cruisers *San Francisco*, *Helena* and *Juneau* and seven destroyers to cover the landings on Guadalcanal.

On the eleventh, Turner's TF 67.1 and Callaghan's TF 67.4 linked up and began the final run into Guadalcanal. That same night, Admiral Kinkaid, with the hastily repaired *Enterprise*, cruisers *Northampton* and *San Diego* and seven destroyers, left Noumea to provide long-range cover. Kinkaid was joined by Admiral Lee with battleships *South Dakota* and *Washington*.

Meanwhile, the Japanese had stepped up their supply runs. On the night of the eleventh, six hundred men, the vanguard of the Thirty-eighth Division, were landed on Guadalcanal. The balance of the division was loaded onto eleven transports and sent off down the Slot escorted by Admiral Tanaka's destroyers.

Like the American effort, the Japanese operation was an all-out final gasp. Admiral Kondo sailed from Truk on the ninth to cover the operation. His plan called for Admiral Abe to cover the troop landings by bombarding Henderson Field on the night of the 12–13 with battleships *Hiei* and *Kirishima*, cruiser *Nagara* and fifteen destroyers. The following night, Admiral Nishimura would repeat the exercise with cruisers *Maya*, *Suzuya*, *Tenryu* and four destroyers. Admiral Mikawa would cover all three operations with cruisers *Chokai*, *Isuzu*, *Kinugasa* and two destroyers. Kondo, meanwhile, would hover northeast of the Solomons with battleships *Kongo* and *Haruna*, carriers *Hiyo* and *Junyo*, cruisers *Sendai*, *Atago*, *Tone* and *Takao* and five destroyers, ready to intervene wherever needed.

November 11 found Scott's force off Lunga Point. The American troops began to land. During the operation enemy planes from Rabaul attacked and managed to damage one of the transports.

The following morning the combined Callaghan-Turner force arrived off the beaches. Another enemy air attack succeeded in damaging the *San Francisco* and destroyer *Buchanan*. No sooner had the landings begun when word came of the approach of the Japanese. Turner ordered the landing operations suspended and took the transports out to sea escorted by destroyers *Shaw*, *McCalla* and *Buchanan*. At the same time, Scott and Callaghan combined forces and lay in wait off Lunga Point for Abe's force to make an appearance.

At 0124 on the morning of the thirteenth, *Helena*'s radar picked out two groups of ships approaching the American formation. To this day no one knows why Callaghan delayed giving the order to fire. Instead, the American admiral called for a change of course.

The move headed Callaghan's squadron smack into the Japanese formation and the following melee has never been accurately plotted. It was both brief and bloody, perhaps the most vicious night action in history, with armored ships engaging at point-blank range, destroyers raking battleships with automatic weapons and torpedos streaking toward targets so close that the warheads had no time to arm.[2]

The destroyers *Cushing*, *Laffey* and *Sterrett* took on the battleship *Hiei*, mosquitos against a bellowing beast. They raked the Goliath's upperworks with their popguns and were rewarded sadly for their efforts. *Sterrett* was damaged badly and steamed out of the battle. *Cushing* was left dead in the water without power. *Laffey* was pounded unmercifully by the battleship's heavy guns and blew up. The destroyer *O'Bannon* also took on the *Hiei* racing down the enemy ship's side firing her small guns.

Early in the battle the *Atlanta* was mortally hit by salvos from the huge guns of the enemy battleships. With Admiral Scott dead on the bridge, the cruiser staggered out of line. Japanese long-lance torpedos plowed into the cruiser's side and she began to blaze furiously.

Hiei then turned her guns on the *San Francisco*. A few moments later Admiral Callaghan was also dead as heavy-caliber shells landed on the cruiser's upperworks. Despite this, the *San Francisco* managed to hit the *Hiei* with her own guns. Then the *Nagara* and *Kirishima* concentrated their efforts on Callaghan's flagship, but the *San Francisco* managed to absorb a great deal of punishment.

Portland, a great hole in her side thanks to a Japanese torpedo, steamed in a circle with her rudder jammed. Around the same time the *Juneau* took a torpedo in her engine room. With her speed drastically reduced, she limped out of the battle.

The American destroyers fared little better. *Aaron Ward* had her engine room flooded by numerous hits. Early in the battle, the *Barton* had blown up and simply vanished. *Monsenn*, following in the wake of the *Barton*, was deluged by enemy shells. She lasted until noon before blowing up. Of the American ships, only the destroyer *Fletcher*, the last ship in line, escaped without a scratch.

On the Japanese side, the *Hiei*, although thick-skinned and powerful, had suffered countless small-caliber hits on her upperworks that started fires. The battleship reversed course and headed back up the Slot, but a few miles north of Savo the fires began to take their toll. The *Hiei* lost her steering and sailed in circles out of control.

Fifteen minutes after the opening of the battle, the first Battle of Guadalcanal was for all intents and purposes over. The ultimate cost to the Americans was the lives of two admirals, a cruiser and four destroyers. Another cruiser, the *Juneau*, was to suffer a horrible fate the following day.

With her engine room damaged during the battle, the *Juneau* was making its way out of the area headed for Noumea and repairs at a greatly reduced speed. She was accompanied by the damaged *Helena*, *San Francisco*, *Sterrett*, *O'Bannon* and the undamaged *Fletcher*. The Japanese submarine I-26 was waiting for the Americans at the exit of Indispensible Strait. A salvo of torpedos was fired and the *Juneau* simply erupted like a volcano. The cruiser took the five Sullivan brothers to a watery grave with her.

On the Japanese side, the destroyers *Akutsuki* and *Yudachi* had been lost during the battle. The *Hiei*, badly damaged, steamed in circles north of Savo.

During the day both sides licked their wounds. All efforts to save the blazing *Atlanta* failed as Marines watched the struggle from the beach. Eventually, the ship had to be scuttled. During the morning the *Hiei* also lost her struggle. Planes from Henderson Field and the *Enterprise* hit her repeatedly and she went down just north of Savo.

When word was received of the battle, Halsey ordered Kinkaid to detach Lee's battleships. In the morning of the thirteenth, Lee and Kinkaid headed for Guadalcanal. The *Enterprise*, however, was too valuable to risk, so Kinkaid was ordered to keep the carrier well south of Ironbottom Sound. Lee's battleships, though, continued to race to the scene.

That night the *Suzuya* and *Maya* sailed into the sound and pounded Henderson Field. But the Japanese had postponed their landing operation for twenty-four hours to enable Admiral Mikawa to allow Kondo to cover the landings by a nighttime bombardment of American positions.

Early in the morning of the fourteenth the combined forces of Mikawa and Nishimura were discovered withdrawing up the Slot. Planes from Henderson Field, aided by pilots from the *Enterprise*, jumped the formation and damaged the *Chokai*, *Isuzu*, *Maya* and destroyer *Michishio*. Cruiser *Kinugasa* was sunk. But the Americans also located Tanaka's reinforcement force heading for Guadalcanal. Wave after wave of planes from Henderson Field attacked the Japanese force. The first wave sank two transports and badly damaged a third. The next attack accounted for another transport. Two more were sunk in the third attack and the fourth destroyed another. Tanaka's destroyers managed to rescue over five thousand troops from the water and the admiral pressed on with the remaining destroyers and transports.

Late in the evening of the fourteenth, Kondo's bombardment force entered Ironbottom Sound from both sides of Savo Island. Lee was waiting for him. Unfortunately, the outstanding Japanese ability to see at night without the presence of radar allowed them to get in the first blow. The Japanese cruisers and destroyers launched their torpedos. Within minutes the American destroyers *Walke*, *Benham* and *Preston* were hit. Then, to add to Lee's woes, the *South Dakota*'s radar failed. The battleship groped blindly as she was attacked by the *Kirishima*, *Atago* and *Takao* and hit over forty times. But the battleship's hide was tough and she managed to take a great deal of punishment. The destroyer *Ayanami*, attempting a torpedo run on the *South Dakota*, was blasted out of the water.

The Japanese could sense victory in their grasp. Three American destroyers were either sunk or sinking and the *South Dakota* was reeling. But they were ignorant of the presence of the *Washington*.

The *Washington* joined the fray with a vengeance, concentrating her attention on the largest enemy ship, battleship *Kirishima*. Within minutes the Japanese dreadnought was a battered wreck and retreating up the Slot. In addition, both of the Japanese heavy cruisers had been damaged. Kondo decided to break off the action and called for a retreat. As the formation headed back up the Slot, the *Kirishima* suddenly went dead in the water. The battleship was being torn apart internally by explosions caused by the many fires raging below decks. At 0300 Kondo reluctantly ordered the ship scuttled a few miles north of Savo.

The second Battle of Guadalcanal was over.

At daylight, Tanaka's transports were attacked repeatedly by American aircraft. The remaining four ships were beached with heavy loss of life and Tanaka took his ships back to Rabaul.

That the battle was an American victory, no one could dispute. No more would large troop-laden convoys attempt to fight their way through to the island supported by the heavy ships of the combined fleet. The Japanese simply could not afford to pay the price. Tanaka's prophetic words rang loud in the commander-in-chief's ears. Attempting to supply Guadalcanal was an exercise in futility. Nevertheless, those troops remaining on the island simply could not be written off and allowed to starve. Another method of supplying them had to be found.

Two methods of achieving this were finally adopted. First, submarines would be used to run supplies in. These boats could sail to Guadalcanal undetected underwater, surface off the beach at night and return beneath the waves before daylight, thus avoiding detection. Unfortunately, because of the relatively small size of these boats, the amount of supplies they could deliver was restricted.

Tanaka came up with an alternative to the submarine plan. He sent his crews scavenging for old steel drums. Once a sufficient number of these were collected, he directed the men to scrub the interiors until they were spotless. The drums were then filled with rice, other foodstuffs, medical supplies and ammunition, lashed together and placed on the decks of high-speed destroyers. Tanaka then took the ships south under cover of darkness and dropped the drums overboard. The tide would carry them near the beach where troops would wade out into the water and haul them ashore. Tanaka's Tokyo Express rode again.

Thus began a series of nightly runs down the Slot. Taking care to remain out of range of American planes during daylight hours, Tanaka's laden ships dashed in toward Guadalcanal under the cover of darkness. Near the island, crews shoved the drums overboard without the ships having to reduce speed. The destroyers then hightailed it back up the Slot and were usually out of range of Henderson Field's aircraft by daylight. Even if they were detected, the ships could take high-speed evasive maneuvers unencumbered by the responsibility of protecting lumbering transports.

Regrettably, this method was far from foolproof. Many of the drums floated harmlessly out to sea or found their way to American beaches. During daylight hours, unretrieved drums and soldiers attempting to retrieve them were easy targets for marauding American planes.

This was the pitiful state to which the Japanese navy found itself reduced in November of 1942. On the twenty-seventh, Tanaka, with his flag in the destroyer *Naganami*, left Rabaul accompanied by seven other destroyers, their decks piled with drums, over one hundred apiece. Six of the squadron were forced to leave their spare torpedos behind to make room for additional drums. After pausing at the Shortlands, Tanaka led his flotilla to sea in the darkness of November 28.

Meanwhile, the Americans had become wise to the Japanese technique. Admiral Halsey was hell bent on halting the pesky Tokyo Express once and for all. A task force under Carleton Wright was directed to intercept the next run.

When compared to Tanaka's formation, Wright's force was formidable indeed. The American admiral flew his flag in the heavy cruiser *Minneapolis*. Other heavy cruisers in the task force were the *New Orleans*, *Pensacola*, *Northampton* and the light cruiser *Honolulu*, bristling with fifteen six-inch guns. Wright's formation was rounded out by the presence of six destroyers.

On the twenty-eighth, American intelligence reported that Tanaka's destroyers would make a run into Guadalcanal during the night of the thirtieth. Admiral Wright took his task force north to intercept.

Meanwhile, Tanaka himself had received reports of enemy naval forces near Guadalcanal. Radio reports from fleet headquarters warned him of the possibility of encountering American forces. Nonetheless, moved by the plight of the troops on the island, he was determined to carry out his mission.

> Almost daily came radio messages reporting the critical situation on the island and requesting immediate supplies. It was indicated that by the end of November, the entire food supply would be gone, and by the latter part of the month we learned that all staple supplies had been consumed. The men were now down to eating wild plants and animals. Everyone was on the verge of starvation, sick lists increased, and even the healthy were exhausted.[3]

Before leaving the Shortlands Tanaka cautioned each destroyer captain. Informed of the presence of American warships, the admiral ordered the following signal sent to each of his destroyers:

> It is probable that we will encounter an enemy force tonight. Although our primary mission is to land supplies, everyone is to be ready for combat. If an engagement occurs, take the initiative and destroy the enemy.[4]

Shortly after 2300, Tanaka's force rounded Savo Island and began the final run in to the beach. With the exception of the destroyer *Takanami* off to port, the Japanese destroyers moved in a single file led by Tanaka's own *Naganami*. The flagship and *Takanami* were the only two ships carrying a full load of torpedos. Behind *Naganami* trailed *Makinami*, *Oyashio*, *Kuroshio*, *Kagero*, *Kawakaze*, and *Suzukaze*.

Wright's ships were also steaming in single file. Destroyers *Fletcher*, *Perkins*, *Maury*, and *Drayton* led the cruisers *Minneapolis*, *New Orleans*, *Pensacola*, *Honolulu*, and *Northampton*, in that order. The two remaining destroyers, *Lamson* and *Lardner*, brought up the rear.

At approximately 2315, Tanaka approached Tassafronga Point and reduced speed to allow the drums to be pushed overboard. Suddenly, the night erupted.

The *Fletcher*'s radar had picked up *Takanami* guarding Tanaka's flank. A few minutes later, numerous blips appeared on the radar screen of the *Minneapolis*. This was Tanaka's remaining destroyers readying their drops. Incredibly, Wright would not give the order to open fire until he was absolutely sure of the situation. Since none of the American ships was authorized to fire independently, Wright's few moments of hesitation gave Tanaka all the opportunity he needed.

As Wright attempted to decipher the situation, the keen eyes of the lookouts on *Naganami* sighted the American formation. Not one to waste an opportunity when he saw one, Tanaka ordered the supply drop temporarily suspended, straightened his battle line and sailed into the attack.

Takanami, meanwhile, had fired a spread of torpedos at the American line and reversed course. Being the closest Japanese ship to Wright's task force, she now became the target of concentrated American gunfire. The little destroyer was hit repeatedly and fires began to spread throughout her length. But her sacrifice was not in vain.

By drawing attention to herself, *Takanami* allowed the rest of Tanaka's squadron to sail down the port side of the American battle line. *Minneapolis* soon swung her guns around and began to fire at the Japanese flagship. Too late! Tanaka's destroyers had already launched their deadly "long lances."

Five minutes after firing, the Japanese fish began to strike home. *Minneapolis* was the first victim. A torpedo decimated her fire room. A second exploded forward of the bridge. Officers on the bridge stared down incredulously at the peculiar angle of over sixty feet of the American flagship's bow. *New Orleans*, next in lie, swerved to avoid ramming the *Minneapolis* and a torpedo plowed into her forward magazine, blowing the entire bow completely off clear back to the second turret.

Seeing the two ships in front suddenly stop dead, *Pensacola* was attempting to avoid them when a "long lance" blew a huge hole in the cruiser's side, amidships.

Honolulu was more fortunate than her sisters. Her captain wisely took his ship down the disengaged side of the confused American formation. Protected by the three blazing cruisers, *Honolulu* continued to blaze away with all guns. In all the confusion, however, her firing was inaccurate.

Next in line, the *Northampton* was the most unfortunate of all. Two torpedos smashed into her side and set the ship's fuel tanks on fire. Burning like an inferno, the *Northampton* went dead in the water and took on an immediate list to port.

Tanaka assembled his destroyers and headed north at top speed. When he noticed that *Takanami* was not present he ordered *Kuroshio* and *Oyashio* to return to the scene of battle and search for their comrade. They found the *Takanami* burning from stem to stern and sinking. *Kuroshio* and *Oyashio* stood by rescuing survivors until the approach of American destroyers forced them to break off and rejoin the rest of Tanaka's formation for the race up the Slot. The actual battle had lasted for a little over twenty minutes.

No drums of supplies reached the Japanese troops on Guadalcanal that night. That was not to say that the Japanese force had been defeated. Tanaka had truly lived up to his nickname. Three badly damaged American cruisers were left in his wake and would require months of extensive repair. As for the stricken *Northampton*, she rolled over and sank a few hours after the battle. The Battle of Tassafronga was a smashing Japanese victory. Outgunned, outnumbered and ambushed, Tanaka had turned the tables and inflicted a crushing defeat on his enemy. With the exception of the loss of *Takanami*, he took on a highly superior force and emerged without a scratch.

It was typical of Tanaka's generosity that he wished to share the credit. After the war he said, "I have heard that U.S. naval experts praised my command in that action. I am not deserving of such honors. It was the superb proficiency and devotion of the men who served me that produced the tactical victory for us.

"We were able to defeat Admiral Wright's ships in this action only because of *Takanami*. She absorbed all the punishment of the enemy in the opening moments of battle, and she shielded the rest of us. Yet we left the scene without doing anything for her valiant crew."[5]

Yet he had attempted to do something for *Takanami*'s crew. Hadn't he dispatched two of his precious destroyers to the scene in a rescue attempt? To risk them unnecessarily, however, when the American forces approached, would have been foolish.

If Tanaka was reluctant to take credit, others were willing to heap praise on him. One of the greatest of all naval historians, Samuel Elliot Morison, had this to say:

> It is always some consolation to reflect that the enemy who defeats you is really good, and Rear Admiral Tanaka was better than that—he was

superb. In many actions of the war mistakes on the American side were cancelled by those of the enemy; but despite the brief confusion of his destroyers, Tanaka made no mistakes at Tassafronga.[6]

Incredibly, when Tanaka arrived back at base it was not to the acclaim of his superiors. Instead, he was criticized for not delivering the supplies.

Tanaka was undeterred. On December 3, again on the seventh, and once more on the eleventh, the Tokyo Express sailed down the Slot and unloaded their drums into the waters off the island. But the Japanese had overused their tactic.

More and more drums failed to reach the shore. During the sortie of December 11, Tanaka's formation was attacked by American PT Boats. His flagship, the destroyer *Teruzuki*, was torpedoed and sunk by the small enemy torpedo boats. Tanaka was wounded during the action but managed to transfer his flag before the *Teruzuki* sank. Returning to Rabaul, the gallant little admiral was hospitalized for treatment of his wounds.

Yamamoto finally began to realize that the Guadalcanal effort would have to be written off. The very last thing that a commander who is forced to admit defeat wants to hear is, I told you so. This is precisely what Yamamoto thought of every time he heard the name Tanaka glorified and praised. Throughout the entire operation the latter had repeatedly spoken out against the folly of it all. With defeat at Guadalcanal imminent, Yamamoto decided that he could dispense with the services of this insubordinate destroyer commander. Tanaka's days were numbered.

Yamamoto was not foolish enough to get rid of Tanaka while there was still work to be done. The troops remaining on Guadalcanal needed to be evacuated.

Without informing the men in the field of his decision, Yamamoto began to evacuate Guadalcanal. The Japanese troops were being pushed back all along the line by superior American forces under Gen. Alexander Patch* and Yamamoto felt that if the defenders knew that they were shortly to be evacuated, all defenses would break down. Consequently, almost right up until the end, the Japanese troops remained uninformed of the plan to evacuate them.

Small packets of troops were evacuated during nightly trips by destroyers and submarines to Guadalcanal. The formation charged with this operation was the famed Tokyo Express, commanded by Adm. Raizo Tanaka, fully recovered from his wounds.

Guadalcanal was finally declared secure during the second week of February, 1943. Now the Americans could begin their slow but steady advance up the Solomons chain. MacArthur's command had overall responsibility from here on, but, since the campaign was totally reliant on naval personnel, Admiral Halsey exercised direct command in the area. This arrangement seemed to satisfy Admiral King because all future objectives in the islands had already been decided upon. Therefore, for all intents and purposes MacArthur would merely be a spectator while Halsey

*See *Great Commanders of World War II Vol. III: the Americans.*

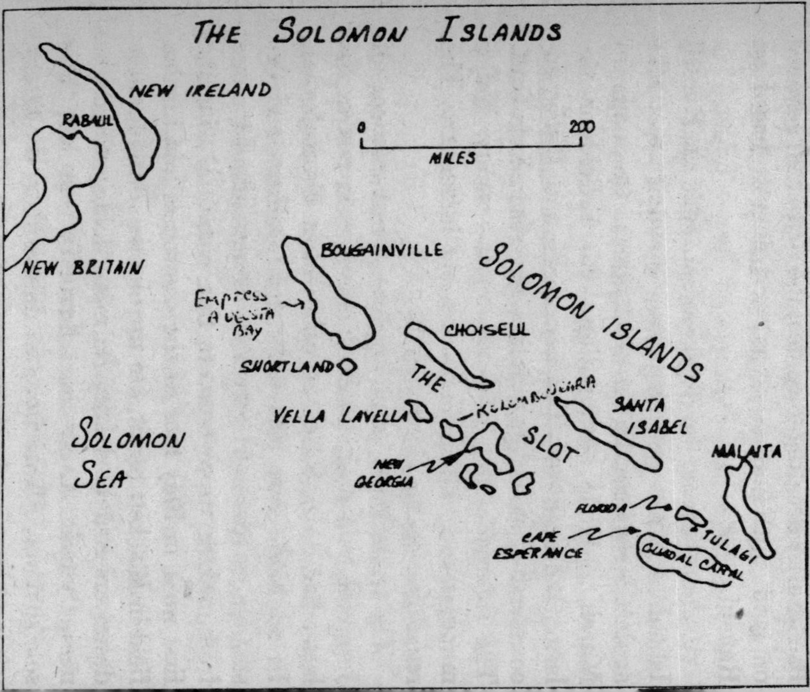
THE SOLOMON ISLANDS
NEW IRELAND
RABAUL
NEW BRITAIN
0
200
MILES
BOUGAINVILLE
Empress Augusta Bay
SHORTLAND
SOLOMON ISLANDS
CHOISEUL
THE
KOLOMBANGARA
SLOT
VELLA LAVELLA
SANTA ISABEL
MALAITA
NEW GEORGIA
SOLOMON SEA
FLORIDA
TULAGI
CAPE ESPERANCE
GUADAL CANAL

handled the day-to-day direction of the campaign. The final objective, however, remained the same for both Halsey and MacArthur. Rabaul.

The advance up the Solomons was marked by a series of small but bitter naval clashes. Admiral Yamamoto had withdrawn his carriers from the south Pacific after deciding to contest the American advance on land, with surface ships, and aircraft based on Rabaul.

On February 21, the Americans invaded the Russell Islands. From there they began softening up attacks against New Georgia, the next stop on the map. On March 6, while bombarding Vila Airfield on the latter, the destroyers *Conway*, *Cony* and *Waller* encountered a force of Japanese destroyers in Kula Gulf. The Americans got the jump on the enemy. Waller managed to sink the *Murasame* and *Minegumo*. The remaining enemy destroyers fled.

The Americans kept up the bombardment of Japanese-held positions on New Georgia just as the latter had done to Henderson Field on Guadalcanal. In addition, they kept a force of cruisers and destroyers on constant guard to prevent the Japanese from making supply runs to that island. During the first week in May four of the destroyers laid a mine field in Blackett Strait. On the eighth, four Japanese destroyers stumbled into the mine field in the darkness. *Oyashio*, *Kagero* and *Kuroshio* were lost. The sole survivor, *Michishio*, was damaged by air attack while attempting to rescue survivors.

On July 21, the first American troops landed on

New Georgia. Rear Adm. "Tip" Merrill's cruisers and destroyers supported the operation by bombarding enemy-held strongholds. During the night of July 4-5, another squadron under Adm. W. L. Ainsworth attacked a force of Japanese cruisers attempting to land troops near Vila in Kula Gulf. This time the enemy struck first.

Japanese long-lance torpedos streaked toward the American formation. The destroyer was sunk almost immediately. The *Chevalier* was damaged by *Strong*'s exploding depth charges. In the confusion the Japanese force made good its retreat.

The following night the Japanese returned with twenty-eight hundred more troops carried in four destroyers. Three more destroyers covered the operation. Ainsworth located the force and attacked with four destroyers and cruisers *Helena*, *Honolulu* and *St. Louis*. The Japanese got in the first blow. Three of the deadly long lances found the *Helena*. Mortally wounded, the cruiser sank quickly. The Japanese paid for *Helena*'s demise with the destroyer *Niitsuki*. The *Nagatsuki* was damaged in the battle and ran aground. The next day this ship was destroyed by aircraft.

The Japanese were certain that Kolombongara was the next American objective after New Georgia. In one sense they were correct. Kolombongara had been the next objective but Halsey had decided to bypass that island and leave its garrison to wither on the vine while his forces attacked the next island up the chain, Vella Lavella. The Japanese, however, had no way of knowing this so they continued to reinforce their garrison on Kolombongara.

On the night of July 12-13 one such Tokyo Express run approached Kolombongara. Ainsworth was waiting for them with *St. Louis*, *Honolulu* and HMNZS* *Leander* (replacement for the *Helena*), and ten destroyers. Despite the Americans having the advantage of radar, the enemy struck first. The cruiser *Jintsu* torpedoed the *Leander* which was forced to drop out of line. The victory of Admiral Tanaka's old flagship was short-lived though. *St. Louis* and *Honolulu* blasted the *Jintsu* to the bottom. At that point, the Japanese destroyers launched their torpedos and broke off the action. No hits were made on the American ships.

After breaking off the action the Japanese ships paused only long enough to reload their torpedo tubes. Then they came steaming back with blood in their eyes. Ainsworth thought that the action was past until torpedos slammed into the *Honolulu* and *St. Louis*. Both ships were severely damaged but managed to remain afloat. The destroyer *Gwin* was not as fortunate. Enemy torpedos destroyed her.

Following the Battle of Kolombongara the naval war subsided for a few weeks. Then, on the night of August 6-7, it erupted again at the Battle of Vella Gulf.

A force of Japanese destroyers attempted to run more reinforcements into Kolombongara. Comm. Frederick Moosebrugger ambushed the enemy formation with destroyers *Dunlap*, *Craven*, *Maury*, *Sterrett* and

---

*His majesty's New Zealand ship.

Stack. Attacking with torpedos Moosebrugger's "Tin Cans" sank the *Kawakaze*, *Arashi* and *Hagikaze*. Only the *Shigure* managed to escape. Finally, the Americans were able to utilize their torpedos in as deadly a manner as the Japanese.

Vella Lavella in the central Solomons was invaded a few days later. In a month's time the enemy garrison was all but defeated. Arundal Island was attacked next followed by Baker Island on September 1.

During the last week in September the Japanese finally began to evacuate their troops from Kolombongara. American destroyers attempted to blockade the effort but met with little success. A week later the evacuation of Vella Lavella began.

On the evening of October 6, an American reconnaissance plane spotted a force of Japanese destroyers making for Vella Lavella. Two American destroyer squadrons under Captain Walker and Commander Larsen were dispatched to intercept. Walker's force coming down from the north was made up of the destroyers *Selfridge*, *Chevalier* and *O'Bannon*. Thanks to their radar the Americans were able to locate the nine-ship Japanese formation. Walker ordered his ships to attack with torpedos. But the sharp-eyed Japanese had fired first. *Chevalier* was hit by a torpedo fired by the *Yugomo*. The American destroyer staggered out of line and collided with the *O'Bannon*. *Selfridge* fought on until she was smothered by the combined gunfire and torpedos of the *Shigure* and *Samidare*. Before undergoing their ordeal, however, the American torpedos managed to hit *Yugumo*.

Commander Larsen's force with *Ralph Talbot*, *Taylor* and *LaVallette* arrived too late for the battle.

Larsen's ships did manage to locate the damaged *Yugumo* and sank the enemy destroyer in quick fashion. *Selfridge* remained afloat and was able to make it back to base. After colliding with *O'Bannon*, *Chevalier* sank.

On November 1, the Americans landed on Bougainville. Halsey knew that any attack against Rabaul would require the support of fighter aircraft. Bougainville was well within range of fighters.

Admiral Samejima, commander of the Japanese Eighth Fleet on Rabaul, ordered every available ship to attack the American landings. Cruisers *Myoko*, *Haguro*, *Agano*, *Sendai* and six destroyers sortied to attack the U.S. landing ships in Empress Augusta Bay.

"Tip" Merrill's Task Force 39 was protecting the American beachhead. The U.S. force was made up of the cruisers *Denver*, *Montpelier*, *Cleveland* and *Columbia* and eight destroyers. The Japanese force, unaware of Merrill's presence, sailed confidently into the bay a little before midnight. Merrill waited for just the right moment before ordering his ships to attack the unsuspecting Japanese with torpedos. None of the American torpedos hit their target but Merrill's ships followed up the attack with accurate gunfire. In a few moments the Japanese formation was in a state of total confusion. The destroyers *Samidare* and *Shiratsuyu* collided while evading the torpedo attack. Both ships limped off toward Rabaul. Meanwhile, the American cruisers concentrated on the *Sendai*. In a few moments the light cruiser was a blazing wreck and sinking fast. Then the destroyer *Hatsukaze* collided with the *Myoko* causing severe damage to the smaller ship.

In the interim, the Japanese had collected their wits and opened fire. Destroyer *Foote* was blasted by a long lance but remained afloat. *Denver* and destroyer *Spence* were hit by enemy gunfire, neither one seriously. But the Americans continued to concentrate their fire on the Japanese cruisers. The Japanese commander, Admiral Omori, was unable to control his ships in the wild melee. He therefore ordered a retreat. *Agano*, *Myoko* and *Haguro* limped back to Rabaul heavily damaged and escorted by the remaining destroyers.

The following morning the *Montpelier* was damaged by enemy planes from Rabaul but only slightly. *Foote* remained afloat and was towed back to base. The remaining American destroyers finished off the helpless *Hatsukaze*. The Battle of Empress Augusta Bay was the final surface battle for the Solomons. Nevertheless, there was more in store for the Japanese fleet.

As the American drive moved closer to Rabaul, Admiral Koga, successor to Yamamoto as commander-in-chief of the combined fleet,* moved the main portion of the fleet to Truk. Following the debacle at Empress Augusta Bay, Koga ordered Admiral Kurita to take the fleet's heavy cruisers to Rabaul. Just as Yamamoto had been determined to hold onto Guadalcanal, so too was Koga equally bent on saving New Britain and Bougainville.

On November 2 Kurita left Truk with the heavy

---

*See *Great Commanders of World War II Vol. IV: The Japanese*.

cruisers *Atago*, *Chokai*, *Maya*, *Takao*, *Mogami*, *Suzuya*, *Chikuma*, light cruiser *Noshiro* and four destroyers. Three days later, around 0700, this powerful force dropped anchor in Rabaul harbor alongside light cruisers *Agano*, *Yubari* and seven destroyers.

Meanwhile, Halsey was planning to neutralize Rabaul with his carriers. When word was received that Kurita's cruisers were approaching the naval base, the prospect became even more inviting. Halsey ordered Admiral Sherman's Task Force 38, containing the carriers *Princeton* and *Saratoga*, to hit Rabaul.

On the morning of November 5, even as Kurita's ships were dropping anchor, Task Force 38 was approaching Rabaul. At 0900 when they were just over two hundred miles away, Sherman turned his ships into the wind and launched over one hundred planes. An hour later the American planes arrived over the enemy naval base. Incredibly, the Japanese never knew the Americans were coming.

Less than half an hour later Kurita's fleet was a smoking wreck. *Atago*'s hull was damaged by 3 near misses. *Maya* raised steam and made for the harbor entrance at the height of the attack. She was pounced on by a flight of dive bombers that ripped out her innards. Unable to navigate, with seventy dead and sixty wounded littering her decks, *Maya* went dead in the water. *Mogami* was struck in the side by a torpedo that started heavy fires. *Takeo*'s number two turret was destroyed by a bomb. *Chikuma* was more fortunate than her sisters; damage from near misses was minor. Most of the destroyers, with the exception of the *Wakatsuki*, escaped heavy damage because the American pilots preferred to concentrate on the larger ships. Not so the *Agano* and *Noshiro*. Unlike their smaller comrades, the two light cruisers took their share of pounding as well.

Kurita stared in horror as the American dive bombers and torpedo planes dove on his vulnerable ships. Less than eight hours after his arrival Kurita ordered the *Atago*, *Chikuma*, *Kumano*, *Mogami* and *Suzuya* back to Truk escorted by six destroyers. *Takeo* and *Maya* were so badly damaged that they were unable to accompany the rest of the fleet.

Six days after Kurita's ordeal, Sherman was back. This time, besides the *Princeton* and *Yorktown* attacking from the south, the *Essex*, *Bunker Hill* and *Independence* attacked from the west. *Agano* and *Naganami* were gutted and the destroyer *Suzunami* sunk. American planes blasted shipping, airfields and installations. Sixty-eight Japanese planes were destroyed on the ground. A hastily prepared counter strike set out after the departing attackers but the Japanese planes never reached their destination. The combat air patrol over the American carriers accounted for an additional forty enemy planes.

The following day, Koga reluctantly ordered the evacuation of all shipping and carrier planes from Rabaul. As a base, the once-mighty fortress was now worthless in the face of American strength in the area. The only force left was the garrison of troops.

Meanwhile, the Americans had decided to bypass Rabaul and leave it to wither on the vine. MacArthur did invade the western portion of New Britain but Rabaul was neutralized by air and sea power. Thus, after numerous naval battles, countless number of lives lost and fierce fighting on the Islands of the

Solomons, the objective of the entire campaign was abandoned. The Americans had decided on a two-pronged offensive against Japan: through the Philippines and across the Central Pacific.

NOTES

1. Lawrence Cortesi, *Bloody Friday Off Guadalcanal*, p. 19
2. Jack Coggins, *The Campaign for Guadalcanal*, p. 131
3. *Ibid*, p. 156
4. Tamiechi Hara, *Japanese Destroyer Captain*, p. 161
5. *Ibid*, p. 164
6. *Ibid*, p. 165

BIBLIOGRAPHY

1. Agawa, Hiroyuki. *The Reluctant Admiral.*
Kodansha International, Tokyo, 1979.
2. Coggins, Jack. *The Campaign for Guadalcanal.*
Doubleday & Co., New York, 1972.
3. Cortesi, Lawrence. *Bloody Friday Off Guadalcanal.*
Zebra Books, New York, 1981.
4. Costello, John. *The Pacific War.*
Rawson Wade Publishers, New York, 1981.
5. Dull, Paul. *The Imperial Japanese Navy.*
Naval Institute Press, Annapolis, 1978.
6. Frank, Benis. *Halsey.*
Random House, New York, 1974.
7. Halsey, W. and Bryann, J. *Admiral Halsey's Story.*
Zenger Publishing, Washington D.C., 1947.
8. Hara, Tamiechi. *Japanese Destroyer Captain.*
Ballantine Books, New York, 1961.
9. Horton, D.C. *New Georgia.*
Ballantine Books, New York, 1971.

10. Hoyt, Edwin. *Guadalcanal*.
    Stein & Day, New York, 1981.
11. Hoyt, Edwin. *The Glory of the Solomons*.
    Stein & Day, New York, 1983.
12. Humble, Richard. *Japanese High Seas Fleet*.
    Ballantine Books, New York, 1973.
13. Pfannes, Charles and Salamone, Victor. *The Great Commanders of World War II Vol. IV: The Japanese*.
    Zebra Books, New York, 1982.
14. Pfannes, Charles and Salamone, Victor. *The Great Admirals of World War II Vol. I: The Americans*.
    Zebra Books, New York, 1983.
15. Rowher, J. and Hummelchen, J. *Chronology of the War at Sea*.
    Arco Publishing, New York, 1974.
16. Smith, Stan. *The Navy at Guadalcanal*.
    Lancer Books, New York, 1963.
17. Winton, John. *The War in the Pacific*.
    Mayflower Books, New York, 1978.

CHAPTER FIVE

THE BATTLE OF THE PHILIPPINE SEA

At the Casablanca Conference of the Combined Chiefs of Staff in January, 1943, Admiral King of the United States first put forth his proposal for attacking the Marianas Islands. The British Chiefs of Staff were opposed initially. Eventually though, after much haggling and maneuvering on the part of the stubborn King, the American proposal was accepted in concept. However, no specifics were discussed at that time.

The upshot of the discussion on the Pacific-Far East operations at Casablanca was a series of limited and contingent agreements. The United States was to conduct a two-way advance in the Pacific through the Central and Southwest Pacific. Plans and preparation were to be made for the recapture of Burma in 1943, but final decision on the operation was to be postponed until the summer of 1943. Increased aid to China in the way of air forces and transports would be provided by the United States. The delegates agreed that the Pacific-Far East operations for 1943 were to be aimed at maintaining pressure on Japan, holding the initiative, and attaining positions of readiness for a full-scale offensive against Japan immediately upon the defeat of Germany.[1]

Though specific strategy was not detailed, a significant keynote was sounded at Casablanca. The British would henceforth have to pay more attention to the Pacific in contrast to their earlier stance. King would see to that.

After returning home King intensified his planning for the Pacific. The problem of Rabaul held a prominent place in this planning. According to an earlier Joint Chiefs decision, Rabaul was to be assaulted by MacArthur's forces. King continued to harbor reservations about this because MacArthur would require naval forces for the campaign and the admiral's views on allowing MacArthur to command naval forces were well known.

The American Joint Chiefs called a conference in March, 1943, known as the Pacific Military Conference. Once again differences in strategic thinking made it necessary to specify Pacific strategy. King was thinking in terms of China and, with this in mind, was planning for the movement of naval forces from Hawaii and the United States mainland directly across the Central Pacific. MacArthur, with a return to the Philippines uppermost in his mind, was planning the capture of New Guinea and the reduction of the Japanese base at Rabaul, to be followed by a movement northwestward toward the Philippines.

Present at this conference were General Sutherland, MacArthur's chief of staff, Adm. Raymond Spruance and Capt. Miles Browning, chief of staff to Admiral Halsey. The final outcome of the meeting was an acceptance of MacArthur's plan for the reduction of Rabaul with the full cooperation of Halsey's naval forces.

By the spring of 1943 signs of victory were evident in North Africa and the Solomons. The Allies were getting ready to invade Sicily. But for operations following the conquest of Sicily, strategy remained in the air. The war in Burma was going absolutely nowhere. The American theater commander there, Gen. Joseph Stilwell, wished to build up a strong ground force for the eventual recapture of Burma while Major General Chennault of the Air Force advocated an increase in air power. The British, on the other hand, wanted a diminution of activity in Burma in order to concentrate everything in future Mediterranean operations. Since so many questions remained unanswered, another major conference of the Combined Chiefs of Staff was deemed necessary. Roosevelt and Churchill arranged for such a meeting to take place in Washington during May. The conference was given the name Trident.

At Trident the British appeared to King to be ready to agree to an intensification of the Pacific war. On May 21, the admiral had his opportunity to explain his Pacific strategy to the British. He reviewed previous studies on Pacific strategy showing the importance of the Philippines and how it dominated American planning. He then went on to discuss three possible avenues of approach toward recovering the Philippines: one from the north, another from the south, and a third across the Central Pacific. At the same time, King emphasized the importance of capturing the Marianas which he called the key to victory. Possession of these islands, he claimed, would sever the enemy's sea lines of communication to the Carolines. Then the Americans could strike westward to the Philippines, China or even Japan itself. An invasion of the Philippines, he went on, would probably serve to draw out the Japanese fleet for an all-out naval battle. From that point on, assuming the enemy fleet were destroyed of course, Japan would suffer strangulation and eventual defeat by the combined use of bombing, blockade and assault. King concluded his presentation by emphasizing the need to accelerate the Pacific war.

The British were suitably impressed but still refused to allow King carte blanche in the Pacific. They wanted restrictions placed on the Pacific effort in order to give first priority to the defeat of Germany. Thus the debate over wording of the official statement continued.

The American chiefs held firm and were ready to appeal to Roosevelt if necessary in order to uphold their position. Finally, thanks to Adm. Sir Dudley Pound, the British naval chief, a compromise was reached. The paragraph that had given the British so much trouble was amended to read that the Combined Chiefs of Staff would give consideration to any major Pacific offensive before it was actually begun.

Though the results of Trident were not startling in themselves as regards to the Pacific war, they did indicate a positive growth of the realization that attention would henceforth have to be given to long-range planning on the combined level. The nebulous Pacific strategy set forth at Casablanca had been replaced by the adoption of new short-range objectives and an effort to analyze the future course of the war in the Pacific. King was satisfied. On May 25, Roosevelt and Churchill approved the final version of the Combined Chiefs' master plan.

Soon after Trident King flew to San Francisco for a meeting with Nimitz to discuss future operations. King was particularly interested in gathering any information about the campaign then taking place on the Aleutian island of Attu which had been assaulted by American forces while the Trident Conference was in session. Unfortunately, little information regarding the attack was as yet available.

Nevertheless, the two admirals forged ahead with plans for a Central Pacific offensive. King stated that the Marshall Islands should be the initial objective. The two also discussed candidates to command the Central Pacific forces. Nimitz nominated Rear Admiral Spruance. King concurred. For the amphibious force commander, Adm. Richmond Kelly Turner, the amphibious commander at Guadalcanal, was chosen. To command the land force Marine Maj. Gen. Holland M. Smith was selected.

After the meeting with Nimitz, King returned directly to Washington. He was anxious to initiate the Central Pacific drive fearing British ambivalence. King did not want to give the latter the opportunity to renege on their Trident agreement. On June 11, the admiral submitted his proposals to the Joint Chiefs. The Army rejected King's proposals, feeling that they slighted MacArthur. King had gone so far as to recommend that there should be only one supreme commander for the Pacific and that the Central Pacific drive be given priority over MacArthur's.

Meanwhile, MacArthur was clamoring for more resources in order to facilitate the capture of Rabaul. A real interservice battle loomed and a compromise was needed.

A compromise was found. MacArthur would not assault Rabaul but merely surround and bypass it before continuing along the north coast of New Guinea toward the Philippines while at the same time releasing the Second Marine Division to Nimitz. For tactical reasons, it was decided that Nimitz's forces should capture the Gilberts before tackling the Marshalls.

Thanks to American industrial output, the Joint Chiefs did not have to choose between MacArthur and Nimitz. Instead, Japan was to be approached on two fronts, two giant pincers, each mutually supportive of the other and aimed at a common goal: the total destruction of the Japanese war machine.

The Joint Chiefs approved the recommendations of the Joint Staff planners on July 20. King made one change by shifting the Gilberts invasion from November 1 to November 15. Finally, his long sought after Central Pacific offensive was about to begin.

When the Trident Conference ended in May, many important issues were left unresolved. For example, there was still the question of what course to take after Sicily was invaded. Should Italy be attacked or should the Allied effort be concentrated on the cross-channel invasion? There was also the question of the China-Burma-India Theater. The Americans feared that the British were stalling. In addition, further clarification was needed regarding long-term Pacific objectives. Therefore, another conference was deemed imperative. This one convened in Quebec in August, 1943, at the beautiful Chateau Frontenac overlooking the St. Lawrence River. Code name for the conference was Quadrant.

The British came to Quebec prepared to do battle with the Americans. They wanted an invasion of Italy. King was appalled. He was of the opinion that such an operation would prove more a liability than an asset. Foremost in his mind was still the Pacific and he was unhappy with the resource allocation for that theater. Only fifteen percent of available resources were still being sent to the Pacific. King wanted that number doubled. As such, he was prepared to use the Quadrant Conference to stage a showdown with the British. The admiral was insistent that the British live up to their Trident promises regarding their support in opening up the Burma Road. Keeping China in the war was vital, for if she collapsed, millions of Japanese troops would be free to defend those Pacific islands which were to be shortly assaulted by Nimitz's forces. As a sign of good faith, therefore, King wanted the British to designate a supreme commander for Burma.

The Joint Chiefs met with the president on August 10 to firm up the American position. It was universally agreed that the cross-channel operation, Overlord, must be finally agreed upon as the major operation for 1944. No more British delays would be tolerated. The Joint Chiefs also urged Roosevelt to push the British into fulfilling their promises for the China-Burma-India (CBI) Theater.

To the British, King and his "damned Pacific policy" was an obstacle. "Admiral King was determined not to have a single additional warship, so badly needed in the Pacific operations, diverted to any extra operations."[2]

The Quadrant Conference convened on August 14 with the British reviewing the European war. After lunch, the Americans presented their views. King gave his usual scenario about the inadequate means to fight Japan and the neglect of the China-Burma-India Theater. The British were on the defensive but did not respond to King immediately.

Two more days of meetings finally brought about an agreement. A target date for Overlord was firmly established for May 1, 1944. The cross-channel attack would have priority of resources over the Mediterranean. As for Italy, the Allies would maintain "unremitting pressure" on the German forces there. Regarding the Pacific and the Far East, there were still problems, primarily over Burma. The British did, however, nominate Admiral Mountbatten to be supreme commander, Southeast Asia. King quickly endorsed the selection.

The Combined Staff planners took all the various ideas and plans expressed during the conference and put together a paper expressing the various positions. The outcome was a masterpiece of compromise.

In summary, Quadrant affirmed giving first priority to Overlord and reducing the Mediterranean to a secondary theater. An invasion of Southern France simultaneous to Overlord was agreed to. Regarding the Pacific, King could expect additional resources. In addition, the Combined Chiefs agreed to the seizure of the Gilberts, Marshalls, Carolines, Palaus and the Marianas. MacArthur's bypassing of Rabaul and his drive along northwest New Guinea was approved.

On September 25, the admiral flew to Pearl Harbor to talk with Nimitz. With the Central Pacific offensive about to begin, King wanted to review strategy on Operation Galvanic, the seizure of the Gilbert Islands. During a meeting with Nimitz and Spruance, discussions centered on which islands in the Gilberts should be invaded and which should be bypassed. Tarawa and Makin were selected for assault. Originally, King had wanted Nauru Island but Spruance talked him out of it because of its distance from Tarawa. Instead, Spruance suggested Makin because, he felt, it was closer to the Marshalls, was large enough for an airfield and was close enough to Tarawa so that the fleet could support both assaults at the same time. King agreed that the arguments made sense.

Nimitz's Central Pacific offensive commenced with an assault of Tarawa and Makin on November 20. The battle for Tarawa was bloody with the Marines suffering heavy casualties. Meanwhile, the Army's Twenty-seventh Division which had assaulted Makin were criticized for proceeding too slowly against relatively light opposition. Friction between the services was inevitable.

On January 3, 1944, King flew to San Francisco to meet with Nimitz and Halsey and review with them the implications of the Cairo-Teheran conferences. King emphasized the importance of the Mariana Islands. Capture of these, he said, would pierce Japan's inner defensive circle, block the line of communications between the homeland and her major naval base at Truk in the Carolines, and open the Chinese coast for exploitation. King was determined to exploit the vast manpower resources of China and to use that country as a staging area for a final assault on Japan itself. He left assured that Nimitz and his staff realized the importance of the Marianas.

Quite the contrary, however, was the case. MacArthur's staff, represented by General Sutherland, argued for the pooling of all Pacific resources for a drive to the Philippines which could then be used as a staging area for an assault on China. Nimitz and his staff seemed more sympathetic to Sutherland's proposals than to King's enthusiasm for the Marianas. When he saw the minutes of the January 27-28 Pearl Harbor meeting where Sutherland had presented his case, King was furious at Nimitz and said so in a scathing letter the contents of which again emphasized the importance of the Marianas. Besides reiterating his previous reasons, in hopes that he could obtain Army Air Force support, King stated that the islands could be used as a staging area for the B-29 bombing offensive of the Japanese home islands.

MacArthur's and King's strategy thus seemed to fly in each other's face. In a February 2 dispatch to Marshall, MacArthur emphasized the importance of his approach to the exclusion of the Central Pacific. The general argued that one strong thrust was infinitely preferable to two weak ones.

King quickly responded to MacArthur's note with one of his own, stating that apparently, "General MacArthur had not accepted the Combined Chiefs of Staff decisions at Cairo that there would be a dual drive across the Pacific and that the Central Pacific took priority in scheduling and resources."[3] King concluded by asking Marshall to tell MacArthur to stick to the rules.

In mid-February, King was still unhappy with Nimitz. The latter wanted to capture Truk while King wanted this island bypassed. In addition, Nimitz procrastinated about making a firm commitment on the Marianas. Meanwhile, the Marshall Islands were successfully assaulted during February and March. In Washington, however, the struggle to determine Pacific strategy continued. The Joint Chiefs favored the already agreed upon dual thrust but MacArthur was not satisfied and continued to harass Marshall.

Nimitz arrived in Washington in early March to meet with the Joint Chiefs in hopes of pinning down Pacific strategy. MacArthur was also invited but as usual declined, saying that he could not leave his headquarters while his forces were engaged in action. Sutherland attended instead. MacArthur's chief of staff could not withstand the arguments of the Joint Chiefs. King's theories dominated.

The admiral found a ready ally in Arnold who wanted the Marianas for a different reason than King. Nevertheless, Arnold's support swayed Marshall and Leahy. The final decision was that MacArthur could complete the isolation of Rabaul and proceed westward along the New Guinea coast before jumping to Mindanao in the Philippines on November 15. Nimitz would bypass Truk, seize the southern Marianas on June 15 thereby isolating the Carolines, and seize the Palaus on September 15 in order to provide a fleet base for support of MacArthur's attack in the Philippines. Following that, Nimitz was to seize Formosa on

February 15, 1945 while MacArthur took Luzon. After Formosa would come the China coast. Finally, after months of haggling, the American commanders had a blueprint to follow.

In the meantime, King began to give serious thought to the Japanese fleet which had remained inactive for over a year. Would this fleet finally make an all-out attack when the Marianas were invaded? He hoped so. As the months slipped by, it appeared that the Japanese would do just that. King was apprehensive about the ability of Spruance's Fifth Fleet to stop the enemy fleet. Nimitz reassured him that Spruance was capable and ready. Spruance, however, understood his primary concern to be the protection of the Saipan beachhead, not the destruction of the Japanese fleet. This accounted for the subsequent escape of the Japanese fleet despite heavy losses. King had done all he could do, the rest was up to Nimitz and Spruance.

The Japanese also recognized the value of the Marianas and felt that they had to be held at all costs. These islands represented the main bastion of their inner defensive ring. If they fell, the home islands would be placed in jeopardy. Consequently, Admiral Toyoda was determined to use every available resource to keep the Americans from capturing them.

Nimitz's intelligence system had intercepted and deciphered Japanese plans calling for an all-out naval counteroffensive should the Americans penetrate as far west as the Marianas-Carolines line. Originally called Operation Z, the Japanese plan was now codenamed operation A-Go. It looked as if the long-awaited opportunity to confront the Japanese carrier fleet, which had remained inactive since late 1942, had arrived.

Meanwhile Task Force 58, built around the new, powerful Essex-class carriers, roamed throughout the Pacific. The Japanese never knew where the American carriers would strike next.

Toyoda ordered what remained of the Japanese fleet to assemble at Tawi Tawi, the Sulu Island base in the southern Philippines. Basing his A-Go plan on the assumption that the next major American offensive would occur in the vicinity of the Marianas, Toyoda's strategy was to strike at the American fleet first. If he could inflict a serious defeat, the Japanese ships could then destroy the American landing forces. To carry out the operation, not only were Ozawa's carriers available, but swarms of planes from Japan itself would be sent south via Okinawa to bases in the Marianas. Thus a twin-pronged force would be used to defeat the Americans.

Even before the U.S. invasion of Saipan, Ozawa was ready to take his fleet to sea. The waters around Tawi Tawi were rapidly becoming too hot. American submarines roamed freely throughout the area and prevented the Japanese from conducting exercises safely. Between May 24 and June 4, Ozawa's force was reduced by five destroyers and three tankers, all losses coming as the result of enemy submarine activity. After the *Tanikaze* was sunk on the eighth by the submarine *Harder*, Ozawa ordered the fleet to sea in an effort to escape the restricted waters around the Philippines.

By mid-May the designs for the American attack were complete. The Marianas would present the attackers with an entirely different type of objective. Whereas the Gilberts and Marshalls, the most recent conquests, were low-lying coral atolls, the Marianas were large, rugged islands, covered with thick vegetation and contained towns with large civilian populations, many of whom were Japanese.

The Fifth Fleet's first objective was Saipan. Admiral Turner, along with Gen. Holland Smith would direct the northern attack force made up of the Second and Fourth Marine Divisions with the Twenty-seventh Infantry Division in reserve. D-day was scheduled for June 15, 1944. After Saipan was secured, Tinian, just to the south would be attacked.

A southern attack force, under Adm. Richard Connolly and Marine Gen. Roy Geiger, consisted of the Third Marine Division and the First Marine Brigade. In reserve was the Seventy-seventh Infantry Division. Their target was Guam. The date for this attack was tentatively set for June 18.

One major question that haunted the American planners was would the Japanese fleet, which had remained quiescent since late in 1942, come out to fight for the Marianas? Spruance doubted that they would. Nevertheless, he prepared for the eventuality.

On May 26 Spruance left Pearl Harbor aboard his flagship and headed for the Marshalls where the Fifth Fleet had assembled for the operation. Task Force 58 had the responsibility for eliminating any Japanese air threat in the Marianas. Mitscher's force was to hit the islands from June 11 onward.

Meanwhile, the Japanese fleet was making its own

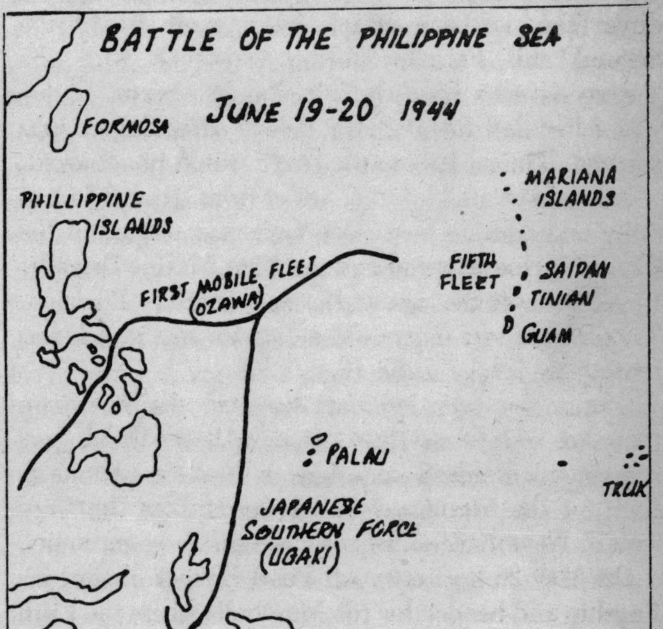
BATTLE OF THE PHILIPPINE SEA
JUNE 19-20 1944
FORMOSA
PHILLIPPINE ISLANDS
MARIANA ISLANDS
FIRST MOBILE FLEET (OZAWA)
FIFTH FLEET
SAIPAN
TINIAN
GUAM
PALAU
TRUK
JAPANESE SOUTHERN FORCE (UGAKI)
NEW GUINEA

preparations. Since the beginning of the war it had been the desire of the Japanese navy to destroy the American fleet in a major naval engagement. In preparation for an American move toward the Marianas the Japanese planned just such an engagement, Operation A-Go. The basic concept of A-Go was to lure the American fleet into battle.

Even though he was virtually certain that the Marianas represented the next American objective, Toyoda could not be absolutely certain. Adopting a tactic used unsuccessfully during the Midway operation, he ordered a picket line of submarines established between Palau and Truk. If the American fleet was indeed making for the Marianas, one of the Japanese submarines was bound to spot it and inform Toyoda's headquarters. What followed was one of the most incredible feats of the entire war.

American intelligence sources reported that a Japanese submarine was making a supply run from Truk to Buin. A squadron of destroyer escorts* under Comm. Hamilton Hains was ordered out from the Solomons to intercept the sub. Hains' Escort Division 39 included the destroyer escorts *George*, *Raby* and *England*. On May 19, the squadron made contact with a Japanese sub. After several unsuccessful attacks by *George*, the *England*'s depth charges sank the I-16.

Meanwhile, the submarine RO-117, running on the

---

*A smaller, more lightly armed version of the destroyer. The destroyer escort's primary function was that of a submarine hunter.

surface, was discovered by an American plane. Admiral Halsey suspected that the Japanese had placed a picket line athwart the route to Saipan and ordered Hains to investigate. Early in the morning of May 22, Escort Division 39's radar located RO-106 running on the surface in the pre-dawn darkness. As the three little ships raced in for the attack, the submarine dove beneath the surface. *England* dropped depth charges where the sub had last been seen and was rewarded by the destruction of a second enemy submarine. But she was just beginning.

The next day, Hains' force located RO-104. *George* failed in five attempts to sink the submarine. *England*'s second run was rewarded by a tremendous undersea explosion. Bits of wood, supplies and human bodies bobbed to the surface marking the end of RO-104. An hour later, *England* made contact with yet another submarine. By then her crew were becoming experts with depth charges. RO-116 joined her sister submarines at the bottom of the Pacific.

Hains was now certain that he had indeed stumbled across a Japanese picket line and continued the hunt. His diligence paid off. On the evening of the twenty-sixth, just before midnight, RO-108 surfaced to charge her batteries. *England*'s radar located her immediately and the DE raced in for the kill. The Japanese submarine executed an emergency all-out dive, but to no avail. *England*'s depth charges found her. Scratch RO-108.

Five days passed before another contact was made. By then the *England*'s crew were becoming rather cocky about the whole affair. Then, on the thirty-first, *George* made contact with RO-105 running on the surface a little after midnight. Hains decided to allow his other two ships to share the glory. *George* exhausted all her depth charges in a series of unproductive runs over the submarine which had hastily submerged. Then *Raby* attempted in vain to make the most of its opportunity. Finally, Hains told *England* to go ahead. From that moment on, RO-105 was doomed. A short time later pieces of wreckage bobbed to the surface following an underwater eruption. Scratch RO-105. Scratch one Japanese picket line. The final submarine in the line was sunk by an American plane off Truk. There would be no warnings of an American fleet sailing north.

Task Force 58 arrived off Saipan on June 11. That same day, Ozawa was ordered to send the giant battleships *Musashi* and *Yamato* along with the cruisers *Aoba*, *Kinu*, *Haguro* and *Noshiro* and a force of destroyers to support the third of a series of Japanese landings on Buin (Operation Kon). Following that, the ships were to attack MacArthur's landings on New Guinea.

On the second day of the American carrier strikes against Saipan, ten cargo ships of various types were sunk. By now Toyoda was aware that the advance warning he was expecting was not forthcoming. Nevertheless, Task Force 58's activity confirmed his suspicions. The Marianas it was. Ozawa set a course toward Saipan and ordered the Kon* ships to abandon their task and rendezvous with the rest of the fleet at sea.

*Operation Kon—Japanese effort to reinforce Biak

The striking power of Ozawa's fleet was vested in nine carriers, split into three divisions of three carriers apiece. It was his intention to split his force once they reached the vicinity of the Marianas by sending a third of the carriers toward the American fleet under heavy escort. This van force was under the command of Admiral Kurita and contained the battleships *Musashi*, *Yamato*, *Kongo* and *Haruna*, cruisers *Atago*, *Takao*, *Chokai*, *Maya*, *Chikuma*, *Tone*, *Kumano*, *Suzuya*, *Noshiro*, fourteen destroyers and six oilers. The light carriers *Chitose*, *Chiyodo* and *Zuiho* were the offensive force.

Ozawa's main body comprised the First Carrier Division with the fleet carriers *Taiho* (flagship), *Shokaku* and *Zuikaku*, the last two the lone survivors of the Pearl Harbor attack. The Second Carrier Division under tactical command of Admiral Joshima was made up of the fleet carriers *Junyo*, *Hiyo* and *Ryuho*. As escort Ozawa had the cruisers *Haguro*, *Myoko*, *Mogami* and *Yahagi*, battleship *Nagato* and nineteen destroyers. Counting the planes of Kurita's carriers under the tactical command of Admiral Obayishi, Ozawa's fleet carried a total of 450 planes.

Since his own planes had a greater range than the Americans', Ozawa planned to stand off, out of range, and attack the U.S. carriers with the longer range planes of his two carrier divisions. Kurita, however, controlled the bulk of the heavy escorting forces and these would be a hundred miles forward during the battle. For a large fleet containing such valuable ships as the carriers, Ozawa's screen was relatively weak. The shortage of destroyers was particularly acute but heavy losses during the previous months could not be made good.

While the Japanese submarines were unable to provide reports regarding the activity of the enemy forces, just the opposite was true of the Americans. Their submarines were patrolling along the entire proposed route of the Japanese advance.

Near 0900 June 15, Admiral Toyoda sent the following message to Ozawa:

> The combined fleet will attack the enemy in the Marianas area and annihilate the invasion force. Activate A-Go Operation for a decisive battle.[4]

Ozawa was already en route. Ten minutes after receipt of Toyoda's directive, the Second and Fourth U.S. Marine divisions swarmed ashore on Saipan following a softening-up bombardment by a force of American battleships.

From the very beginning, lack of communications between commanders doomed the Japanese effort to failure. Admiral Takagi never saw fit to report the loss of his submarines. Neither had Admiral Kakuta bothered to inform Ozawa that Task Force 58's three days of bombing had resulted in the loss of many Japanese planes and heavy damage to key airfields on Guam, Tinian, Rota and Saipan. In addition, Takagi elected not to bring all his planes in from Yap and Peleliu. Ozawa was not only counting on these planes, he was planning to use the air bases to refuel his planes so that they could be sent back into battle immediately, thus avoiding the time-consuming return flight to the carriers.

On the evening of the fifteenth the submarine

Flying Fish reported that a large Japanese naval force, including carriers and battleships, had entered the Phillippine Sea via San Bernadino Strait, north of the Philippine island of Samar. At its current rate of speed the Japanese fleet could be expected to reach Saipan in three days.

Spruance's initial reaction was to order the scattered carrier groups of Task Force 58 to assemble near Saipan by June 17. For efficiency of command, the task force had been broken into four carrier task groups and a support group of battleships. Two of these groups, however, were en route to a mission against the airfields on Bonin and Volcano islands. Spruance did not order them to return immediately to Saipan but he did direct them to limit their strike to one day. This would allow them to return to the vicinity of Saipan by the seventeenth.

On the morning of the sixteenth the submarine *Sea Horse* made contact with another enemy task force two hundred miles north of Mindanao. This force was also sailing into the Philippine Sea. A frightening specter now stared Spruance in the face. The western Philippine Sea seemed to crawl with Japanese ships. Obviously the Japanese were ready to risk their fleet in the long sought after major engagement. Spruance's first reaction was to postpone the Guam landings and call for an immediate conference with Turner and Smith. What he did not know, however, was that the two Japanese formations were headed for a rendezvous with each other.

At a conference with his subordinate commanders, Spruance told them of the Japanese advance. His immediate concern was for the vulnerable transports.

He asked Turner if they could be moved to the east, out of harm's way. Turner answered that this was impossible in light of the fierce fighting ashore. The transports, he said, with their vital supplies, could not be spared from the beachhead. Mitscher would have to keep the Japanese at bay with his carriers.

Task Force 58 was an awesome force. Under the command of Adm. Marc Mitscher, the force was split into five sections, four of which were powerful carrier forces. The fifth section was Adm. Willis Lee's formation of modern fast battleships. At the Marianas, the composition of the fleet was as follows.

Task Group 58.1—Rear Adm. Joseph J. (Jocko) Clark
fleet carriers *Hornet** and *Yorktown*
light carriers *Belleau Wood* and *Bataan*
4 cruisers, 14 destroyers and 267 planes

Task Group 58.2—Rear Adm. Alfred E. Montgomery
fleet carriers *Wasp* and *Cabot*
light carriers *Bunker Hill** and *Monterey*
4 cruisers, 12 destroyers and 244 planes

Task Group 58.3—Rear Adm. John W. Reeves
fleet carriers *Enterprise** and *Lexington*
light carriers *Princeton* and *San Jacinto*
5 cruisers, 13 destroyers and 228 planes

*Flagship.

Task Group 58.4—Rear Adm. William K. Harrill
    fleet carrier *Essex*
    light carriers *Langley* and *Cowpens*,
    4 cruisers, 14 destroyers and 163 planes
Task Group 58.5—Rear Adm. Willis Lee
    battleships *Washington*, *North Carolina*, *Iowa*, *New Jersey*, *Indiana*, *South Dakota* and *Alabama*
    4 cruisers and 14 destroyers

Mitcher was in the *Lexington* and Spruance's flag flew from the masthead of the cruiser *Indianapolis* in Task Group 58.3.

On the seventeenth Spruance's scout planes began to search for the Japanese fleet. No contact was made. He wrongly assumed that the enemy's primary target was the transports. Since the Japanese were advancing from two different directions, or so he thought, Spruance feared that they might attempt to turn his flank and descend on the helpless transports. He was thus wary of any move that would draw him out and allow the Japanese to side slip him. He would not deviate from his position that his primary objective was the protection of the transports. The destruction of the Japanese fleet, though desirable, was secondary to the primary objective. The transports could not be jeopardized.

Spruance composed his battle plan. "Our air will knock out enemy carriers as operating carriers . . . then will attack enemy battleships and cruisers to slow or disable them."[5]

This plan was based on the assumption that the Japanese would approach close enough for a fleet engagement. But what if the Japanese limited their attack to long-range carrier air strikes?

Their carrier planes outranged the Americans'. Since Spruance was obsessed with protecting the transports, would he allow the carriers to move westward within range of the Japanese fleet and leave the transports without air cover? Those questions were left unanswered in the battle plan.

Thus his plan was ambiguous. What was Mitscher's primary objective? Sink the Japanese fleet or protect the transports? The vagueness of the plan would raise controversy later on. However, on June 17 the two objectives did not seem incompatible. Nevertheless, when battle finally did ensue, their incompatability became obvious. "The two missions seemingly would become impossible to achieve simultaneously."[6]

Ozawa knew Spruance by reputation. The Japanese commander guessed that his opponent would elect to fight a defensive battle. In fact, this was precisely what Spruance was planning. Unlike the Japanese, the Fifth Fleet commander was less concerned with the destruction of the enemy fleet than he was with the protection of the American landing forces. With this in mind and unaware that Ozawa's primary objective was the destruction of the American carriers first and the beachhead second, Spruance adopted a formation designed to provide the maximum defense and prevent an end run. In addition, Spruance initially labored under the impression that two Japanese forces were approaching Saipan. This misconception was brought about by reports from the submarine

Seahorse which had sighted the Kon force prior to its linking up with Ozawa's main body on the sixteenth.

The Japanese force sailed into the Philippine Sea on the eighteenth. All through that day Admiral Kakuta sent his planes roaring from bases on Guam, Saipan, Tinian and Rota against the U.S. fleet. The inexperienced Japanese pilots were no match for Mitscher's highly trained veterans. Wave after wave of Japanese planes were intercepted far from their targets by Task Force 58's Combat Air patrols and beaten back with incredible losses to the attackers. By evening, Kakuta's powerful air force was but a skeleton of its former self. Those planes that had escaped destruction on the ground during the previous three days were easily outmaneuvered by the more experienced American pilots.

On the other hand, Kakuta never did have the quantity of planes that Ozawa was counting on. Instead of committing every plane in his fleet, Kakuta decided to hold back some planes for the defense of other areas such as the Palaus. Kakuta compounded this error by not informing Ozawa of the heavy losses or the fact that many planes never did arrive in the Marianas. Confident that sheer weight of numbers would overwhelm the Americans, Ozawa continued on.

Spruance positioned Lee's battleships twenty miles to the west. Behind this line were the carriers with the four task groups operating independently on a north/south axis. The rationale for this information was threefold. First of all, the battle line could blast the Japanese planes with anti-aircraft fire as they passed overhead en route to their main target. Secondly, the enemy planes, seeing the battleships, might be tempted to hit the expendable surface ships instead of the valuable carriers. Finally, if the enemy surface ships approached the American battle line, an old fashioned broadside battle could take place with the heavily armored surface vessels able to protect the thin-skinned carriers.

Meanwhile, on land the fighting raged savagely and the casualties mounted steadily. Over fifteen hundred Americans were killed during the first three days alone.

The Japanese fleet continued to baffle Spruance. During the night of the seventeenth he received reports of its whereabouts but dared not move his own fleet. Thus he passed the initiative to his opposite number, the Japanese Admiral Ozawa. They would have to make the first moves, to the disgust of the American aviators.

On the eighteenth, search planes scouting to the west continued to send back negative reports. The Japanese were still beyond range. Spruance decided to allow Mitscher's carriers to move westward until midnight, but not a minute longer. If no contact were made until then, they were to reverse course and head back to Saipan. Mitscher radioed the Fifth Fleet commander that he would like to continue the advance beyond midnight but Spruance reaffirmed his original order. His fear for the transports continued to dominate strategy and would cost the Americans an overwhelming victory.

Around 0600 on the eighteenth, Ozawa began to launch his search planes. Sixteen planes searched for the American fleet but failed to make contact. A few planes did, however, run across search planes from Task Force 58. Three of the search planes fell victim to the American guns.

Around noon, Ozawa launched another search of fifteen planes. This flight fared a little better as one of the pilots located the American fleet three hours later. The first sighting was followed three quarters of an hour later by another. What the Japanese scouts had stumbled across, though, was not the entire American force but merely the northern task groups. Once the location and course of the enemy fleet was determined, Ozawa set his own course to keep his fleet approximately four hundred miles from his opponent. The Japanese commander was not about to throw away the advantage of the longer range of his aircraft. In addition, if necessary, he could shuttle his planes to bases on Saipan and Guam. Ozawa elected to wait until first light the next morning before launching his attack. After all, to the best of his knowledge, his fleet remained undetected.

A few of his subordinates did not agree with Ozawa's decision to wait. Admiral Obayishi of the Third Carrier Division, for one, prepared to launch his planes immediately following the receipt of the sighting reports. One flight of planes from the carrier *Chiyoda* was already airborne when Ozawa ordered them recalled, much to Obayishi's disgust. The aggressive carrier commander railed at the decision but to no avail. Ozawa steamed north, as did Kurita.

On the morning of the nineteenth Mitscher launched his search planes once more. Again nothing was found. Then, a few minutes before 0900, Spruance received a delayed sighting report from a long-range seaplane based at Saipan. It had made contact with a large enemy force at the exact spot to which Mitscher had asked permission to advance to. Still Spruance refused to give Mitscher the go ahead. The other Japanese force was still unaccounted for. Spruance had no way of knowing that the two had actually merged into one large formation before splitting once more, but to be mutually supportive of each other, not to act independently. Unless he could account for every enemy naval force within range of Saipan, Spruance would not risk exposing the beachheads by sending the carriers away.

Up to that point, Ozawa had indeed remained undetected. At least for the last few days. Late that evening though, he made an incredible blunder. Wishing to ensure a coordinated attack the next day, Ozawa ordered a radio transmission made to Kakuta directing the latter to synchronize his attacks with those of the carriers. The Americans fixed on the Japanese transmission and reported their findings to Spruance. For the first time, the Fifth Fleet commander was reasonably certain of the location of the Japanese fleet.

Spruance pondered the question of whether to maneuver for attack or continue with his present defensive posture. There was always the possibility that the calculation of the radio interceptors was in error. The Japanese still had plenty of time to execute an end run in an attempt to get at the American landing areas. Protection of the latter was Spruance's prime objective. No. He would not close with the Japanese. The Fifth Fleet was to lay back and let the enemy come to them. Verification of Ozawa's location came two hours after midnight. The submarine *Finback* made contact with the enemy fleet and dutifully reported its findings immediately.

Ozawa's fateful transmission was a wasted effort. Kakuta had few planes left with which to attack the Americans. The heavy air raids of the three previous days had taken their toll of Japanese air bases and planes. On the eighteenth, the Japanese attackers had suffered unusually high losses. To compound the inaccuracy, not only did Kakuta fail to report his heavy losses, but he informed Ozawa that his attacks had been an unqualified success. Many American planes had been destroyed along with damage to several carriers, according to Kakuta. It remains unfathomable why Kakuta acted in this manner unless it represented an attempt on his part to save face.

Half an hour after midnight, Ozawa made a move which typified the Japanese operations throughout the war. He divided his forces. Kurita took his van force and moved one hundred miles closer to the enemy. Not only was Kurita not a carrier expert, his force contained the bulk of the heavy ships. This move also necessitated diluting the already weak destroyer screen since both formations required destroyers to screen them.

In the early morning hours of the nineteenth, Ozawa ordered his ships to take up battle stations. Unlike Nagumo at Midway, he was determined to avoid the pitfalls of using too few search planes. At Midway the lack of adequate search planes was decisive. Accordingly, at the Philippine Sea, in a two-hour period beginning around 0415 Ozawa's fleet launched over forty scout planes. An hour and a half later, Mitscher began to launch his.

Three and a half hours after the first search plane climbed into the sky, Ozawa was rewarded with a sighting report. Although his planes were armed and fuelled on the decks of the carriers just waiting for the order to take off, Ozawa hesitated until reports of a second sighting could confirm the first.

One hundred miles ahead, the impulsive Admiral Obayishi refused to wait. Instead of biding his time to coordinate his attack with the main force from Ozawa's six carriers, an hour after the initial sighting, seventy of Obayishi's planes were winging their way east from the decks of *Chitose*, *Choyoda* and *Zuiho*. Thirty minutes later, Ozawa, having exhausted his own patience, launched twenty-seven torpedo planes, fifty-three bombers, forty-eight fighters and one plane carrying Window (strips of tin foil which, when dropped, confused enemy radar). Meanwhile, while Ozawa was stalking Spruance, the submarine *Albacore* was stalking the Japanese admiral.

Just before 1000, the USS *Alabama*'s radar in Lee's force picked up the first Japanese strike over one hundred miles out. In the meantime, Mitscher had ordered all his planes to return from their raids on Guam and Rota. In addition, he directed each task group to launch their torpedo planes and dive bombers to clear the decks for use by the fighters and reduce the possibility of having the attack planes destroyed on the decks. The torpedo and dive bombers were ordered to hover a distance from the fleet, out of harm's way. Then Mitscher ordered all carriers to launch their fighters. Five minutes before 1030, the carriers began to comply. Fighters from the

Princeton, *Essex*, *Hornet*, *Cowpens* and *Monterey*, however, were already in the air returning from raids. These groups turned to intercept the enemy.

As envisioned, the Japanese planes concentrated on the first targets, Lee's battle line of surface ships. The American battleships were like magnets, drawing swarms of the enemy planes toward them. The sky was black with flak.

Into this melee dove American planes. Even as Mitscher's remaining carriers were launching their fighters, *Essex*'s fighters waded into the Japanese formation. The American planes had a field day with their inexperienced opponents. Like autumn leaves, Japanese aircraft spun flaming from the sky and splashed into the sea. Between the American planes and the anti-aircraft fire of the battleships the Japanese lost fifty-nine planes.

Ten minutes after the first Japanese wave headed back for their carriers, the next flight arrived over Lee's task group. Once more American fighter pilots pounced on the Japanese formation. One enemy plane smashed into the side of the *Indiana* but merely succeeded in scratching the battleship's paint. Half a dozen others made it through to attack Task Groups 58.2 and 58.3. *Wasp* and *Bunker Hill* suffered slightly from near misses but that was the extent of the damage inflicted by Ozawa's large strike. Only thirty-one Japanese planes returned from the attack.

Despite the lack of adequate destroyers, Ozawa elected to commit as many planes as possible to the attack instead of retaining a few to bolster his anti-submarine patrols. This was his most costly decision. Shortly aftrer 0900, six torpedos from the *Albacore* streaked toward the Japanese flagship. One pilot who had just taken off from the *Taiho*'s deck dove his plane into one of the fish. Four others missed. One, however, smashed into the side of the huge ship, rupturing fuel lines and jamming the forward elevator. Competent damage-control parties secured the damage and the carrier was able to maintain course and speed.

An hour later, the Second Carrier Division launched its first strike, the third for the Japanese that fateful day. Half of this flight was misdirected en route to the target and failed to find the American fleet. The other half was jumped by *Hornet*'s combat air patrol and driven off with heavy loss.

Impatiently marking time a short distance away from Task Force 58, the American torpedo and dive bombers requested permission to get involved in the battle by attacking the Japanese air bases. Mitscher quickly gave his consent and for the second time that day, the airfields on Guam and Rota came under heavy attack.

The fourth Japanese strike fared even worse than its predecessors. Kurita's van force was busy recovering planes when Ozawa dispatched the next force. Consequently, the former's three carriers were unable to add their planes to the weight of the attack. This flight missed the Americans completely and, after a lengthy search, all but eighteen planes headed for the air bases on Guam and Rota, hoping to replenish their fuel tanks before setting off once more in an effort to find the American fleet. In the midst of landing, the Japanese aviators suddenly found the sky filled with American planes. All but a handful were destroyed either on the ground or in the air.

Shortly after launching his fourth strike, Ozawa stared in horror as the Pearl Harbor veteran, *Shokaku*, seemed to erupt in a ball of flame. After eluding the weak destroyer screen, the American submarine *Cavella* had fired four torpedos at the Japanese carrier. All four struck home. Within an hour, the carrier's bow was under water and her captain gave the order to abandon ship. Fierce fires blazed throughout the carrier and she took on a heavy list. Yet she remained afloat, although it was obvious that the great ship was doomed.

Ozawa's shock over the fate of the *Shokaku* was nothing like his bewilderment over the fact that few planes seemed to be returning from the raids. Misled by Kakuta's glowing reports, Ozawa could only conclude that his planes were shuttling back and forth between the Japanese air bases and the American fleet. Never in his wildest imagination could he fathom the huge losses of aircraft. The Japanese had completely underestimated the enormous striking power of Task Force 58.

Three hours after being hit by *Cavella*'s torpedos, the *Shokaku* was engulfed by a tremendous explosion and plunged beneath the waves. On the bridge of *Taiho*, Ozawa was still sorting out the day's events when the entire ship erupted beneath him. Fumes from the ruptured gasoline and oil lines damaged by the torpedo hit had seeped throughout the ship. One spark was all it took. This spark was provided by one officer's decision to activate the exhaust fans in an effort to rid the ship of the noxious fumes. The resulting explosion destroyed the flight deck completely, blew huge holes in the ship's bottom, and doomed the *Taiho*. Ablaze from stem to stern, the carrier slowed to a stop. Nothing could save her now.

Ozawa's staff pleaded with him to leave the burning ship. In turn, Ozawa expressed his wish to follow the example of Admiral Yamaguchi at Midway and go down with his ship. Eventually, however, the staff's views prevailed. Ozawa ordered the Emperor's picture removed from the ship and slid down the *Taiho*'s side to the deck of the destroyer *Wakatsuke*. From the deck of the destroyer, Ozawa watched in sadness as the mighty *Taiho* slipped beneath the waves taking over sixteen hundred men and a dozen planes with her. Added to *Shokaku*'s twelve hundred casualties, the Japanese cost in lives was heavy.

Wakatsuke's facilities were inadequate for Ozawa to conduct the battle. Around 1700 he again transferred ship, this time to the cruiser *Haguro* whose facilities were only slightly better than the destroyer's. Since it was painfully obvious that the day's fighting was concluded, Ozawa ordered Kurita to join up and called a halt to activities.

By midafternoon Spruance's fear of an end run had abated. The great loss of enemy planes convinced him that the transports were relatively safe. He thus ordered Mitscher to search aggressively and attack westward.

By early evening, after the last American plane had landed, Task Force 58 was moving at high speed westward toward the anticipated location of the Japanese fleet. Reports from a submarine indicated that Ozawa's force was approximately 375 miles to the west of Mitscher.

Including the destruction of fifty more of Kakuta's planes and the 22 lost when the *Shokaku* and *Taiho* went down, Japanese aircraft losses for the day totalled 412. On the other hand, Mitscher's losses totalled 31 planes. The Americans dubbed the action "The Great Marianas Turkey Shoot," and rightly so.

By midmorning of the twentieth, the exact whereabouts of the Japanese fleet was still a mystery. Spruance directed Mitscher to close the range and carry out searches throughout the day. If no contact was made by evening, then the fleet would return to Saipan.

Ozawa's force was refuelling when American search planes located it in midafternoon. When the American scouts were detected, Ozawa ordered the refuelling operation suspended and the fleet to take up defensive battle stations. The Japanese admiral knew that his turn had come.

According to the sighting reports, the enemy formation was at the extreme range of attack aircraft and with darkness approaching, recovering the planes would be a risky matter since most of them would be low on fuel. In the darkness, the pilots would be unable to locate their own ships easily. Regardless of the risk, Mitscher wanted to proceed with the attack.

Ozawa launched eighty planes as a combat air patrol. It was a pitiful handful to throw at what was heading the Japanese way. Mitscher threw the entire weight of his fleet against the enemy.

The American planes arrived over Ozawa's fleet and waded in. The enemy combat air patrol was brushed aside and easily handled by the escorting American fighters. The carriers drew most of the attention. *Hiyo* was hit by two torpedos and sank soon after. *Zuikaku* was hit repeatedly by bombs that started the carrier burning throughout. The *Junyo* was also bombed and was left battling raging fires. Three of the tankers were blasted to the bottom. Cruiser *Maya* and destroyer *Shigure* were seriously wounded. Battleships *Nagato* and *Haruna* also took bomb hits but their thick skins protected them from heavy damage.

The approach of darkness caused the Americans to break off the attack. Ozawa gloomily assessed the damage. His fleet was a total wreck. Sixty-five of the eighty planes of the combat air patrol had been shot down. After dark, Admiral Toyoda ordered Ozawa to break off the battle and return to base.

The returning American planes arrived over Task Force 58 in the darkness. Despite the potential threat of Japanese submarines, Mitscher ordered all carriers to turn on their lights to aid the pilots. Flashing different colored beacons to designate individual ships, Mitscher's carriers guided their pilots home. For many it was too late. But for most of the American pilots the sight of that huge force glowing like a Christmas tree was the most welcome sight they had ever seen. Seventy-three planes ran out of fuel and never made it back, but most of the pilots were fished out of the water by destroyers or patrolling submarines. Thanks to the decision to illuminate the fleet, however, the vast majority of the American planes landed safely.

Throughout the next day Task Force 58 continued westward in vain. The Japanese were gone. At 2000, Spruance ordered the force back to Saipan. The Battle of the Philippine Sea was over.

"The enemy fleet had escaped," Mitscher disappointedly wrote in his battle report. Before the ink had even dried, criticism from the aviators of the fleet abounded. Towers went so far as to demand that Spruance be fired for his inept handling of the fleet.

En route home, Ozawa sat down at his desk and penned his letter of resignation. Manfully, he accepted full responsibility for the defeat. But was he really totally to blame?

Kakuta's actions contributed heavily to the American success. His inaccurate but glowing reports of many enemy planes shot down and carriers blazing misled Ozawa from the very beginning. Then, of course, there was his reluctance to report on the conditions of his airfields. Obayishi's impetuous premature launching of his strike instead of waiting to coordinate the attack with Ozawa's, to form one huge formation, certainly contributed to the debacle.

The inexperience of the Japanese pilots also weighed heavily. The veterans of Midway, Pearl Harbor and Santa Cruz were long gone. The newer pilots were no match for their veteran American counterparts and their overzealousness and youthful enthusiasm caused the first two waves to hit Lee's battleships instead of their primary target, the American carriers. Furthermore, there was no way Ozawa could control the fact that half of the third strike and all of the fourth missed the American fleet completely. Blame for that rests with the flight leaders themselves.

Whatever the reasons for defeat, the Battle of the Philippine Sea marked the final time the Japanese carrier fleet was a viable force in battle. The once proud and mighty Mobile Fleet was a wreck. Any remaining hope lay in the hands of the surface forces, the bulk of which were commanded by Admiral Kurita.

Rebuilding the fleet would be, of course, an impossible task. The most pressing problem facing the Japanese was where would the Americans strike next? The Philippines, Formosa, Okinawa or Japan itself? Whatever the next enemy move, it would most certainly be aimed at severing Japan's supply line from the East Indies. Without the natural resources and vast oil reserves of that area, Japan would be unable to wage war at all since she had no resources of her own. Therefore, Admiral Toyoda directed his staff to prepare plans to meet any eventuality.

Despite the criticism, Spruance had accomplished his goal of protecting the transports. The aviators, however, countered this by insisting that he had placed the carriers in jeopardy by holding them back until the Japanese made the first move.

Fortunately, the Japanese planes were destroyed during the air battles of the nineteenth without harm to the carriers. The story might have been a very different one indeed if the enemy had broken through and hit Task Force 58. The aviators lambasted Spruance for not giving Mitscher the go ahead to search out and destroy the Japanese carriers early in the battle before they could launch their planes. Fortunately, the Japanese pilots were not of the same caliber as those of the early months of the war.

Actually, Spruance could have ordered the transports out of harm's way as early as the eighteenth. When he first asked Turner on the sixteenth if the transports could be moved, Turner said no because their presence was urgently required at Saipan thanks to the intensity of the battle. However, though the fighting remained fierce, the presence of the transports was not nearly as critical on the eighteenth as it had been two days previously. They could easily have been moved eastward. Then, with them safe, Mitscher's carriers could have been allowed freedom of action. Acting on the premise that the transports were still needed offshore, Spruance never broached the question during his later meeting with Turner.

Spruance also misread Ozawa's intentions. He thought the Japanese admiral would split his forces, using one as a decoy while the other side slipped and attacked the American beachhead. But Ozawa did just the opposite. He concentrated his fleet and never had any intention of doing otherwise. Unhappily for him, the Japanese pilots were so ill trained that they were devastated before they could accomplish their primary mission, the destruction of the American carriers, not the transports.

Although the surviving enemy carriers made good their escape, they were empty shells. There were few planes or pilots left. Nevertheless, Spruance continued to be criticized. To his dying day he maintained that his actions at the Philippine Sea was the best policy. At the beginning of such a large and important amphibious operation, Spruance felt he could not afford to gamble and place the entire operation in jeopardy. When Admiral King met with Spruance during a visit to Saipan, he told the latter point-blank that his conduct during the battle was above reproach. Perhaps King was just being polite.

NOTES

1. M. Matloff, *Strategic Planning for Coalition Warfare*, p. 36
2. Arthur Bryant, *The Turn of The Tide*, p. 575
3. Thomas Buell, *Master of Sea Power*, p. x
4. William Y'Blood, *Red Sun Setting*, p. 66
5. Thomas Buell, *The Quiet Warrior*, p. 264
6. *Ibid*, p. 266

BIBLIOGRAPHY

1. Bryant, Arthur. *the Turn of the Tide*.
   Doubleday & Co., New York, 1957.
2. Buell, Thomas. *The Quiet Warrior*.
   Little Brown & Co., Boston, 1974.
3. Buell, Thomas. *Master of Sea Power*.
   Little Brown & Co., Boston, 1980.
4. Clark, J. J. (Jocko). *Carrier Admiral*.
   David McKay Co., New York, 1967.
5. Dull, Paul. *The Imperial Japanese Navy*.
   Naval Institute Press, Annapolis, 1978.
6. Hoyt, Edwin. *To the Marianas*.
   VanNostrand Reinhold Co., New York, 1980.
7. Hoyt, Edwin. *How They Won The War in the Pacific*.
   Weybright & Talley, New York, 1970.
8. Humble, Richard. *Japanese High Seas Fleet*.
   Ballantine Books, New York, 1973.
9. King, Ernest and Whitehall, Walter. *Fleet Admiral King*.
   W. W. Norton & Co., New York, 1953.
10. Matloff, M. and Snell, E. *Strategic Planning for Coalition Warfare 1943-1944*.

Office of Chief of Military History, Washington, 1959.
11. Pfannes, Charles and Salamone, Victor. *The Great Commanders of World War II Volume IV: The Japanese.*
Zebra Books, New York, 1982.
12. Pfannes, Charles and Salamone, Victor. *The Great Admirals of World War II Volume I: The Americans.*
Zebra Books, New York, 1983.
13. Potter, E. B., *Nimitz.*
Naval Institute Press, Annapolis, 1976.
14. Reynolds, Clark. *The Fast Carriers.*
McGraw Hill, New York, 1968.
15. Y'Blood, William. *Red Sun Setting.*
Naval Institute Press, Annapolis, 1981.

CHAPTER SIX

THE BATTLE OF LEYTE GULF

Adm. Ernest King's vehement objections to the contrary, the American Joint Chiefs of Staff recognized that Gen. Douglas MacArthur's Southwest Pacific Command needed its own naval force if it were to complete the capture of New Guinea, isolation of Rabaul and an eventual jump to the Philippines.

In the summer of 1943 MacArthur's naval forces consisted of a handful of light warships, obsolete heavy forces and a large number of amphibious ships. To command this outdated hodgepodge fleet, Admiral Nimitz put forth the name of Adm. Thomas Kinkaid. The latter was at the time idle after wresting the Aleutian Islands from the Japanese.

Tom Kinkaid was a fighting admiral with an outstanding record and vast experience. He had fought at the Coral Sea, Midway, Guadalcanal, and commanded carriers during the battles of Santa Cruz and the Eastern Solomons. More recently he had conducted a brilliant campaign in the Aleutians. Kinkaid would take MacArthur's Seventh Fleet and send it soaring to new heights of glory.

In November, 1943, Adm. Thomas Kinkaid reported to General MacArthur's headquarters. He had been promoted to vice admiral during the Aleutians campaign and rated a fleet command. He and Mac-

Arthur hit it off immediately. The general liked the genial Irishman and was impressed with his fighting spirit. Kinkaid's impressive record of achievement spoke for itself. Yes, MacArthur was completely satisfied with the man the Navy had sent to command the Seventh Fleet.

By 1944, the Japanese were being thrown back throughout the Pacific. The isolation of Rabaul was virtually complete, the Solomons were for the most part firmly in American hands and MacArthur's forces were advancing steadily along the coast of New Guinea. The Seventh Fleet was responsible for all naval activity in the Southwest Pacific. As such, Kinkaid successfully directed MacArthur's leapfrog operations in New Guinea. At one point he conducted an invasion over four hundred miles in the enemy's rear at Hollandia. Along the way Kinkaid's fleet successfully participated in the capture of the Admiralties and Cape Gloucester on New Britain. By midsummer 1944, plans were being made for MacArthur's triumphant return to the Philippines. The first target was Mindanao.

The Seventh Fleet had by this time expanded to include many amphibious ships. Battleships, although not the new fast ones, were assigned to Kinkaid along with numerous cruisers and destroyers. The Australian navy added their handful of cruisers and destroyers to the Seventh Fleet. For the projected invasion of the Philippines, Nimitz also loaned Kinkaid a force of small escort carriers to provide aerial cover for the beachheads. By September, 1944, all was in readiness.

Although the CinC of the Japanese navy, Admiral

Toyoda, suspected that the next American attack would come against the Philippines, he had no evidence with which to substantiate it. Formosa was a potential target as was the mainland of Asia. Thus, when Halsey began hitting targets in the Philippines with his entire fleet, Toyoda knew the next objective. It was definitely the Philippines. He therefore ordered the implementation of the grandiose Sho-1 plan.

The Japanese Sho plan was an elaborate one. Like many of their previous operations, most notably Midway and the campaign in the Dutch East Indies, the plan was complicated and repeated a commonly used tactic, splitting the fleet. Throughout the war the Japanese repeated this mistake, frequently with disastrous results. They never did get over their fondness for elaborate operations that relied on the precise timing of widely dispersed forces.

A striking force under Admiral Shima would sail down from the north, link up with a second force under Admiral Nishimura moving up from Brunei in Borneo, and move into Leyte Gulf from the west to attack the American transports and beachhead. This combined force was but one arm of a gigantic pincer. The second arm of the pincer was a more powerful fleet under Admiral Kurita, also based at Brunei. Kurita's force would move through the Sibuyan Sea, pass through the San Bernadino Strait, make its way down the east coast of Samar and attack the Americans off Leyte in conjunction with the forces of Shima and Nishimura. Meanwhile, Admiral Ozawa would bring the remaining Japanese carriers down from the north, trail his coat about two hundred miles east of Luzon, and lure Halsey's carriers north.

Thus the elaborate timing with Shima linking up with Nishimura—and both rendezvousing with Kurita. But if Ozawa's decoy role was successful, there would be no American force left powerful enough to thwart the operation.

The Japanese were determined to hold onto the Philippines whatever the cost. They knew that if the Americans were successful in their efforts to wrest those islands from the Japanese grasp, total defeat would be simply a matter of time. Therefore, the Japanese high command felt that they had little choice but to commit all available resources to the defense of the Philippines.

Of all the Japanese forces involved, Kurita's was the most powerful by far. Five battleships—*Kongo*, *Haruna*, *Nagato* and the mammoth sisters *Yamato* and *Musashi*—were the backbone of the formation. The navy's finest heavy cruisers—*Atago*, *Takao*, *Chokai*, *Maya*, *Myoko*, *Kumano*, *Suzuya*, *Chikuma* and *Tone*—were present. Fifteen destroyers were led by the light cruisers *Noshiro* and *Yahagi*.

Two additional battleships, *Fuso* and *Yamashiro*, constituted the heart of Nishimura's fleet. They sailed in company with the heavy cruiser *Mogami* and four destroyers. Shima was to add the weight of heavy cruisers *Nachi*, *Ashigara* and *Abukuma* and seven additional destroyers. Thus, seven battleships, thirteen heavy cruisers, two light cruisers, and twenty-six destroyers converged on the American landing beaches.

MacArthur was scheduled to invade Mindanao on October 20 and Leyte the following month. In view of the relatively light Japanese naval resistance encountered since the Battle of the Philippine Sea, Adm. William Halsey suggested cancelling the Mindanao attack and advancing the invasion of Leyte to October 20. At the same time he urged Nimitz to cancel the proposed Peleliu and Morotai invasions so that the troops designated for these attacks could be diverted to MacArthur's use.

Nimitz agreed with the Leyte proposal and forwarded the recommendations to King who also agreed. The latter in turn urged the Joint Chiefs to do likewise. However, Nimitz would not agree to the cancellation of the Palaus operation, stating that it was too late to cancel the attack. This was unfortunate because the Palaus battle became one of the bloodiest of the entire Pacific war.

The Joint Chiefs added their endorsement to Halsey's proposal. The invasion of Leyte was officially moved up to October 20.

To deceive the Japanese regarding the true intentions of the Americans, Halsey began a ten-day raid against Formosa on October 6. The Third Fleet then made a high-speed run back to the Philippines where it began to soften up enemy positions on Leyte while at the same time attacking enemy air bases throughout the islands.

As commander of the Seventh Fleet, Kinkaid had overall responsibility for the landings. For aerial support he borrowed a force of small escort carriers from Nimitz. These were used in direct support of the assault forces. Halsey's fleet carriers would lay off the east coast of the Philippines, add their weight to that of the escort carriers, keep the enemy air forces pinned down and protect MacArthur's forces from intervention by the Japanese fleet.

On October 18, Kinkaid sent his battleships and cruisers under Adm. Jesse Oldendorf into Leyte Gulf. For two days the ships bombarded enemy positions near the landing beaches. Three groups of escort carriers sat off the east coast of Samar and Leyte. Planes from them flew hundreds of sorties against Japanese installations on Leyte.

On the morning of the twentieth, Kinkaid's amphibious forces, under Adm. David Barbey, began landing American troops at two beaches on Leyte, one near Tacloban and the other further south near Dulag.

"On the first day it was a matter of getting the troops ashore, about seventy thousand or eighty thousand that first day. Then two days later about thirty thousand or so more went ashore."[1]

The American plan called for Kinkaid to exercise overall command until the beachhead was firmly secure. He would then turn command over to the Sixth Army commander, Gen. Walter Krueger. Initial Japanese opposition was light but a few enemy planes managed to get through. One put a torpedo into the light cruiser *Honolulu* and another crashed aboard the cruiser HMAS *Australia*. Kinkaid had to order both ships to the rear for repairs.

That afternoon, General MacArthur waded ashore at the beachhead even though enemy snipers were still active in the area. Once ashore the general, ever the showman, made his dramatic statement, "I have returned."

Meanwhile, standing off the east coast of Samar, Halsey's carriers provided support for the advancing

American troops. Throughout the islands, Japanese targets were hit and hit again. Adm. Marc Mitscher, commanding the carriers, had split the four carrier task groups. Adm. Frederick Sherman's TG 38.3, with carriers *Essex*, *Lexington*, *Princeton* and *Langley*, was off Luzon attacking enemy air bases and positions in and around Manila. Off the south coast of Luzon was Adm. Gerald Bogan's TG 38.2. This group contained the *Intrepid*, *Hancock*, *Bunker Hill* and *Independence*. Further south was the *Franklin*, *Enterprise*, *San Jacinto* and *Belleau Wood* of TG 38.4 under Adm. Ralph Davison. This group pounded targets on Samar and Leyte.

Enemy opposition was relatively light since Admiral Fukodome, the Japanese commander in the Philippines, had only a handful of planes remaining in his command. But it was here that the dreaded kamikaze made its first appearance.

Since the Third Fleet had been at sea continuously for months, and in view of the light opposition, Halsey felt it was time to begin resting his units. Adm. John McCain's TG 38.1 with the *Wasp*, *Hornet*, *Monterey*, *Cowpens* and *Cabot* was ordered to Ulithi for rest and replenishment. If events continued as they were, Davison's group would follow a few days later.

At 1700 on the day of the invasion, Admiral Ozawa gave the order to his fleet to weigh anchor and set sail for the Philippines. The following day Shima left the Pescadores. Then it was Kurita's turn. With his powerful force of surface ships he sailed from Brunei on the morning of the twenty-second. A few hours later Nishimura followed from the same anchorage.

Halsey was operating under instructions from

Nimitz to support and cover the forces of MacArthur. However, his orders conflicted in that Halsey was also directed to destroy enemy shipping whenever and wherever it was found.

Prior to the attack on the Philippines, American submarines were dispersed and ordered to patrol all sea lanes through which a Japanese fleet might pass en route to Leyte. Two of these submarines, *Darter* and *Dace*, were on patrol east of Palawan. In the early morning darkness of October 23 the two boats were sailing side by side on the surface while their captains compared notes via megaphone. Suddenly, a few minutes after 0100, the *Darter* made contact with a force of surface ships approaching. Steaming directly towards them was Kurita's fleet. After getting off a sighting report, the subs raced ahead and submerged to wait for the enemy ships. It was a submariner's dream.

After the war Admiral Kurita confided to his interrogators that he fully expected to lose half his ships during the operation. From the outset he did not approve of the plan but there was little he could do about it short of asking to be relieved of command.

Kurita was no novice to the striking power of the American fleet, having fought in the Solomons, at Midway and at the Philippine Sea. Aboard *Atago*, his flagship, the admiral paced the bridge impatiently, his mind filled with thoughts. He was in a foul mood that morning since he was still not fully recovered from a bout with Dengue fever. Kurita was no fool. He knew that whatever the outcome of the forthcoming battle, the price to the Japanese navy would be a high one. Which of his ships would he leave behind at the

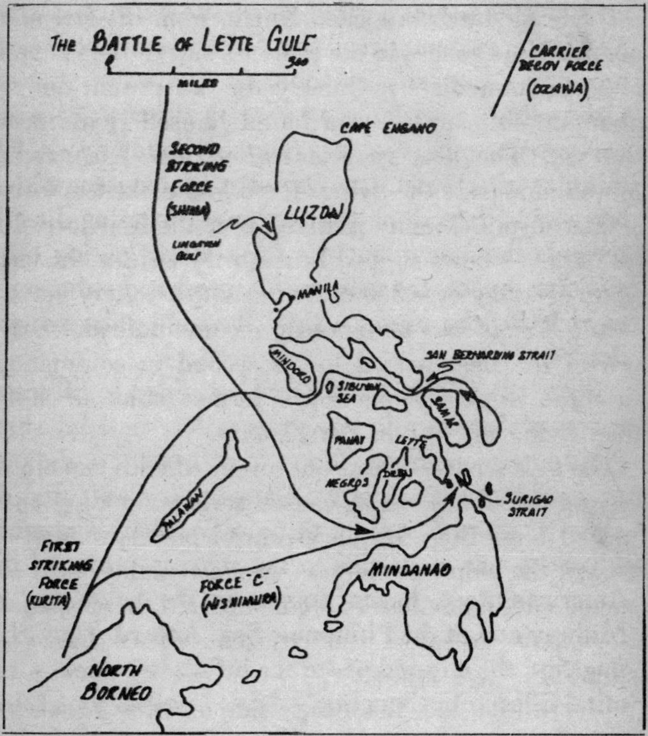
THE BATTLE OF LEYTE GULF
300
MILES
CARRIER DECOY FORCE
(OZAWA)
CAPE ENGANO
SECOND STRIKING FORCE
(SHIMA)
LUZON
MANILA
MINDORO
SAN BERNARDINO STRAIT
SIBUYAN SEA
SAMAR
PANAY
LEYTE
NEGROS
CEBU
SURIGAO STRAIT
PALAWAN
FIRST STRIKING FORCE
(KURITA)
FORCE "C"
(NISHIMURA)
MINDANAO
NORTH BORNEO

bottom of the sea, even if the operation proved successful? His answer was not long in coming.

Just before 0530 *Darter* and *Dace* attacked. *Darter* launched a full spread of six torpedos from her forward tubes at an inviting target before turning 180 degrees and firing all four of her stern tubes at another. Moments later two torpedos slammed into the side of *Atago*, knocked Kurita from his feet and opened huge gashes in the cruiser's side. *Atago* began to settle immediately. Quickly the order went out to abandon ship and Kurita found himself floating in the sea. The destroyers *Asashimo* and *Kishanami* moved alongside the dying *Atago* and picked up over 500 survivors. Twenty minutes after the first torpedo hit, *Atago*'s bows slipped beneath the sea for the last time, carrying over 360 of her crew to a watery grave. While Kurita was temporarily incommunicado, control of the fleet passed to his second in command, Admiral Ugaki, Yamamoto's former chief of staff then flying his flag in the *Yamato*.

Darter's second spread was rewarded with two more hits on the *Takeo* which caused serious flooding and started huge fires. Damage-control parties managed to save the ship but she was unquestionably unfit to participate in any battle. Ugaki ordered the destroyer *Naganami* to escort the stricken cruiser back to Brunei.

Meanwhile, on the other side of the Japanese formation, *Dace*'s attack was crowned by four direct hits on the cruiser *Maya*. A few minutes after 0600 *Maya* exploded in a huge ball of flame and carried 340 of her crew to the bottom with her. Over 700 survivors were plucked from the water by escorting destroyers. In the brief span of three quarters of an hour, Kurita had lost his flagship and seen his force reduced by three heavy cruisers and a destroyer. Drying off on the deck of the *Yamato* where the rescuing destroyer had deposited him, the admiral's mood was worsened by the ignominious events thus far. Nevertheless, he maintained course for Leyte and entered the Sibuyan Sea around 0630.

Neither of the American subs were capable of matching speed with Kurita's surface ships. Therefore, once the Japanese drew out of range the *Darter* and *Dace* set off in pursuit of the wounded *Takao*. A few hours later the *Darter* ran aground on some uncharted shoals. All efforts to free the ship failed. *Dace* removed her crew and the cause was suspended.

Darter's sighting report forced Halsey to alter his plans. Davison's group, which had departed for Ulithi a few hours earlier, was recalled and all three carrier groups were consolidated. At the same time McClain, who was halfway to Ulithi, was ordered to reverse course and return to the Philippines. However, this task group was many hours away by that time.

Orders went out from Halsey's flagship, the *New Jersey*, for each group to detach the fast battleships from their screen. These were consolidated into a task group (34) under Adm. Willis Lee. Halsey sent Lee to guard the exit from the San Bernadino Strait. At the same time the admiral ordered all task groups to launch search planes at first light. Finally, the carriers were directed to move closer to shore and be prepared to launch full strikes as soon as the exact whereabouts of the enemy ships were known.

Halsey's order to Lee was intercepted by Kinkaid's

flagship in Leyte Gulf. As a result the first seeds of confusion were sown. Kinkaid misinterpreted the message and concluded that no matter what, Lee would be guarding the San Bernadino Strait.

At 0812 one of the *Intrepid*'s scout planes located Kurita's force. The *Intrepid* and *Cabot* immediately sent their planes winging toward the reported position. Other carriers quickly followed suit.

The first attack of the day came against not Kurita, but Nishimura. *Enterprise* planes managed to drop a bomb on the battleship *Fuso*. The battleship's thick skin saved it from serious damage.

In the meantime the *Intrepid* and *Cabot* planes arrived over Kurita's fleet a few minutes before 1100. The American planes concentrated on the *Musashi* who, along with her sister ship *Yamato*, was one of the most powerful battleships in the world. In this attack the cruiser *Myoko* was also hit. The cruiser's damage was serious enough for Kurita to order it back to Brunei.

Following the attacks of the *Intrepid* and *Cabot*, planes from *Essex, Franklin, Enterprise* and *Lexington* arrived on the scene. The *Musashi* acted as a magnet drawing the American planes to her. The more she was hit, the more she was attacked. By early afternoon the Goliath had been hit by nineteen torpedos and seventeen bombs. The battleship's speed was drastically reduced and her bow was under water. Nevertheless she was still able to proceed under her own power. Kurita ordered the *Musashi*'s captain to beach the ship but before he could carry out the order the ship rolled over and sank.

In addition to the *Musashi*, the *Yamato* and *Na-*

gato were also hit by bombs. But the Japanese battleships were capable of absorbing a great deal of punishment.

There was still plenty of daylight left. The American planes shuttled between their carriers and Kurita's force which was devoid of aerial protection. Kurita felt as if he were steaming into the lion's den. Therefore, around 1530 he ordered the fleet to reverse course. His intentions were not to retreat but merely to draw out of range of the American carrier planes until darkness could cover his run through the San Bernadino Strait.

Meanwhile, Admiral Fukodome struck back with his meager force. The few remaining Japanese planes attacked Sherman's task group. The *Princeton* was hit by a bomb which penetrated the flight deck before exploding below and starting fires. The cruiser *Birmingham* moved alongside the stricken carrier to aid in the fire fighting efforts. At 1523 a huge explosion racked the carrier, sending huge chunks of steel and debris high into the air and through the crowd of men and wounded on the *Birmingham*.

> The spectacle which greeted the human eye was horrible to behold. . . . Dead, dying and wounded, many of them badly and horribly, covered the decks. The communication platform was no better. Blood ran freely down the waterways, and continued to run for some time.[2]

Following the explosion, the *Princeton* began to burn furiously. Admiral Sherman had no choice but to order her abandoned. Then the escorting destroyers were told to finish the ship off with torpedos.

Throughout the morning Halsey had been puzzled by the absence of the Japanese carriers. He knew that the Japanese had committed everything they had but where were the elusive flattops? Surely they were somewhere nearby.

Ten minutes after Kurita reversed course, one of Davison's scout planes sighted the Japanese carriers making for Cape Engano, far to the north. Halsey was faced with a dilemma. Should he break off the attack and head for the enemy carriers or should he continue to guard the San Bernadino Strait? Throughout the day the admiral paced the deck pondering his options. Finally, at 2022, believing Kurita to be retreating, he ordered Sherman, Davison and Bogan to concentrate and made off at high speed to the north. But Halsey had made a drastic mistake by ordering Lee's fast battleships to accompany the fleet.

> As it seemed childish to me to guard statically San Bernadino Strait, I concentrated TF 38 during the night and steamed north to attack the Northern Force at dawn. I believed that the Center Force had been so heavily damaged in the Sibuyan Sea that it could no longer be considered a serious menace to Seventh Fleet.[3]

Ozawa's decoy role had worked to perfection. But for a time it appeared as if it would be a failure. The Japanese carriers steamed leisurely east of Cape Engano hoping to be discovered. Ozawa subsequently sent seventy-five of his one hundred planes to Luzon to aid Fukodome in his attacks against the Americans. Ozawa hoped that the arrival of his planes would make the Americans aware of his presence in the vicinity. This ruse failed and Ozawa was left with two dozen planes. Finally, in desperation, Ozawa sent a small portion of his fleet south in hopes that it would lead to the discovery of his fleet. This maneuver proved successful.

Ozawa's pitifully weak carrier force was comprised of the lone remaining survivor of Pearl Harbor, *Zuikaku*, light carriers *Zuiho*, *Chitose* and *Chiyoda*, converted battleships *Ise* and *Hyuga*, cruisers *Oyoda*, *Tama* and *Isuzu* and nine destroyers. The *Ise* and *Hyuga* held a particular fascination for Halsey. These two ships were originally battleships whose rear turrets had been replaced by small flight decks.

In the meantime, Kurita's force had reversed course once more. Shortly after this maneuver the Japanese ships were sighted by one of the *Independence*'s scout planes. The latest sighting was reported to Admiral Mitscher but Mitscher was miffed at Halsey for assuming direct control of operations. Therefore Mitscher did not pass the report on to his superior.

Admiral Lee was uncomfortable with the latest turn of events. Shortly after the fleet set out after Ozawa, he sent a message to Halsey stating his opinion that Kurita would still attempt to traverse the San Bernadino Strait. No reply was received from Halsey.

Halsey was certain that he had made the correct decision. At first he considered taking on Ozawa and Kurita simultaneously but this would have meant splitting his attention between two targets separated by hundreds of miles. The overly optimistic reports of the American pilots regarding their attacks on Kurita indicated that the Japanese had suffered more heavily than they actually had. Kurita did nothing to dispel this myth when he turned back temporarily to take his fleet out of range of the American carriers. This maneuver caused Halsey to place more credence in the reports of his pilots. Finally, Halsey felt that even if Kurita elected to come on, Kinkaid's Seventh Fleet would be more than capable of handling the few remaining Japanese ships.

On the other hand, Ozawa's force was fresh and unbloodied. When he left Japan, however, his carriers could only count one hundred planes present. Seventy-five of these had already left to join the forces on Luzon. Unfortunately, Halsey had no way of knowing that the Japanese carriers were capable of putting only twenty-five planes in the air.

Thus, after mulling over all the options and the latest information, Halsey made the only decision any fighting admiral would have done in his place. But unfortunately, Halsey failed to notify the Seventh Fleet that he was leaving the San Bernadino Strait unguarded. Kinkaid continued to operate under the impression that Lee's fast battleships were still guarding the exit to the strait.

Far to the south, out of range of Halsey's carriers, three Japanese fleets approached Leyte Gulf. Kurita, Shima and Nishimura were getting ready to close the pincer.

Kinkaid was in his command post on the transport *Wasatch* when word came of the approach of Nishimura's force. Although his mind was preoccupied with the landings and fighting ashore, Kinkaid had little trouble guessing Nishimura's intentions. He quickly ordered General Kruger to go ashore and assume command of the ground troops. Then he passed the word for all non-combat ships to haul off and be prepared to sail at a moment's notice. If the Japanese broke through, Kinkaid would not have the vulnerable transports exposed.

Tom Kinkaid prepared a hot reception for Nishimura and Shima. It was one of the most brilliant ambushes in naval history, worthy of a Drake, Nelson or Dewey. Every type of warship in his command was pressed into service.

In the mouth of and at the approaches to Surigao Strait, Kinkaid positioned thirteen squadrons of PT boats strung out so that the approaching Japanese fleet would have to pass each one in turn. Lining both sides of the upper portion of the narrow body of water were four squadrons of destroyers. At the head of the strait steaming back and forth was a battle line under Oldendorf. Six old battleships, *Mississippi, West Virginia, Tennessee, California, Pennsylvania* and *Maryland*, the latter five salvaged from the mud of Pearl Harbor, were the heart of this force. Slightly forward and at each end of the battle line were two groups of cruisers, *Phoenix, Boise* and the Australian *Shropshire* on the right, *Portland, Minneapolis, Denver, Columbia* and Oldendorf's flagship *Louisville* on the left. MacArthur had asked permission to join the battle line in his flagship, the cruiser *Nashville*, but a flabbergasted Kinkaid would not hear of it.

Admiral Nishimura missed his rendezvous with Shima. The latter had deliberately reduced his speed so that he would not have to operate under Nishimura. There was an intense jealousy between the two. Consequently, Shima's force was a good two hours behind the more powerful force of his fellow admiral.

Three quarters of an hour after midnight the first PT boats sighted Nishimura's force and raced in for the attack. The Japanese ships successfully eluded the American torpedos but they were entering the gauntlet. For the next two hours the story was the same. A squadron of PT boats would suddenly dart out of the darkness and fire their torpedos. Japanese fire was effective and the small boats were driven off without causing any damage but the experience was unnerving to the Japanese sailors. The warships' crews had to be constantly on the alert, peering out into the darkness. As Nishimura's ships passed each successive PT squadron, their advance was reported to Oldendorf and Kinkaid.

Around 0300 Nishimira was in the heart of the strait when the destroyer attacks began. Hidden against the background of land, the American ships were all but invisible and had the advantage of surprise. Desron 54 was the first to attack.

From the east side of the strait destroyers *McGowan*, *Remey* and *Melvin* raced in, fired their torpedos and sped off again. One or more hit the *Fuso* which began to circle out of control and on fire. The battleship circled for half an hour before the fires reached the magazines. At 0330 the *Fuso* erupted in a ball of fire and split in half. Both parts of the ship remained afloat for a while before sinking.

Ten minutes after the first destroyer attack, the *McDermut* and *Monsenn* attacked. Nishimura's flagship *Fuso* was hit by one torpedo but managed to continue on. Destroyers *Yamagumo* and *Michishio* were not as fortunate. The former was hit and blew up at once. *Michishio* went dead in the water and began to settle. At the same time, destroyer *Asagumo* had her bow blown off.

Despite the loss of over half of his force Nishimura continued on. At 0320 Desron 24, *Hutchins*, *Beale*, *Bache*, *Killen*, *Beale* and HMAS *Arunta*, sped in for another attack. *Yamashiro* was hit once more and was forced to reduce speed. Nevertheless, the Japanese formation sailed doggedly on.

Just before 0330 the final American destroyer attack came. *Bryant*, *Halford*, *Robinson*, *Bennion*, *Leutze*, *Edwards*, *Grant*, *Leary* and *Newcomb* fired a full spread of torpedos. The *Grant* managed to put two more fish into the *Yamashiro*. With her bottom ripped open the battleship slowed to a crawl. Then the American battle line opened up.

The *Mogami* and *Yamashiro* were quickly smothered in a hail of heavy-caliber shells. Nishimura was killed almost immediately and the *Yamashiro* began to list heavily. The battleship sank shortly thereafter.

Mogami, with her upper decks a wreck and littered with dead, reversed course and headed back down the strait escorted by the *Shigure*.

Unfortunately, the radar on the American ships could not distinguish between friend and foe. The final destroyer attack was almost over when Oldendorf gave the word for his battle line to open fire. Along with the *Yamashiro* and *Mogami*, the destroyer *Grant* was hit a dozen times. Mortally wounded by her own warships, the *Grant* was towed out of the battle.

The survivors of Nishimura's force altered course away from the hell they had just experienced. *Portland*, *Denver* and *Louisville* set out in pursuit. Then the lumbering American battleships joined the chase. Oldendorf was anxious to finish the job.

Meanwhile, after running the gauntlet of PT boats, Shima was just entering the Suragio Strait. At 0430 his flagship, *Nachi*, sighted the retreating *Mogami*. Shima took his ship closer just as the *Mogami* swerved. Her bow sliced into the side of the *Nachi*, causing heavy damage. Before entering the strait the PT boats had managed to torpedo the cruiser *Abukuma* and Shima was forced to order that ship back to base. Now, with two cruisers damaged and unable to contact Nishimura, Shima turned his ships around and headed home.

The American cruisers caught up with the *Mogami* and *Asagumo* later in the day. The destroyer was sunk in quick fashion but the *Mogami* managed to survive even more punishment before Oldendorf recalled his cruisers to protect the beachhead. Eventually, American planes located the gallant Japanese cruiser and finished it off.

The Battle of Suragio Strait was but one segment of the Battle for Leyte Gulf. It was, however, the most decisive. Nishimura lost six of his seven ships, including two battleships and a heavy cruiser. He also lost his life. Another heavy cruiser, Shima's *Nachi*, had been damaged along with the *Abukuma*. Other than some damage to the *Grant* and a few PT boats, Kinkaid's fleet remained intact. His positioning of Oldendorf at the head of the strait had resulted in the latter being able to execute the time-honored naval maneuver; "capping the t." One arm of the Japanese pincer was totally destroyed.

Morning of October 25 dawned gray and overcast. Undetected and unopposed, Kurita had moved through the San Bernadino Strait during the night and was moving south along the east coast of Samar. The only force standing between him and the beachhead were three formations of escort carriers known as Taffys.

Adm. Thomas Sprague's Taffy 1 was off Mindanao. This force contained escort carriers *Sangammon*, *Suwanee*, *Santee*, *Petrof Bay* and seven small escorts.

Taffy 2, commanded by Adm. Felix Stump, was off Leyte Gulf. Stump had the *Natoma Bay*, *Manila Bay*, *Marcus Island*, *Savo Island*, *Ommaney Bay* and *Kadashan Bay*. Three destroyers and four destroyer escorts formed the screen.

The group furthest north was Adm. Clifton Sprague's Taffy 3. Sprague was off Samar with the *Fanshaw Bay*, *St. Lo*, *White Plains*, *Kalinin Bay*, *Gambier Bay*, *Kitkun Bay*, destroyers *Hoel*, *Heermann* and *Johnston*, and DE's *Butler*, *Dennis*, *Raymond* and *Roberts*.

Kurita's force now closed on Taffy 3. Halsey was far to the north chasing Ozawa so there was little to fear. The fox was in the henhouse.

A few hours after midnight Kinkaid had ordered the Taffys to launch search planes in addition to their routine anti-submarine patrols. Unfortunately, for whatever the reason, this order was not followed.

At first light all three Taffys had their anti-submarine scouts in the air and were busily readying their first strikes against Japanese positions on Leyte.

Lulled into a false sense of security brought about by Halsey's presence on their northern flank, Sprague's force had ignored a message from Kinkaid.

The night before (twenty-fourth) I had directed Sprague to have attack groups ready on deck (of the jeep carriers), looking forward to what might be the morning situation. I'd directed him to send one attack group down to Mindanao to get any stragglers or escapees from the night action, which he did. I'd also directed him at daylight to send a search northward along the San Bernadino Strait. I did that mostly out of curiosity to know what had gone on up there, because I thought that Lee was there with Task Force 34, and I didn't expect to find anything that we had not planned. I was quite wrong in that.

Unfortunately, that search did not get off. Sprague got off his anti-submarine patrols, and he got off an attack group against stragglers from the night action.[4]

On the bridge of the escort carrier *Fanshaw Bay*, Adm. Clifton Sprague was observing the activity when he was handed an urgent radio dispatch at 0645:

Enemy surface force of four battleships, seven cruisers and eleven destroyers sighted twenty miles northwest of your task group and closing on you at thirty knots.[5]

Sprague remembers thinking, "Now there's some

screwy young aviator reporting part of our own forces."⁶

Unaware that Halsey had slipped anchor and was off chasing Ozawa, Sprague ordered the scout plane to check the identification. Two minutes later he received the shock of his life.

"Ships have pagoda masts."⁷

Lookouts aboard the Japanese ships sighted the Americans around the same time. Sprague had no choice. He was unable to turn his ships into the wind to launch his remaining planes so he did the next best thing. Hoping that his planes would be able to take off in a crosswind, he set a course due east toward a rain squall. At the same time he ordered all ships in the formation, including the escorts, to make smoke.

Sprague sent a message to Kinkaid requesting permission to close on Leyte Gulf. Unwilling to risk his transports or the beachhead, Kinkaid refused. With Oldendorf still far down the Suriago Strait pursuing the Japanese, there was no force available to oppose the enemy.

On board the *Yamato*, Kurita was straining out over the bows of the mighty ship hoping to get a glimpse of the enemy ships. At 0700 he ordered his ships to open fire with their forward turrets as they came in range. One minute later, the huge eighteen-inch guns of the *Yamato* belched fire and smoke, sending her awesome projectiles toward Sprague's six helpless carriers. Then Kurita ordered the "General Chase" signal hoisted. This directive meant that each ship or squadron of ships was free to act independently. Thus, any advantage of a disciplined fleet action was thrown away.

When he was refused permission to close on Leyte Gulf, Sprague made off at his best possible speed away from the beachhead. Unfortunately, his best speed was only half of what the enemy was capable of. In a short time heavy-caliber shells began to straddle Taffy 3.

Running at high speed toward the rain squall, Sprague watched in horror as multicolored shell splashes ringed his small fleet. The enemy shells were equipped with colored dye, thus allowing each ship to spot its own particular fall of shot. Furious orders issued forth from the flag bridge of *Fanshaw Bay*. Make smoke. Launch all available planes. The latter order was difficult to carry out since most of the squadron's planes were already in the air over Leyte. Frantic calls for help went out to Kinkaid's headquarters.

South of Taffy 3, Admiral Stump, on Taffy 2's flagship, *Natoma Bay*, heard Sprague's urgent call for help. Stump ordered those planes already airborne to abort their mission and alter course for the Japanese force. That order was also received by Taffy 3's planes who promptly complied.

For ten precious minutes Sprague's ships were covered by the nearby rain squall. When the clouds passed the Japanese ships began to find the range. *White Plains* was hit numerous times by heavy-caliber shells. *Fanshwa Bay* was hit twice and the *Kalinin Bay* once. Then more enemy ships began to find the range on *Kalinin Bay*. The closest ship to the Japanese was the *Gambier Bay*. The unfortunate carrier was hit repeatedly by heavy- and small-caliber shells. Fires broke out below decks and the *Gambier Bay*'s machinery began to break down.

The distance between the opposing forces was closing rapidly when, out of the smoke, firing their guns, raced the destroyers *Heermann*, *Hoel*, and *Johnston*. The latter took on the *Kumano* at close range with gunfire and managed to launch ten torpedoes. One of these hit the *Kumano* at 0727. The gallant little destroyer then broke off the action and had begun to retreat when she was smothered by the fourteen-inch shells of the Japanese battleships. In a short time *Johnston* slipped beneath the waves.

Hoel selected the *Kongo* as an opponent. Racing down the side of the battleship the *Hoel* fired her popguns at point-blank range. She was so close that the Japanese were unable to depress their guns far enough to hit the destroyer. *Hoel* missed with a torpedo attack on the battleship, then turned and fired at the *Kumano*. These torpedos also failed to find their target.

Right behind the *Hoel* sped the *Heermann*. The destroyer tackled the *Haguro* and missed with her torpedos. Then she picked on the *Kongo* which replied with all guns. *Heermann* managed to elude the enemy shells and escape. The same was not true for the *Hoel*. As the destroyer raced away from the scene almost every enemy ship concentrated its guns on her. Battered beyond imagination the *Hoel* was pounded to the bottom.

To Kurita it seemed as if the Americans were throwing everything they had at his ships. Stump's planes aided Sprague's and attacked the enemy with a fury. Those planes that were unable to land aboard their own fleeing or damaged carriers shuttled back and forth between the Japanese fleet and a hastily prepared airfield at Tacloban. Stump's planes also relied heavily on the Tacloban Field since the round trip to their own ships consumed precious time.

The American planes sank the cruisers *Chikuma* and *Suzuya*. The *Chokai* ventured too close to the stricken *White Plains* and had her engines wrecked by the incredibly accurate fire of the carrier's five-inch guns. Aircraft finished what the *White Plains* had begun. The *Chokai* joined her sisters at the bottom of the sea.

Not to be outdone by their larger colleagues, Taffy 3's destroyer escorts now raced into the attack. *Roberts* followed *Heermann* and *Hoel* into the fray. A few moments later, *Butler*, *Raymond* and *Dennis* came racing out of the smoke. *Raymond* missed *Haguro* with her torpedos before retiring. *Dennis* also missed the *Chokai* with her fish. As the small boys retired, the *Roberts* was smothered in a hail of fire at 0850. Ten minutes later the DE rolled over and sank. The attack of the escorts was so obviously one-sided that it resembled gnats taking on elephants. But their sacrifice and bravery had a distinct influence on the battle. Their attack had thrown the entire Japanese formation into chaos as ships maneuvered violently to avoid torpedo attacks.

From his vantage point at the rear of the battle line, Kurita was unable to keep abreast of the situation. His ships were steaming in all directions in an effort to avoid the American destroyers and aircraft. As the planes shuttled back and forth between the Japanese fleet and Tacloban, Kurita saw only a constant stream of attacks. Since he no longer had control of the battle, the Japanese commander ordered his ships to reform but this was virtually impossible in view of the constant pressure by the Americans. At 0911, therefore, Kurita broke off the action and ordered his ships to retreat.

Sprague could not believe his eyes. Just when the Japanese were within killing distance, they pulled off. "At best I expected to be swimming by this time, saw the enemy ships disappear into the smoke haze to the north."[8]

For his part, Kurita was unaware that his ships had been in action against a mere handful of escort carriers. As far as he knew, the battle was against Halsey's mighty Task Force 38. As a veteran of the Marianas Turkey Shoot, Kurita was all too aware of the awesome striking power of that formation. There was no way the admiral could have known that at that very moment, Halsey was far to the north chasing Ozawa's decoys. The latter made no report to inform Kurita of what was transpiring at that very moment. In addition, there was no word of Nishimura's and Shima's fleets, forces that were supposed to rendezvous with his own fleet.

After sailing north for an hour and a half, pursued every minute by the pesky American aircraft, Kurita decided to make one last effort. The fleet altered course toward Leyte Gulf once more. A few minutes later a strong air strike from Taffy 2 arrived on the scene. That settled the issue once and for all as far as Kurita was concerned. Ordering the cripples to retire on their own, Kurita set sail for the San Bernadino Strait and made the following signal to Admiral Toyoda:

First striking force has abandoned penetration of Leyte anchorage and is proceeding north to search for enemy task force. Will engage decisively, then pass through San Bernadino Strait.[9]

At Pearl Harbor, Nimitz was following the progress of the huge battle closely. The admiral had monitored Kinkaid's and Sprague's urgent calls for help and was puzzled by Halsey's absence.

Far to the north, on the bridge of the *New Jersey*, Halsey found himself besieged by frantic calls for help. Just before 0700 Seventh Fleet asked if TF 34 was guarding the San Bernadino Strait. An hour and a half later word came that a force of cruisers and battleships was attacking Taffy 3. This message was followed a few moments later by one calling for help from Lee's battleships.

Halsey knew that this was impossible. Lee was with the rest of Task Force 38. The admiral was excited since the Third Fleet had driven north all night at top speed. Two hours after midnight scout planes had located Ozawa. Shadowers followed throughout the night reporting the enemy's exact course and speed. On board the American carriers pilots breakfasted, were briefed and climbed aboard their planes awaiting word to take off.

At 0710 180 American planes roared off the flight decks. In less than an hour they were over Ozawa's helpless formation. The *Zuikaku*, *Chitose* and *Zuiho* were hit hard in the first attack.

At 0945 the second American wave arrived. *Chiyoda* was left burning to sink later on. In this attack the cruiser *Tama* was also hit.

Mitscher's third wave concentrated on the burning carriers *Zuiho* and *Zuikaku*. Both ships were hit repeatedly. Around 1430 the *Zuikaku* slipped beneath the waves, thus settling the account for Pearl Harbor once and for all.

The fourth wave polished off the *Zuiho* and hit the hybrid carrier *Ise*. Although they could launch planes via catapult, *Ise* and her sister *Hyuga*'s flight decks were too short to allow for landings. For this battle Ozawa's critical shortage of planes precluded the former battleship's having planes at all.

As Task Force 38 continued to pound Ozawa's helpless ships, the frantic messages continued to arrive from Leyte Gulf. Halsey sent a message off to McCain ordering him to attack the enemy ships as quickly as possible, but McCain was still not within range.

Halsey was torn between two storms. He was too far north to offer immediate assistance and Ozawa's fleet was teetering on the brink of total annihilation. Finally, a message was received from Seventh Fleet requesting immediate assistance from Lee. Since the message had been sent in the clear, Halsey knew that the situation in the south was critical. Shortly thereafter the admiral was handed one of the most electric messages of the entire war and it made his blood boil.

In order to deceive enemy cryptographers, American messages were usually padded at the beginning and end with nonsensical phrases. It was the duty of the receiving radio operator to strike out this gibberish before giving it to the addressee. In this case, however, the padding seemed to be part of the message and was left in. When Halsey was handed the urgent message from Admiral Nimitz it read, "Where is Task Force 34? The world wonders."[10]

The last three words were actually the padding. Innocently, the radio operator at Pearl Harbor had added them to the message. It is easy to see though, how the operator on the *New Jersey* could have misconstrued them to be part of the message.

Halsey was incensed. How dare Nimitz insult him in this manner. More out of spite than common sense he ordered Lee's Task Group 34 and Task Group 38.2 (Bogan) to reverse course and head at full speed back to Leyte. Halsey knew that they would not reach the area before the next morning and could therefore be of little assistance. Mitscher, with Sherman's and Davison's groups, was left behind to finish off Ozawa. Nimitz later apologized for the misunderstanding.

Late in the afternoon what remained of Ozawa's fleet headed back to Japan. Mitscher dispatched a squadron of cruisers, *Santa Fe*, *Mobile*, *Wichita* and *New Orleans*, to pursue and polish off any stragglers and cripples. Then he turned his ships around and followed Halsey back to Leyte.

Ozawa's decoy operation was almost a total success. He had been unable to keep the American ships from harassing Kurita in the Sibuyan Sea but eventually he gave Kurita a free run to the Leyte beachhead. Only the failure of the latter's nerve saved the American Navy from a disastrous defeat.

But had Kurita lost his nerve? Perhaps he had his own perfectly good reasons for acting as he did.

That he had his flagship sunk under him by

underwater attack, had been without sleep for three days and had suffered a day and a half of almost incessant massed air attack, losing the splendid *Musashi* and two heavy cruisers in the process, must inevitably have clouded his judgment and played its part in bringing him to a decision to retire at 12:20 on October 25.[11]

Later, Kurita confided to Captain Hara, "I made the retirement out of sheer physical exhaustion."[12]

Even though his mind was irrevocably made up, Kurita knew that his ordeal was far from over. He was absolutely certain that the American planes would allow him no respite. He couldn't have been more prophetic. Halsey had taken steps to cover his tracks.

Steaming full tilt to the Philippines was Admiral McCain's Task Group 38.1, hastily recalled from their scheduled rest at Ulithi. As soon as he was in range, McCain launched almost 150 planes from the decks of the *Wasp*, *Hornet* and *Hancock*. Kurita's fleet was discovered in midafternoon. Fortunately, the only additional damage incurred was bomb damage to the *Tone*. The renewed American attacks, however, served to convince Kurita that he had indeed reached the correct conclusion. If he was harboring any thoughts of aiding Ozawa, these were quickly cast aside as he took his fleet full ahead for the San Bernadino Strait.

Kinkaid had been lucky. Now, with the battle over it was time for fixing the blame for the near disaster off Samar. Who was to blame? Kinkaid or Halsey?

Actually, neither was. Kinkaid had rightly assumed that Halsey was protecting his rear. He had no reason to believe otherwise. As for Halsey, he had erred in not notifying anyone that he was moving north but even had he done so, the dual command picture did not necessarily mean that he would have notified Kinkaid of his decision anyway. Halsey was operating under a conflicting set of orders to protect the American beachhead but to seize every opportunity to destroy the Japanese fleet. The latter was just what Halsey had done when Ozawa was discovered.

Admiral King, a friend and admirer of Halsey, attempted to shift the blame to Kinkaid whom he did not care for. He attributed "the element of surprise in the Battle of Samar not only to Halsey's absence in the north but also to Kinkaid's failure to use his own air squadrons for search at a crucial moment."[13]

But as already stated, Kinkaid had issued orders for an air search to be carried out; the orders were simply not complied with.

The largest naval battle in world history was now over. The Japanese navy was in ruins.

NOTES

1. Edwin Hoyt, *The Battle of Leyte Gulf*, p. 33
2. Samuel E. Morison, *History of U.S. Naval Operations in World War II Volume XII: Leyte*, p. 181
3. *Ibid*, p. 193
4. Hoyt, *op. cit.*, p. 206
5. S. E. Smith, *The U.S. Navy in World War II*, p. 864
6. *Ibid*, p. 864
7. *Ibid*, p. 864
8. *Ibid*, p. 864
9. Donald MacIntyre, *Leyte Gulf-Armada in the Pacific*, p. 127

10. *Ibid*, p. 135
11. *Ibid*, p. 150
12. Tamiechi Hara, *Japanese Destroyer Captain*, p. 270
13. Thomas Buell, *Master of Sea Power*, p. 580

BIBLIOGRAPHY

1. Buell, Thomas. *Master of Sea Power.*
Little Brown & Co., Boston, 1980.
2. Cannon, M. Hamlin. *The Return to the Philippines.*
Office of Chief of Military History, Washington, 1954.
3. Dull, Paul. *The Imperial Japanese Navy.*
Doubleday & Co., New York, 1978.
4. Falk, Stanley. *Decision at Leyte.*
W. W. Norton & Co., New York, 1978.
5. Halsey, William and Bryann, J. *Admiral Halsey's Story.*
McGraw Hill, New York, 1947.
6. Hara, Tamiechi. *Japanese Destroyer Captain.*
Ballantine Books, New York, 1961.
7. Hoyt, Edwin. *The Battle of Leyte Gulf.*
Weybright & Talley, New York, 1972.
8. Hoyt, Edwin. *How They Won the War in the Pacific.*
Weybright & Talley, New York, 1972.
9. MacIntyre, Donald. *Leyte Gulf-Armada in the Pacific.*

Ballantine Books, New York, 1969.
10. Manchester, William. *American Caesar*.
Little Brown & Co., Boston, 1978.
11. Morison, Samuel E. *History of U.S. Naval Operations in World War II Vol. XII: Leyte*.
Little Brown & Co., Boston, 1958.
12. Pfannes, Charles and Salamone, Victor. *The Great Admirals of World War II Vol. I: The Americans*.
Zebra Books, New York, 1983.
13. Pfannes, Charles and Salamone, Victor. *The Great Admirals of World War II Vol. III: The Americans*.
Zebra Books, New York, 1982.
14. Pfannes, Charles and Salamone, Victor. *The Great Admirals of World War II Vol. IV: The Japanese*.
Zebra Books, New York, 1982.
15. Reynolds, Clark. *The Fast Carriers*.
McGraw-Hill, New York, 1968.
16. Smith, S. E., ed. *The U.S. Navy In World War II*.
William Morrow & Co., New York, 1966.
17. Watts, A. J. and Gordon, B. G. *The Imperial Japanese Navy*.
Doubleday & Co., New York, 1978.

THE WORLD-AT-WAR SERIES
by Lawrence Cortesi

COUNTDOWN TO PARIS (1548, $3.25)
Having stormed the beaches of Normandy, every GI had one dream: to liberate Paris from the Nazis. Trapping the enemy in the Falaise Pocket, the Allies would shatter the powerful German 7th Army Group, opening the way for the . . . COUNTDOWN TO PARIS.

GATEWAY TO VICTORY (1496, $3.25)
After Leyte, the U.S. Navy was at the threshold of Japan's Pacific Empire. With his legendary cunning, Admiral Halsey devised a brilliant plan to deal a crippling blow in the South China Sea to Japan's military might.

ROMMEL'S LAST STAND (1415, $3.25)
In April of 1943 the Nazis attempted a daring airlift of supplies to a desperate Rommel in North Africa. But the Allies were lying in wait for one of the most astonishing and bloody air victories of the war.

LAST BRIDGE TO VICTORY (1393, $3.25)
Nazi troops had blown every bridge on the Rhine, stalling Eisenhower's drive for victory. In one final blood-soaked battle, the fanatic resistance of the Nazis would test the courage of every American soldier.

PACIFIC SIEGE (1363, $3.25)
If the Allies failed to hold New Guinea, the entire Pacific would fall to the Japanese juggernaut. For six brutal months they drenched the New Guinea jungles with their blood, hoping to live to see the end of the . . . PACIFIC SIEGE.

THE BATTLE FOR MANILA (1334, $3.25)
A Japanese commander's decision—against orders—to defend Manila to the death led to the most brutal combat of the entire Pacific campaign. A living hell that was . . . THE BATTLE FOR MANILA.

Available wherever paperbacks are sold, or order direct from the Publisher. Send cover price plus 50¢ per copy for mailing and handling to Zebra Books, Dept. 1887, 475 Park Avenue South, New York, N.Y. 10016. Residents of New York, New Jersey and Pennsylvania must include sales tax. DO NOT SEND CASH.